FIRST PERSON

Conversations on Writers & Writing

FIRST PERSON

CONVERSATIONS ON WRITERS & WRITING

· WITH ·

GLENWAY WESCOTT

JOHN DOS PASSOS

ROBERT PENN WARREN

JOHN UPDIKE

JOHN BARTH

ROBERT COOVER

·

edited by Frank Gado

1973

UNION COLLEGE PRESS
SCHENECTADY NEW YORK

3/1974
Eng.

For

Arlin Turner

Published in 1973 by Union College Press, Schenectady, New York
12308, U.S.A.

Distributed by Syracuse University Press, Syracuse, New York
13210, U.S.A.

International Standard Book Number 0-912756-03-9 (cloth)
0-912756-04-7 (paper)
Library of Congess Catalog Card Number 73-84601

Contents

Preface

Each of the interviews in this collection represents the final stage in a long process. Initially, of course, there was the discussion itself, in which a group of Union College faculty and students met informally with the author. Then a tape recording of the session was redacted and subjected to a preliminary editing. Next, in all cases but one, the author received this typescript for his emendations, additions and clarifications. (Glenway Wescott had made exemption from refinement of the text the one condition for his participation.) After incorporation of the revisions, further editing, and the author's approval of galley proofs, the text was published in a pamphlet as a special issue of *The Idol,* the student literary magazine at Union College. (The Robert Coover interview, conducted while this book was being prepared for the press, is the sole exception: its publication here marks its first appearance.)

For the most part, the texts in this volume correspond to those in the pamphlets. Aside from correction of obvious errors which escaped the proofreaders, the only general difference lies in the elimination of the introductions and of the attribution of the questions to the participants in the discussions—details which would be of no interest to readers beyond the Union College campus. The Wescott interview alone has undergone an extensive alteration, mostly cutting and rearrangement of sections, made necessary by the fact that *The Idol* had inadvertently printed an early, virtually unedited draft.

A brief statement about the process of preparing a tape recording for publication may be in order. No one who has engaged in such work can ever again approach a printed interview with the illusion that *all* the words represent an *exact* report of what was said, for the first thing an editor realizes is that a verbatim transcript creates difficulties in reading and understanding. Sentences frequently change direction in mid-course, tenses shift, predicates lose their subjects, and, at times, the written record, lacking the qualifications of the voice, betrays the meaning intended. Therefore, even before sending the manuscripts to the author for his revisions, I resorted to the editorial pen wherever it served to clarify the text. In some of the interviews, very few such intrusions were necessary; in others, sense occasionally had to be rescued from the muddle of the transcript. Throughout, however, I sought to remain as faithful as possible to the manner of speech and still render a readable text.

To several people, I owe an expression of my gratitude for having helped make this volume possible. Harold C. Martin, president of Union, lent his support for publication of this book at a time when budgetary shears, honed to a keen edge, threatened its existence. Bernard R. Carman of the Publications Office repeatedly gave me his advice and assistance. Students too numerous to mention by name worked diligently preparing themselves for the interviews. Janet Pearce and Marge Clark uncomplainingly typed drafts of the manuscript. Michael Shinagel, the first to encourage me to plan this collection, in this instance as in all others proved to be, more than a colleague, a friend. Finally, I wish to acknowledge my debt to Glenway Wescott, who launched the series with his graciousness and friendship, and to John Dos Passos, Robert Penn Warren, John Updike, John Barth, and Robert Coover; their cooperation in this project was generous beyond expectation.

Introduction

Midway through this series of interviews, when it was suggested that they might eventually be published in one volume, I began searching for an organizing principle which would make the book something more than a gathering of fugitive pieces. It struck me that, by chance, each of the writers who had already participated could be regarded as mirroring the sensibilities of a different decade. Wescott, in his literary perspectives as well as in his participation in the swell of temporary expatriation that followed the Great War, represents the spirit of the 'twenties. Dos Passos first achieved a measure of success in 1921 with *Three Soldiers,* a novel typical of that period's anti-war sentiments, but his aesthetic innovations were not fully developed until the trilogy *U.S.A.,* which began appearing in 1930; it was the 'thirties that championed him as its most sympathetic voice and that gave him his greatest audience. Warren, who had made his debut as a novelist in 1939, secured his position as one of our leading writers with *All the King's Men* in the mid-'forties.

Consciously making a decision of what, up to that point, had been fortuitous, I sought to complete the series with writers who would reflect the evolution of fiction in the post-war years. To be sure, the major works of Updike, Barth, and Coover cannot as easily be apportioned by decade as those of the earlier writers; yet, despite the contemporaneous publication of their books, each author manifests attitudes rooted in a successive phase of the period. *The Floating Opera* (1956) and *The Poorhouse Fair* (1959), both first novels, show basic thematic similarities; but Barth, even in his initial work, prefigures the new energies that recharged fiction in the 'sixties, while Updike, no less a craftsman, has remained a citizen of the 'fifties. Robert Coover was intended to typify the current *avant garde.* Coover won the 1966 Faulkner Prize with *The Origin of the Brunists,* and his subsequent books of fiction, *The Universal Baseball Association* and *Pricksongs and Descants,* have been critically well-received, but one senses that his talent is still in the process of defining itself amid aesthetic questions posed by the 'seventies.

The aggregation, therefore, spans approximately half a century of American fiction, and while it would be foolish to contend that these authors represent the full range of its narrative art, the sample does, I believe, identify some of its most characteristic features.

For the most part, literary historians, with Malcolm Cowley at the fore, have focussed on the literature of the 'twenties as an isolable phenomenon, bounded by Wilsonian optimism and the disenchantment of the Wall Street crash. The concept of a Lost Generation more or less united in a common adventure has a certain romantic appeal. Most of that generation's members entered adulthood while serving in war—several, indeed, in the same unit, the Norton-Harjes ambulance corps—and virtually all inferred from direct experience with the idiocies of nations that the individual's concluding a separate peace was not only condonable but also morally necessary. Resort to a private code was equally evident in their sexual attitudes: cut off from the proscriptions of their upbringing, they explored the ways of sexual freedom and, to the shock and delectation of their American audiences, reported their discoveries in their literary works. Aesthetically as well, they emphatically proclaimed change: the prevailing image of the young writers in the post-war years is centered on their fervid response to Ezra Pound's imperative to "make it new." Anecdotists, eagerly refining the smallest details, have lent further support to the notion of a collective enterprise of expatriates with accounts of literary friendships and quarrels pursued in the winey ambiance of Third Republic Paris.

Generally accurate as this composite of the 'twenties writers is (despite discrepancies presented by a number of individual careers), it tends to distort the significance of the period's literature by localizing its context to the war and the war's aftermath. After all, the first blows for aesthetic Modernism had already been struck before the assassination of an archduke in Sarajevo—as a quick glance at the bibliographies of Pound, Joyce, and Gertrude Stein, or, for that matter, at any history of twentieth-century art, shows. And the Depression, though it brought a spate of Marxist-influenced writing into short-lived ascendancy, did not cause fundamental revision in literary conventions; indeed, those conventions usually associated with the 'twenties continued to dominate the 'forties and most of the 'fifties. Perhaps understanding the forces that animated our modern literature until recent years is better served by taking a broader view than one fixed on the effects of battle and the influence of expatriation.

Of the writers who set the pace for more than three decades after the war, almost all were born within a few years of the turn of the century. The importance of this fact is that they passed childhood and adolescence in a period of profound transformations. Technologically, scientifically, politically, sociologically, and culturally, quantitative change which had been accelerating in rate since the middle of the preceding century had begun to affect men's qualitative perception of the world. Suddenly the reassurances of the familiar did not suffice. In his brilliant autobiography written in 1905, Henry Adams reeled from his discovery that "as the mind of man enlarged its range, it enlarged the field of complexity, and it must continue to do so, even into chaos, until the reservoirs of sensuous or supersensuous energies are exhausted, or cease to affect him, or until he succumbs to their excess." After concluding that "Chaos was the law of nature; Order was the dream of man," Adams developed his dynamic theory of history, then retreated for spiritual comfort to the stability of the thirteenth century. Nowhere is the mood of the writers who were to follow more eloquently announced. Children of nineteenth-century American values forced to confront the moral chaos of the twentieth, they produced a literature deeply conscious of the disjunction between past and present.

So pervasive is this theme in the fiction of the interbellum period that one would be hard-pressed to name a major figure who avoids it entirely. The protagonist of what is probably Sherwood Anderson's most accomplished novel, *Poor White,* is an almost mythic blend of nineteenth-century American virtues; he ends as the baffled victim of the twentieth-century forces he has unwittingly loosed. Fitzgerald's characters "beat on, boats against current, borne back ceaselessly into the past." Hemingway's hero, caught in the "messy" conditions of modern life, tries to invoke a sense of order through the rituals of pristine existence. Faulkner's saga-like progression of novels and stories is concerned not only with the rise and fall of families but also with our fall from grace. Wolfe's two personae, forever "lost," look homeward in vain. West depicts the nightmare of an entropic America. Steinbeck's dispossessed bands search for their pastoral heritage.

The three representatives of this generation in this collection come from different backgrounds, employ different approaches to literature, and have had different kinds of careers; yet, like their contemporaries, they exhibit a common fascination with history as guide in the quest for individual identity. Brief examination of their works should not only help inform the interviews but also provide a selective chart of responses to an America which had lost the illusion of its innocence.

GLENWAY WESCOTT

Wescott's large, raw-boned frame, his heaviness of jaw, and especially his walk—a purposeful step, not quite a stride, always a little behind the forward movement of a slightly stooped figure—bring to mind the farmer grandfathers we knew or imagined in childhood, the forebears of his books who move over the stubborn Wisconsin soil. The impression which emerges from conversation with him, however, is rather different. The wit and effusive charm of a man who takes obvious delight in the art of talk are what one would expect of the cosmopolite whose natural habitat is the convivium.

Curiously, both aspects of the man project into his fiction, and each in turn has been recognized by the critics. He was first acclaimed as a regionalist and realist, a successor to Hamlin Garland in portraying life on the Middle Border; then, in the period between *The Babe's Bed* and *The Pilgrim Hawk*, he was viewed as an expatriate who forsook the coarseness and sorrow of native materials for a finely wrought aestheticism. Both of these observations are to some extent justified, but neither strikes at the essence of an art poised between provinciality and worldliness.

Wescott discussed his commitment to literature in the introduction to *Images of Truth*. As text for that essay, he chose the beginning of the eleventh book of the *Odyssey*, in which Odysseus sits on the Cimmerian shore and calls up the shades to ask the way back to Ithaca. Although the allusion was not meant to refer specifically to himself, Wescott's own conjuring of the ghost of the great world traveler is particularly appropriate. Throughout almost all of his major fiction, the process of anagnorisis begins with the protagonist's awareness of the distance between the values represented by his current state and the values which have shaped him. Perhaps the central image in the Wescott canon is that of his persona, Alwyn

Tower, in the company of European friends on the Riviera, reaching for quality of truth in the meaning of his American home. The collision of European epicureanism and America's puritan legacy reverberates through the literature and cultural criticism of our country, especially during the 'twenties; Wescott's art derives from that shock, but unlike so many others concerned with the same theme, he is not content with the easy triumph of one set of values over the other. His works recognize that a man can wholly defeat neither the yearnings implanted by the Ithaca which formed him nor those stimulated by the intoxicating freedom from it.

Wescott, who once defined style as "whatever may make it worthwhile to restate a platitude," is primarily story-teller, and his stories, as he has himself described them, have to do with "the private life: the education of the young, the religion of the old, love-affairs, deathbeds;" in short, with the cyclical drama of the land and its people. *The Apple of the Eye* (1924) is his first attempt at portraying this "private life."

The story divides into two parts, representing past and present. The first concerns Hannah Madoc, or "Bad Han," a drunkard's daughter who unintentionally kills her father in defending herself from his attack. Impelled to leave her farm, she takes a job as a barmaid in town and meets Jule Bier, the industrious son of German immigrants. They become lovers and expect to marry, but the Biers' social ambitions intervene and Jule instead weds a girl from a respectable family. The betrayed Han becomes a prostitute. Then, after the passage of years, she returns to her homestead where, ministering to those in trouble until her death, she earns a legendary reputation as a secular saint. The second part of the novel deals with the next generation. Rosalia, Jule's daughter, falls in love with the appropriately named Mike Byron, a young malcontent whose college experience has led him to reject the old moral and religious order. They have a brief affair before Mike, bowed by Mrs. Bier's hostility, disappears. Rosalia, grieving over her abandonment, convinces herself that she is pregnant and runs away. Months later, her dog- and crow-eaten body is found in the swamp.

This simple chronicle is transformed by the introduction of Dan Strane, Jule's nephew, into the novel's second half. In groping for a moral standard among the events unfolding before him, he unifies the past and present segments of the story. Initially as staunchly puritan as his family, he is won over to young Byron's religion of "joy, delight, pleasure." Rosalia's death, however, abruptly ends

Dan's admiration for his friend's pagan celebration, and it is not until Jule invokes the Demeter-like Han that his crisis of faith is resolved. The story of Han's mystical acceptance of life, so "like a Greek myth," gives him a new basis for his own life.

That the resolution is more imposed than earned is only one of several defects in the novel traceable to the fact that its author, writing between the ages of 17 and 23, was struggling to schematize a world view. And, in the manner of most first novels, it is transparently imitative—in this case, of Lawrence's earthiness and Sherwood Anderson's notion of the land as the repository of all truths. Even so, the book has an impressive power born of Wescott's own urgent need to come to terms with his heritage. Like Dan Strane, the first of his personae, he comes to understand the role of communal myth in defining the individual identity. The West, traditionally imbued with an Edenic character in the American imagination, acquired added significance in the post-war years when the intelligentsia, bitterly anti-Puritan, strove to displace a New England *mythos* of damnation with a frontier *mythos* of original innocence. Although Wescott's mythic purposes in *The Apple of the Eye* are not yet national in dimension, the outline of what was to come is already discernible. The "Bad Han" segment of the novel has a Genesis-like quality: the unyielding marsh of Han's childhood is no paradise, but it does seem to belong to pre-history. Then, with the killing of her father, Han in a sense bears the mark of Cain and comes to know the anguish of disappointment before the palliation of surrendering all ambitions. The death of Rosalia in the next generation, for which Dan feels a vicarious responsibility, marks the end of his innocence, and he is utterly confused and estranged from life until he hears Han's story. Thus becoming her spiritual heir, he recovers a past free from a puritan burden and is enabled "to go on just to go on."

The melding of past and present becomes even more pronounced in *The Grandmothers* (1927). *The Apple of the Eye* was the work of a gifted apprentice; Wescott's second novel reveals the mature artist who has found his own voice and mastered point of view to the degree that it is, throughout, an integral part of the content. Like the Quentin Compson of *Absalom, Absalom*, a Southerner in an alien North, Alwyn Tower, an expatriate, attempts to tell the history of his people to a group of foreign friends. From his distant European prospect, he begins to understand the meaning of his relationship to his past:

> For a moment all Europe seemed less significant than the vicis-

situdes of pioneers, men who were anonymous unless they were somebody's relatives. He did not quite like their suffering, their illiterate mysticism, their air of failure; but he understood them, or fancied that he did. It did not matter whether he liked them or not—he was their son.

The whole of the novel flows from Alwyn's grasping for the meaning of this kinship. He starts with two documents: one, an essay on America he had written at school, is too grandiloquent, too beautiful to convey the human experience of his pioneer family; the other, his grandfather's incomplete attempt at a record of their migration from the East, lacks the perspective necessary to invest the ordinary with significance. The quest, he now realizes, will necessitate dressing the past with flesh. Thus, just as an ancestor had collected cuttings from her family's heads into an album of hair wreaths, Alwyn gathers old tintypes, assorted heirlooms, and gossip handed down through two generations, then weaves a tradition of the motives that went into the composition of the family saga—"greed and sensuality and courage and compassion and cruelty and nostalgia; all the destinies there were—manias, consolations, regrets." In the process of discovering what it means to be a Tower, Alwyn shapes an allegorical fable of America itself.

Our society, Wescott has stated, has been matriarchal from its inception. It is not surprising, therefore, that Alwyn's grandmother, Rose Hamilton, occupies a central place in the mythopoeic novel. She typifies the Middle West which, for her generation, was the seat of our national character. It was the Rose Hamiltons who stamped the prairies with their image; driving out the hunters and trappers, they made a "woman's country out of it."

Grandmother Tower's America was Anglo-Saxon Protestant. The character of the new America is represented by her grandson, Orfeo Craig. Born of a French-Italian mother, he is emblematic of the immigrant infusion. "He was not like a member of the family nor even like an American; he had no appearance either of the country or of the sort of city Alwyn knew." A "strange boy," he is "dark" (the author repeats the word three times within two short sentences) and Catholic. To underline the symbolic implications, Wescott stresses that in Orfeo's friendship with Alwyn, "Something more important than good relations between sons of the family were [sic] at stake." What is "at stake" of course is the ethos to result from the interplay between two cultures—one peopled with pioneer stock, economically agrarian and morally Calvinist; the other immigrant, industrialist, and Latinate—that the two boys represent.

Wescott views this change in the American character with both optimism and sadness. In the person of Alwyn, he clearly identifies himself with Grandmother Tower's America and regrets its passing. It had levelled a wilderness and transformed it into farms and communities; its work was done. But the promise inherent in the spartan life the task had demanded was destined not to be realized. Poverty, not riches, Wescott continually re-iterates, was the harvest of the pioneers.

The future would belong to others: to the immigrant groups, whose industry Wescott both admired and distrusted, who would choose to ignore "the part [of America which] was by nature tragic;" and to the inheritors of the West, as rich, to the point of prodigality, as the Middle West had been poor.

Although *The Grandmothers*, with a complexity of theme and structure too intricate for extensive comment here, is a much more fully orchestrated work than *The Apple of the Eye*, its use of myth is similar. Dan Strane's journey at the end of the novel, symbolically a journey into adulthood, is made possible by his having been infused with the mythic knowledge of the past. Alwyn's research begins with the grandfather's manuscript history, broken off with the account of the uncompleted road that was to approach the Tower land; it ends with him trudging along what might be the same road, using his memory of landmarks mentioned in the old stories told him as a boy to guide his family to new quarters.

The image of the journey in *The Grandmothers*, as in *The Apple of the Eye*, signifies the attempt to escape from the "humbler griefs" of the Wisconsin experience. Wescott's next two books of fiction, however, indicate that the liberation his two personae thirsted for was difficult to achieve. *Good-bye, Wisconsin* (1928), a collection of ten short stories and a title essay, illustrates the problem. The essay, written by Wescott on a return journey from Europe to visit his mother, reflects on an America that is a wasteland: "the flower [of its youth] turns out to be seedless;" its future is the "riddle of a sphinx with the perfect face of a movie-star, with a dead-leaf complexion." It concludes with a good-bye to "my origins." Yet expatriation, the alternative to living in the Wasteland, is less than a salvation. His description of a character in one of the stories who has also returned from abroad seems to express his own dilemma: "Terrie was lonesome for temptations and regrets, for sharp contrasts, for distance good and evil—in other words, for Europe—but at the same time he hated these things from the bottom of his heart because they had made a fool of him." This Odyssean position of Wescott somewhere between the Land of the Lotus-Eaters that is Europe and the hard realities of his America also governs *The Babe's Bed* (1930), a privately published story he called "a melancholy fantasy upon Western themes, upon what if it were music would be folk-tunes." The fantasia issues from the protagonist's oscillations between his direct experience of life and his artistic imagination: ultimately, he must choose between the "ephemeral western town in himself" and his "distant ambition."

In the preface to *The Babe's Bed*, Wescott expressed the hope that, after the dangerous second adolescence of a writer had passed, he would learn to content himself with lesser realities in place of infinite possibilities. *The Pilgrim Hawk*, ten years later, was the apparent fruition of this hope, an abandonment of an art striving to embrace the "confusion" of his Wisconsin experience for the "lesser reality" of an art isolated from national themes. The novella, set in France, once again employs Alwyn Tower as the central character. Unlike *The Grandmothers,* however, it is a tight story, confined to Alwyn's perceptions of five other characters and a peregrine falcon kept by one of them. A creator of fictions, Alwyn weaves an ever more complex fable around the hawk as the symbol of the relationships among the characters until he suspects he has been so taken with the process that he has lost sight of the actualities. At that point, he reverses the process and the falcon which had obtruded as so forbiddingly unreal devolves into a clumsy, homely, ordinary creature. While Alwyn's—and the reader's—attention was being diverted to adorning the hawk with abstract meaning, the dynamics of the more common-place mystery of love, sustained by suspicion, uncertainty, and mutual destructiveness, were being revealed.

This technical tour-de-force has nothing to do with Wescott's "western town himself"—except when set in the context of his earlier works. Like Joyce's Daedalus, his protagonists had sought to fly by the nets of family and nationality. In *The Pilgrim Hawk*, Alwyn has finally achieved his expatriation and the artistic freedom from "humbler griefs" with which it is associated, but at a great human cost: the novella's last lines suggest he should "envy" those characters whose passions his art has made the occasion for "vengeful lyricism."

Wescott has told me that the book was written in a very short time and without the laborious revision which had accompanied his earlier fiction. Heartened by the ease of his composition, he proposed writing several novellas of the same type. *The Pilgrim Hawk* is a masterpiece, an exemplum for students of the literary craft, and it is tantalizing to speculate on the effects a succession of similar novellas would have had on his reputation. Unfortunately, his publisher discouraged him on the grounds that there was no market for such esoteric fiction. A very different novel followed instead.

The setting of *The Pilgrim Hawk* is less France than a private stage where the roles of the self join in conflict; the setting of *Apartment in Athens* (1945), ostensibly Greece, is in fact the theater of history. For the first time in his novels he abandons the device of the persona, and, deliberately removing himself from the familiar, he turns to didacticism.

> So many Americans were having to fight and to sacrifice in ignorance. I first attempted a tale of the fall of France, but I found that unwritable. . . . Then I happened to meet a hero of the Greek underground . . . and although I had never been to Greece, even as a tourist, I was inspired by his account of the German occupation of Athens to begin all over again, with Greek everyman and everywoman and everychild instead of my familiar, too familiar French.

Unlike his earlier fictions in which the line of narrative is frequently convoluted, *Apartment in Athens* proceeds along a simple outline. The Germans have occupied Greece and billeted one of their officers, a Captain Kalter, in an apartment inhabited by the Helianos family. The family at first resists their imposed subservience, but gradually they are reconciled to it by the favored position the officer's presence offers. Then, in the middle of the war, Kalter goes to Germany on leave. On his return, he appears to have been softened by the death of his wife and sons. Mr. Helianos is led by the changed climate to enter into discussions on the war with the man who shortly before had been so tyrannically arrogant. The venture proves fatal. He carelessly insults Hitler and is arrested. While Helianos is in prison, Kalter commits suicide in a way that will incriminate his host. Shortly after, Helianos is executed. The moral of the novel is sprung on the reader from Helianos's grave in the form of a letter warning his heirs to avoid his mistake of trusting the Kalters of the world and urging that his "message" be made known in America.

The author attempts to give dimension to his otherwise commonplace characters and actions by making them archetypal. Mr. Helianos represents the traditions bequeathed by classical civilization to Western culture. A former publisher and editor, he is an individualist, a man of ideas who shares the frequent failing of the intellectual mind—the reluctance to act. His adversary emerges from the dark underside of Western civilization. Kalter's very name—"the cold one"—implies a northern intrusion into Hellenic rationality. As a functionary of a corporate state, he possesses no identity outside of it. In his discussions with Helianos, Kalter plays Naphta to Helianos's Settembrini and, like Naphta, he destroys himself when his concept of life is jeopardized.

The minor characters also have a significance beyond themselves. Helianos's daughter, Leda, is throughout the novel in a state of shock, in analogy to the condition of Greece and Western Europe. Just as her mythical namesake fascinated Zeus, so she fascinates Kalter, the "Zeus" of the Helianos household. And, as the earlier Leda was raped by Zeus, so the Kalters ravish the civilization Leda Helianos represents. Leda's brother Alex also has greater symbolic than substantial importance. Like Alexander the Great, his essentially non-Hellenic namesake, Alex bears a hating, vengeful nature. From the first, his ambitions are to join the underground, to become part of a movement greater than himself and, in its name, to kill indiscriminately. When, upon Helianos's death, his mother not only retracts her opposition to his service in the underground but dedicates him to it, Wescott seems to be implying the defeat of the Greek ideal. If Greeks adopt fascist attributes, their position philosophically becomes no more desirable than that of their oppressors.

For personal reasons, Wescott has decided that *Apartment in Athens* would be his last venture into fiction making. A novelistic career which began by searching in the mythic power of a local legend for an antidote to a life-defeating Puritanism thus concluded with a mythic story of Western Civilization threatened by the temptation to surrender the self to an abstract cause. This similarity between such ostensibly dissimilar works is no coincidence, for throughout his writing Wescott has been concerned with the self's struggle for definition, amid the confusions of the present, in terms of the lesson of the past. Robert Penn Warren once defined the philosophic novelist as "one for whom the documentation of the world is constantly striving to rise to the level of generalization about values, for whom the image strives constantly to rise to symbol, for whom images always crawl into dialectic configuration, for whom the urgency of experience, no matter how vividly and strongly experience may enchant, is the urgency to know the meaning of experience. . . . For him the very act of composition [is] a way of knowing, a way of exploration." There is no better description of Wescott's practice as novelist and story writer.

JOHN DOS PASSOS

Few writers of their generation would be more likely to chafe at being paired than Wescott and Dos Passos. Aside from the quarrel to which Wescott alludes in his interview, too much seems to separate them—especially in their literary attitudes—for any comparison to be meaningful. Wescott's career has been that of a man of letters devoted to art as a fixative of transcendent truth; his fictions, in transmuting experience—usually personal—into symbols, propend towards anagogic allegory. In contrast, Dos Passos, a self-professed naturalist, has employed various forms of narration as means of social criticism and the novel particularly as a corporate chronicle. That the Marxist-influenced 'thirties disparaged Wescott while elevating Dos Passos to a position of virtual pre-eminence among living American novelists signifies the extent of their differences.

Yet, without intending to minimize the divergence in their approaches to literature (as well as to politics), I believe some striking similarities in their response to their times should be noted. Antagonism toward the Puritan view of life and toward the notion that Puritanism was the crucible of the American nation, so characteristic of the 'twenties writers, is of course a central theme throughout Wescott's works, but it is also a chord sounded repeatedly by Dos Passos. Aestheticism, its appeal as a refuge from reality and its dangers, figure prominently in *The Babe's Bed* and *The Pilgrim Hawk*— and in the young Dos Passos's fiction as well. The interplay between the lyric self and an epically portrayed society is fundamental to the two "collective novels," *The Grandmothers* and *U.S.A.*, which are their major works. In journeys to the Old World, both sought, in part, freedom from the constrictions of their homeland, and ironically discovered that the roots of their identity required the nurture of their native soil. Above all, they shared a sense of the need to revivify the experience that has made us a people. "Every generation rewrites the past," Dos Passos stated in 1941,

> We need to know what kind of firm ground other men, belonging to generations before us, have found to stand on. . . . In times of change and danger when there is a quicksand of fear

under men's reasoning, a sense of continuity with generations gone before can stretch like a lifeline across the scary present. . . .

The same sentiment is implicit in the greater part of Wescott's work.

Commentaries on Dos Passos's career generally divide it into three distinct phases. The first—from his Harvard days to the mid-'twenties —is that of the Art Novelist. In a 1937 essay, Malcolm Cowley nominated Dos Passos as one of the chief practitioners of the post-World War I fiction which argued the case of the Poet against the World. The thesis of this genre was that the sensitive young artist, after entering the world with hope and then contending against its inanities, was doomed to be crushed. To varying degrees, the protagonists of Dos Passos's first four novels fit Cowley's paradigm. Martin Howe, the venerator of stained glass amid the explosions of an ugly war in *One Man's Initiation—1917* (1920), earnestly states, contrary to all evidence, "We are too young, too needed to fail. We must find a way . . . or life is a hollow mockery." John Andrews of *Three Soldiers* (1921), who had enlisted in the army to "take refuge from the horror of the world that had fallen upon him," is carried off as a deserter at the end of the novel while the pages of music he has composed are taken by the breeze. Wenny and Fanshaw, the aesthetes of *Streets of Night* (1923), both eventually acknowledge defeat, one by committing suicide, the other by surrendering to a Prufrock-like existence. Even in the transitional novel *Manhattan Transfer* (1925), Jimmy Herf, a would-be writer, is leached of his aspirations by a dehumanized society and then cast off. All these characters are to some extent personae of the author and the judgment rendered through them is that modernity is too consumed in its carnival of mechanized savagery to heed finer sensibilities.

The works of the second phase of his career leave behind the previous tendency toward quietism, and the mood shifts from lament to vitriolic attack. The depiction of the corruption of American materialism in *Manhattan Transfer* is given broader scope in the three volumes of *U.S.A.* (1930, 1932, 1936). Formally, the triology is a more successful work, largely because Dos Passos was at last able to separate his portrayal of the aesthetic self from his panoramic view of society. Personally, too, he took to the offensive. He helped found the leftist magazine *New Masses*, was very active in committees for the defense of Sacco and Vanzetti and of "political prisoners," and associated himself with the Harlan County miners in their bitter labor dispute (which led to his being indicted for "criminal syndicalism"). For a time, the Communist Party claimed him as its own—

and lay claim to his distinctive form of novel as well. Marxist critics had been clamoring for the "collective" fiction their ideology dictated long before they had a clear conception of how such fiction would operate. When Dos Passos, who, for non-ideological reasons, had been evolving the multi-stranded narrative ever since his first novel, finally perfected the formula in the first book of *U.S.A.*, it was hailed as the model which demonstrated the theory. The combination of Party sanction and personal activism in causes embraced by the left fixed in the public mind Dos Passos's image as a Communist fellow-traveler.

In fact, he had made an expedient alliance with the C.P.U.S.A. and with others sympathetic to it, but he remained very much his own man—as he began to show his startled admirers on the left with his indictment of the Party mentality in the final segment of the triology. If, as Dos Passos repeatedly maintained, his principles remained constant, their application changed dramatically during the third phase of his career. From 1936 on, the presidential preferences of the man who had voted for the Communist candidate in 1932 move steadily rightward—Roosevelt, Dewey, Eisenhower, Nixon, Goldwater. His writings during the period follow a similar course towards conservative positions. The adverse effect this shift of allegiances had on his following was compounded by his difficulties with adopting a narrative strategy which would avoid merely copying the form of *U.S.A.* The components of the *District of Columbia* triology, for example, careen almost as wildly in their novelistic modes as they do in their subject matter: *Adventures of a Young Man* (1939) traces Glenn Spotswood's infatuation and disillusionment with Communism in a literary manner reminiscent first of Joyce and finally of Floyd Dell; for brother Tyler Spotswood's parallel disenchantment with a Huey Long-like demagogue in *Number One* (1943), Dos Passos resorted to a conventional novel; *The Grand Design* (1949), which completes the family conceit by dealing with father Herbert Spotswood's enmeshment in the bureaucratic New Deal, marks a part-way return to the tactics of *U.S.A.* All the D.C. books are weak, primarily because their nakedly didactic purposes override the demands of characterization, and although *Chosen Country* (1951) and *The Great Days* (1958), his autobiographical subsequent novels, are more convincing, it was not until *Mid-Century* (1961) that he recovered a measure of his former reputation.

Unquestionably, the course Dos Passos followed after *U.S.A.* severely damaged his reputation. He seemed to be a turncoat who had broken faith with the twentieth century and, more unforgivably, with the causes he had championed. Closer inspection of his writings, however, reveals that the reactionary current had been there all along. Like the rebellion of the early nineteenth-century Romantics, Dos Passos's battle against the conditions of his world was fueled more by the yearning for an ideal past than by the dream of perfecting the future.

To appreciate the depth of the psychological force which impelled him toward the past requires a brief consideration of the circumstances of his young life. The insecurity fostered by the trauma of illegitimate birth and the disruptions of being "carted around a good deal as a child" was exacerbated by a difficult relationship between the clumsy withdrawn boy and his driving father. A divided family background heightened his sense of not belonging. His mother, whose father had served in the Confederate Army, represented the Southern tradition of Maryland; his father, the son of a Portuguese immigrant shoemaker, rose through the practice of corporation law to hob-nob with President McKinley. What, he wondered, did this make him? School added to the confusion: with European classmates, he felt he was a "double foreigner;" in America —where, because of his illegitimacy, he was enrolled as John Roderigo Madison until his third year at Choate—he could not even be sure of his name. The effect of this "horrible childhood" was to make national ties all the more important. Not surprisingly, when *The Man Without a Country* was first read to him, he imagined himself to be Philip Nolan ("and the judge sentenced me and they took me to foreign lands"), the stateless "poor young man" who worshipped his country in secret.*

At a very early age, fatherland and father became inextricably bound together. The elder Dos Passos, something of an amateur historian who argued America's Manifest Destiny in a book called *The Anglo-Saxon Century,* preached patriotism as more than a virtue, a creed. The son's response was ambivalent. Just as he needed to believe in an ideal father, he needed to affirm his faith in an ideal America; yet, he also saw the interests his father served use

---

*Dos Passos, during his visit to the Union College campus, walked by a building named after the son of the author of *The Man Without a Country.* When I called the fact to his attention, he said, "That story meant a lot to me when I was a boy." It was not until I re-read Camera Eye 14 in *U.S.A.* and *Chosen Country* that I realized how much.

the name of American principles to trample people like his immigrant forebears.

One of his most interesting books in this regard is *Rosinante to the Road Again* (1922), a somewhat fictionalized record of his travels on the Iberian peninsula from which the Dos Passoses came. Significantly, he gave the name Telemachus to his persona. The book begins: "Telemachus had wandered so far in search of his father he had quite forgotten what he was looking for," and indeed no Odysseus is mentioned subsequently. Instead, the search for Odysseus is transvalued into a search for the meaning of the Iberian tradition and the perspective it furnishes on America. "Father" also enters in a second guise. In conjunction with the title, Telemachus sees himself as Don Quixote, "the individualist who believed in the power of man's soul over all things;" his Sancho is Lyaeus, an intelligent man of the world modelled on the author's conception of his father as a young man. This conversion of father into companion and confidant—in *One Man's Initiation,* the idealistic Martin Howe's hedonistic friend even bears as his surname the senior Dos Passos's middle name—occurs repeatedly in the early novels. Both representations of the father are intended to serve as guides who can lead the aesthete-hero down from his ivory tower toward an active role in life, but true to the Art Novel design, the hero, either unable to descend or unconvincing in his decision to do so, remains ineffectual.

As a mural of a nation, *U.S.A.* appears to avoid the private dilemma Dos Passos had inconclusively sought to resolve in its predecessors; in fact, it marks the first successful attempt to come to grips with it. Midway through the writing of the trilogy, Dos Passos postulated that the novelist should be the "architect of history." The metaphor of course reflected his earlier ambitions to study architecture, but it was also appropriate in another way. The term aptly describes his father's intention in *The Anglo-Saxon Century,* and *U.S.A.* is fundamentally the son's version of the father's book. After a succession of personae who failed because they could be only half of what was in a sense a divided self, Dos Passos at last managed to bring sensibility and action to a point of fusion by assuming his father's role.

The malaise the author had been expressing in a decade of writing was the result of the disunity of three elements: the introspective self, the tumultuous history of his time, and his sense of nationhood. *U.S.A.* represents a deliberate effort to align them. A triple biography of sorts, the trilogy begins with the three approximately simultaneous "births" of the author (the Camera Eye) himself, the century, and, in the Spanish-American War, the new Imperial America which was such a radical departure from the precepts of the early Republic. In separately developed narrative strands, maturing private lives are gradually shaped by public events until the climax is reached with the execution of Sacco and Vanzetti. Here the strands cross, indicating a whole people's complicity in this historic moment which is the culmination of the attitudes and events attending the birth of "U.S.A.," and Dos Passos, no longer the shy, intellectual spectator but an active participant in the campaign to save the Italian anarchists, delivers a bitterly eloquent denunciation of the new, conscienceless, conglomerate state. "We stand defeated America," he concludes in Camera Eye 50, but this defeat, unlike those of his earlier protagonists, is to be the beginning of future struggle against "the men of the conquering nation."

The "two nations" Dos Passos discerns in this passage are those of the oppressed and the oppressors, but they are also the eighteenth century America of his father's rhetoric and the modern perversion of the ideal. Camera Eye 50 implies that the old nation will be reinvigorated when we have restored the meaning of "the old words." Although almost everything Dos Passos produced after the Sacco-Vanzetti executions states the same theme, the point is most explicitly made in plays written "to reach a larger public" with his message. *Airways, Inc.* (1928), a drama mythically linking the executions and the Lindbergh flight, presents Americans as so bemused by the achievements of technology that they forget the past. And in *Fortune Heights* (1933), the hero reminds us, "Resistin' oppression was how this country was started," and the play closes with the words, "We got to find the United States."

Significantly, Dos Passos was himself to spend much of the rest of his life finding the United States by writing a series of histories and biographies which renewed his acquaintance with "the architects of the young republic." As a Harvard senior in 1916, he had fired a broadside at technology in an essay entitled "A Humble Protest." That protest against the demeaning of the individual by a system driven by the wealth-producing potential of its machines set the tone for all of his future works. In devoting his latter years to the company of Jefferson and his contemporaries, he was discovering and affirming political and cultural values expressive of an agrarian society. Appropriately, much of this time he was domiciled on his father's grand Virginia estate. Telemachus had concluded his search.

ROBERT PENN WARREN

Born in 1905, Robert Penn Warren is virtually a contemporary of the novelists who dominated the period between the World Wars, yet he is almost never associated with them. Too young for service in World War I, he does not record that experience which was for a literary generation as well as for a nation a rite of passage. His apprenticeship was spent in Nashville and at Oxford, not in the bistros of Paris; his mentor was Ransom, not Pound; and his circle consisted of self-conscious regionalists, not of men who fled from the constrictions of American culture to the emancipation which Europe seemed to offer. Most important, he came to fiction late, making his debut with a historical novel at a time when costume romances dominated the best-seller lists; it was not until the 'forties that critics recognized his as an outstanding talent. Further, in combining scholarship and teaching with the writing of poetry and fiction, Warren anticipated the university pattern of post-World War II writers.

In fact, his affinity with his contemporaries is far stronger than these differences seem to suggest. No writer had more to do, directly and indirectly, with reshaping the American novel after 1920 than Joseph Conrad, and Warren is perhaps the last major American novelist cast in the Conradian mold.* Like Fitzgerald and Faulkner, he has made use of the Marlovian narrator in his masterwork, and like most of the "Lost Generation" authors, he has been a "philosophic novelist," a term which he himself defined by using Conrad as the prime example. The chief resemblance, however, is thematic. Typically, Conrad's protagonist, upon discovering imperfection in himself or the world, withdraws from the contentiousness that is life into a state of negation of self; the illusion of this return to innocence, however, is eventually violated by the insistence of experience, and the protagonist (or the observer whom he serves as mentor), finally accepting an essentially tragic vision of life, resumes his place in the world. Warren, in a *credo* entitled "Knowledge and the Image of Man," describes the movement towards achievement of identity in very similar terms.

---

*Warren, in the interview which follows, says, "I don't think he influenced me," but he also acknowledges that he had read Conrad's books as "a boy of fifteen or sixteen" and that, "after Conrad, novels could never be quite the same." Comparison of Warren's novels and his critical writing on Conrad should leave little doubt about their relationship.

. . . Man's process of self-definition means that he distinguishes himself from the world and from other men. He disintegrates his primal instinctive sense of unity, he discovers separateness. In this process he discovers the pain of self-criticism and the pain of isolation. . . . In the pain of self-criticism he may develop an ideal of excellence, and an ideal of excellence, once established, implies a depersonalized communion in that ideal. In the pain of isolation he may achieve the courage and clarity of mind to envisage the tragic pathos of life, and once he realizes that the tragic experience is universal and a corollary of man's place in nature, he may return to a communion with man and nature. . . . The return . . . is the discovery of love, and law. But love through separateness and law through rebellion. Man eats of the fruit of the tree of knowledge, and falls. But if he takes another bite, he may get at least a sort of redemption.

The price of this redemption is the realization—which Warren has identified as central to Conrad—that "Man is precariously balanced in his humanity between the black inward abyss of himself and the black outward abyss of nature."

In its imagery as well as in its general outline, the first Warren novel, *Night Rider* (1939), is strikingly reminiscent of *Heart of Darkness*. Like Kurtz, Percy Munn is a man who discovers the darkness within himself and within human nature. The book opens with Munn on a train; this motif of the journey, in its metaphoric extension as a movement towards self-definition, continues throughout the story, and indeed, throughout the corpus of Warren's fiction.

Resentful of his farmer fellow-passengers, of the "pressure that was human because it was made by human beings," Munn is a typical Warren protagonist, a man who prefers the abstractions of life to life itself. Yet, fascinated by what he is not, he is attracted to the swarm of the crowd and its capacity for action. When, during a meeting of tobacco farmers organized to press for fair prices, he is called on to speak, he senses the power of the crowd and becomes its creature. Initially, his commitment is to a grand idea. As he watches the farmers adding their names to the association's roll, he feels "the grip of an absolute, throbless pleasure in which he seemed poised out of himself and, as it were, out of time." But the corruption of men, principally evinced in the betrayal by his mentor, Senator Tolliver, shatters that illusion and leads him into activities which, ironically, reveal his own corruption. He forms a Klan-like band of night riders who terrorize recalcitrant farmers, kills a man he had once saved from a murder charge, and turns from his wife, a reflection of his original ineffectualness whose face he studies as though it were a mirror, to an affair with the earthy daughter of one of his sponsors. Now confirmed in his evil, he resolves to kill Tolliver, who has been twice a kind of "father" to Munn, first at his "birth" as a noble man of action and then at his "rebirth" as a vengeful brute. Munn's obsession throughout the novel has been to be more than he is; face-to-face with Tolliver, a revolver in his hand, he makes one desperate last attempt. Responding to Tolliver's statement that Munn doesn't even know who he is, Munn says: "I do know. I'm nothing. . . . But when I do it [kill Tolliver], I won't be nothing. It came to me, Do it, do it, and you'll not be nothing." To his amazement, he cannot pull the trigger. He seems to see something of himself in the betrayer's face, and in a moment of redemption he is reconciled to their common humanity before a posse, hunting him for a murder he did not commit, brings him down in a hail of bullets.

Although the violent scene in which the explorer of darkness confronts his adversary only to meet himself is almost obligatory in a Warren novel, it is most sharply defined in his first four novels, where it is the culmination of each dramatic agon. (That these are also generally superior artistically to his later novels may not be unrelated.) In *World Enough and Time* (1950), the relationship between Jeremiah Beaumont and Cassius Fort essentially replicates the complex ties between Munn and Tolliver; in fact, when Beaumont vows to kill his former sponsor for having once seduced his wife, the words used to justify the murder—"the perfect act . . . the perfect justice self-defining and since defining self defining all else"—nearly paraphrase Munn's under similar circumstances.

In the two earlier novels, these roles are not as distinct, but the dialectic they illustrate lies at the core of the conflict. Presiding over the world of *At Heaven's Gate* (1943) is Bogan Murdock, a parallel figure to Tolliver in his "abstract passion for power, a vanity springing from an awareness of the emptiness and unreality of the self," but the function of the protagonist is divided among several characters who, like Munn, must define themselves in terms of their relationship to an embodiment of evil: Jerry Calhoun, susceptible to Murdock's manipulations because he wants to sever himself from the human misery of his past and become the apotheosis of the American dream of success; Sue Murdock, who rebels against her father's Platonic inhumanity in a series of carnal adventures; Duckfoot Blake, finally roused from his spectator's somnolence to accept and participate in life.

All the King's Men (1946), Warren's most notable achievement in fiction, also represents his fullest exploitation of the Munn-Tolliver conflict. In its simplest, architectonic form, it appears in the relationship between Adam Stanton, a man who insists that the world conform to the purity of an idea, and Willie Stark, who, to Adam, incarnates the foulness of which the world must be cleansed. Warren's implication, during his interview at Union, that the embryo of the novel was the scene in which Adam stands with a gun waiting for Stark indicates the generative force of the image he initially presented at the end of *Night Rider*. In developing that image, however, Warren chose a more complicated strategy than he had employed in his first novel. Adam, unlike Munn, pulls the trigger and he experiences no redemptive vision of himself before being shot by Stark's guards. Instead it is Jack Burden who achieves knowledge because of that act. Burden also assumes Munn's position in another, similarly vicarious way; Stark's climb to power recalls Munn's rise in the tobacco growers' groups, but it is his deputy, Jack Burden, who, like Munn, must ponder what this reveals about man and about himself.

Categorizing Conrad as a philosophic novelist, Warren called attention to his striving for "a great, massive, multi-phase symbol that would render his total vision of the world, his sense of individual destiny, his sense of man's place in nature, his sense of history and society." The structural pattern of the early Warren novels—and, to a lesser extent, the variations on it in the later works—describes his own fundamental metaphor for the human adventure. The fate of the "Munn prototype" is prepared when some quasi-deiform figure nominates him for a heroic role which elevates him above ordinary men. After devoting himself to this new life, he discovers the human clay in himself and, worse, in the Great Man to whom he owes what is, in a sense, his re-conception. He then turns on his now-tarnished patron, expecting that, by destroying him, he can salvage the idea of perfectability. But in that confrontation, or in its consequences, he comes to appreciate the truth in the aphorism Warren states through Willie Stark: "Man is conceived in sin and born in corruption and he passeth from the stink of the didie to the stench of the shroud." No father, real or surrogate, can deliver him from his heritage.

The American writer with whom Warren is inevitably bracketed is Faulkner. Both are Southerners (although they come from very different "Souths") who use their region as synecdoche for the whole of human experience. In their technical and stylistic approaches to fiction as well, there are correspondences: several Warren novels approximate Faulkner's contrapuntal narrative and both authors show a proclivity for discursive passages and lush rhetoric. The radical similarity, however, lies in their image of man as a creature trapped in history.

Both authors are doubly "mythic" in their portrayal of this theme. Apparent digressions into past events, like the Cass Mastern story or the research into the McCaslin ledgers, acquire the force of myth when they later prove to illuminate the nature of the present and future. More fundamentally, an entire novel, indeed even most of the canon, seems a modern restatement of a classical myth. Faulkner, concentrating on the imposition of civilization on a wilderness, draws on the epic story of Cadmus; Warren, more interested in the dialogue between the individual and the past that has made him, creates analogues to *Oedipus Rex*.

One of the several puns suggested by "Oidipos" (the Greek form of the name) is "I know," and although Freud has obscured the fact for us, the *hamartia* of Oedipus is not his incest with Jocasta but his relentless pursuit of the truth which ends in devastating self-knowledge. Warren, who several times has offered the equation that "Life is Motion towards Knowledge," presents a succession of characters similarly obsessed: the most recurrent question in the body of his work is "Oh, who am I?"

As in Sophocles' play, self-knowledge is often joined with some form of parricide in Warren's books. Both Percy Munn (a character conveniently linked with Thebes, Kentucky) and Jeremiah Beaumont associate the realization of their identity with the decision to murder surrogate fathers. A more elaborate example of this motif is found in *All the King's Men*, where Jack Burden's strategy for cheating his fate, like Oedipus's, ironically insures he will meet it. His quest causes the death of Judge Irwin (who he then learns is his father) and paves the way for the murder of his adopted "father," Willie Stark. "The truth," Burden reflects, "always kills the father."

In other works, the Sophoclean pattern is less direct but nonetheless present in some guise. The story about a father unwittingly murdering his son which furnished the plot for "The Ballad of Billie Potts" is American folklore; yet Warren, despite the inversion of the Oedipus story in his source, draws a Little Billie who recalls Oedipus first in fleeing his Kentuckian "Corinth" to escape his history and then in tracking his way back toward his origins. In *The Cave* (1959), Isaac Sumpter, through his responsibility for the death of his friend, gains the self-knowledge sought by his victim and thus becomes his heir. The club-footed Adam Rosensweig in *Wilderness* (1961), equipped with boots designed to hide his deformity, leaves his native Bavaria to establish a new identity fighting for the idealistic cause of the Union Army. But after a runaway slave who is in a sense a "twin self" kills their boss (a father of sorts) and, later, Adam himself shoots a Confederate soldier, he laces on his old boots, realizing that there is no escape from the congenital moral flaw which he shares with all men.

Why the Oedipus archetype has so compelled Warren is a question to which probably not even Warren knows the answer, but the thematic justification is plain. His abiding concern has been with the idealist who nourishes the illusion that he can avoid contamination from the evil of the past by floating free of time. The figure of the father, the immediate reminder that no life exists independent of history, thus becomes the chief obstacle to rebellion against the fettered conditions of his being, and it is with him that metaphysical accounts must be settled.

Warren has also made capital of the fact that the Oedipus motif of attempting to outrun knowledge of innate corruption in a new land is admirably suited to the wilderness which, for most of America's history, lay just beyond the town's chimneys. For many of our writers in the first half of our century, the attraction to deal epically with the frontier or its legacy as the basis of the American experience has been irresistible. Unlike the majority, however, who depict the frontier as an Eden and celebrate innocence, Warren has used the frontier for the opposite purpose of showing that a society's beginning, no less than an individual's, is conceived in sin. Willie Proudfit's tale in *Night Rider* of wandering in a West which is not idyllic but depraved (and then settling in Thebes, Kentucky) marks only the first phrasing of what would become a refrain in later works. The most overtly mythopoeic use of the frontier theme, however, is to be found in *Brother to Dragons* (1953). Here, Jefferson is both spiritual father to a nation and spiritual son of the frontier. He has based his life on human perfectibility, but a murder by his kinsman in western Kentucky dashes the dream of which his West was to be the realization and initiates a descent into self. Eventually, he acknowledges that the murderer had acted out of a fear that Jefferson also carries within himself; that discovery enables him, like Jack Burden, to "go into the convulsion of the world, out of history into history and the awful responsibility of Time."

Towards a New Aesthetic

Until the late 'fifties, our writers, with few and minor exceptions, were essentially realists. The subject could range from the innermost recesses of the self or, as with the naturalists, to a society from which the self was excluded as a matter of "scientific" principle, but the setting of the fiction had to be palpable and the code by which to judge actions intrinsic to the author's informing vision. Whether the reality the writer sought to illumine lay in the world or in the mind's perception of it, he presumed an iclastic correspondence between experience and the conventions of fiction.

The fatigue in this aesthetic attitude began to show in the post-World War II period. Certain that parallel great events should produce parallel artistic effects, critics jockeyed for position in sighting successors to the outstanding figures of the previous generation. Ironically, what accounts for the undistinguished literary profile of the early post war years is that most new writers were creating precisely what the critics expected: works clearly derivative from Hemingway, Faulkner, and Wolfe—but without the originals' vitality. Although the universe of the 'fifties was emphatically different from that of the 'twenties, the stories about ourselves remained essentially copies of copies.

By the end of the decade, when the shortfall in expectations was evident, the typical response was to blame the world for failing to respect the protocols of literature. Philip Roth's 1960 essay, "Writing American Fiction," is most instructive in this respect.

> [T]he American writer in the 20th century has his hands full trying to understand, and then describe, and then make *credible* much of the American reality. . . . The actuality is constantly outdoing our talents, and the culture tosses up figures almost daily that are the envy of any novelist. Who, for example, could have invented Charles Van Doren? Roy Cohn and David Schine? Sherman Adams and Bernard Goldfine? Dwight David Eisenhower? . . . [And the machination of the Nixon-Kennedy debates—] so fantastic, so weird and astonishing, that I found myself beginning to wish I had invented it.

This astonishing panorama, Roth went on to state, created "a serious occupational impediment" for the writer.

> For what will be his subject? His landscape? It is the tug of reality, its mystery and magnetism, that leads one into the writing of fiction—what then when one is not mystified, but stupefied? not drawn but repelled? It would seem that what we might

get would be a high proportion of historical novels or contemporary satire—or perhaps just nothing. No books. Yet the fact is that almost weekly one finds on the best-seller list another novel which is set in Mamaroneck or New York City or Washington, with people moving through a world of dishwashers and TV sets and advertising agencies and Senatorial investigations. It all *looks* as though the writers were still turning out books about our world. . . . But what is crucial, of course, is that these books aren't very good.

Several commentaries on the contemporary novel have quoted from Roth's forceful exposition as though it were a manifesto for the new fiction. In fact, the prescription offered was a more potent dose of realism applied to produce a more convincing affirmation of traditional humanistic values. No prognosis for the fiction of the next decade could have been more inaccurate.

What Roth neglected to notice throughout the essay was that his familiarity with the characters and events that assaulted his credulity was through television. The "incredible" figures he named are hardly rivals to the imaginary creations of even the writer for the pulps, and they seem very pale indeed beside the miscreants writers earlier in the century had to contend with (what, after all, are a Goldfine and a Cohn compared to a Ponzi and a Rasputin?). The electronic camera, however, provided a new kind of intimacy with "the grander social and political phenomena of our times," and it was this shortened perspective that startled a traditional acculturated sensibility. Had Roth directed his "astonishment" toward his reaction instead of toward the phenomena, he might have proved a better analyst of what the future held. Although the cathode ray has not been responsible for the momentous changes in our lives and values, it has had a profound effect on our perception of the world and thus on the fictions which render the world intelligible to us.

Realism, paradoxically, relies upon a clear demarcation between life and its representation.* Television has blurred the dividing line. First, in its documentary role, it serves up a diet of the remote and improbable. Second, even while investing everything it surveys with immediacy, it increases our sense of distance from the world by making us spectators of what we receive, almost literally, as the drama of our times. Third, as a medium which juxtaposes the real and the patently unreal, it tends to erase the distinction. (If this

---

*One point which illustrates this condition: a realistic writer, who trades in the probable, would not dare present a series of amazing coincidences in fiction even if they had occurred in life.

seems far-fetched, consider the implications in the fact that "Marcus Welby" gave the commencement address at a medical school this year, or that, a decade ago at Richard Nixon's law school, the students invited "Perry Mason" to lecture.) Fourth, the authority of the TV screen has given new meaning to Bishop Berkeley's *esse est percipi*. (I am reminded here of a girl's distress because a demonstration she had participated in was not shown on the evening news. "I might just as well not have gone down there," she said, weeping. "It's as though nothing happened.")

In addition to affecting our attitude toward reality, television has also influenced contemporary writing by pre-empting the realistic mode in fiction. On any one day, a viewer receives more "stories," ranging in duration from the thirty second commercial dramatization to the two hour film, than the average reader once absorbed in a year. That most of this fare is obviously not of very good quality matters far less than its quantity. The audience which once sought vicarious experience in realistic fiction now finds it in varied and superabundant supply, available at the twist of a knob.

These pressures of the presumption underlying realism and on its competitive position in the market place have stimulated the realistic instinct to seek different subject matter. The recent growth of interest in science fiction—which is actually Naturalistic in its philosophical underpinnings and realistic in its techniques—is one example. Because it lends itself better to the suggestiveness of the written word than to the verisimilitude of the camera, it has had to confront little direct competition from television for its audience. Further, "sci-fi" permits avoidance of the very blurring of the real and unreal that has troubled the writer who attempts to depict contemporary life; in this respect, despite the apparent contradiction in terms, the futuristic fiction phenomenon marks a reactionary trend. Another example is the poaching on the domain of the pornographer, not for the purpose of excitation but to deal more realistically with life. The erotic element in fiction, which once concerned the palpitations of the heart, now concentrates on the throbbing of the genitals. Here, too, although for different reasons, fiction has flourished free from the rivalry of the networks. From an aesthetic standpoint, the most curious permutation within the realistic mode has been the hyper-realism represented by Norman Mailer. Mistakenly described as journalism, Mailer's accounts of the great public events and personalities of our age are in effect grand fictions in which fact is ancillary to symbolic truth. Ever since *Advertisements for Myself*,

Mailer has been demonstrating his inability—or anyone's inability—to write the "big novel" in the great tradition. Instead, he has produced dreamscape paranovels in which the hero is Mailer's mind trying to impose form and meaning on a reality presented as disorganized fiction by the media.

Interesting as these retrenchments are as indications of realism's dilemma, they are overshadowed by the movement away from realism itself among younger writers. Rather than devise ways of accommodating their writing to the altered perceptions of reality, they have abandoned that aspect of mimesis altogether. John Barth, one of the most dazzlingly talented of this group, identified the crucial element of the new fiction when he stated that the way "to come to terms with the discrepancy between art and the Real Thing is to *affirm* the artificial element in art . . . and make the artifice part of your point." The writer's obligation, in short, is not to make credible but to fascinate.

What Barth and his fellow "fabulators"* have achieved is not merely a shift of emphasis but the most fundamental revolution in fiction in the last two hundred years. For the first time since the eighteenth century, narrative has been placed at the service of a comic vision—"comic" not because it reaches for humor (although there is a darkly humorous side to much of the fabulators' writing) but because it strikes away from experience and the notion of order in the world. In contrast to past experimentation which broke from literary conventions to seek a more fateful replication of life, "fabulation" involves sophisticated manipulation of the primitive elements of story-telling. Like the fable—or the joke—the fabulation is autonomous: everything depends upon the expression of a design.

Earlier in our century writers consciously worked within an identifiably American tradition: the fabulators, finding that tradition irrelevant to their purposes, have turned to the dawn of the novel and to the tales constituting the bulk of imaginative prose before Cervantes. This discontinuity with the national literary past, most obvious in the radical alteration in the manner of fictional representation, is also evident in the desertion of characteristically American themes. The quest for the meaning of the self in relationship to a people's heritage, which motivated so many of the previous generation's novels, no longer seems to compel our writers' imaginations: the concept of self has become too problematical and the notion of

---

*Robert Scholes's term for the group.

purposive history too disjoined from a society which has lost faith in its communal gods. The archetypal American Adam, an heroic figure who clung to the illusion of innocence amid incontestible evidence of corruption, survives, without grandeur, mainly as the object of parody (as in Terry Southern's *Candy*) or as a contemporary version of Peter Schlemiel. Most telling of all, the preoccupation with Time, not merely as the agent of mutability but as the metaphysical basis for tragic view of exile from an Edenic past, has virtually disappeared from recent fiction. What these abandonments of traditional ground suggest is the loss of the sense of a unique American experience which we needed to interpret to ourselves. The new fiction of the 'sixties and 'seventies may draw on features peculiar to American life but its attitude, like its tradition, is cosmopolitan.

The three writers in this collection who represent the latest two decades in American fiction have probably not yet reached the midpoint of their careers (Barth was born in 1930, Coover and Updike in 1932); even so, each has exhibited a variety of responses to the literary upheaval of recent years. Updike, the most traditional of them, has nevertheless veered toward playfulness with form in *The Centaur* and *Bech*, books as different from each other as they are from the rest of his works. Coover, at the very time he was writing a rather conventional novel, was also performing the radical experiments with the elements of story which were eventually published in *Pricksongs and Descants*. Barth has ranged from the black humor of his first two novels to the parodistic *Sot-Weed Factor* and *Giles Goat-Boy* to the retelling of myth in his recent groupings of short pieces. This evidence of flux contrasts sharply with the established patterns into which earlier writers settled once their apprentice works were behind them. It reflects the rapidly exploding forces loosed when a new esthetic movement comes into being. To the extent that post-1920 writers reacted to a suddenly transformed world, current writers have had to face the challenge of the sudden transformation of both the world and the imagination with which it is perceived. The signal feature of the last three interviews in this volume is the writers' consciousness of this challenge and of the strategies they have employed to meet it.

JOHN UPDIKE

From the initial comment in Updike's interview that, at thirty-eight, he no longer considers himself a young writer, to his musing near the end whether the truths of modern life are not best rendered by "rotten" novels, there is a leitmotif of dislocation from the current scene; the reader has the impression that the voice belongs to a son of an *ancien regime*.

This seems a curious mood for one whose name must inevitably appear on any list of leading writers of the last twenty-five years, whose new titles stand a better than fair chance of adorning the best-seller lists, and whose pen is as nimble today as at the start of his career when its elegant precision alerted readers to the appearance of a remarkable talent. Why, then, has he adopted the tone of a man prematurely elevated to the rank of elder statesman? Why, in the light of his continuing success and productivity, has he recently projected his own literary experience in the writer Hency Bech, eight years older than his creator, who is adjusting to the exhaustion of his creative energies?

In large measure, the answer lies in his having given allegiance in his early twenties to philosophical and aesthetic precepts which have grown steadily more suspect in his eyes as well as ours. The *zeitgeist* of the 'fifties found its most eloquent spokesman in Camus. His novels and essays humanized the principles of existentialism and offered the promise of meaningful action in a meaningless universe. Man was alienated from his environment, but in that alienation he could summon the strength to affirm his individuality. That the illusion of order in the world was in shambles was cause for rejoicing, not lament, for out of the loss of false security would come the recognition that only the moral order which the individual constituted within himself mattered. Surrender to external authority made man a slave; in revolt lay his freedom.

Camus's notion of the Absurd—a term he used to describe the irreducibility of the world to the moral vision of the individual—has been widely assumed to subtend the many forms of irrealistic literature flourishing in the 'sixties and the 'seventies. In fact, the two rest on opposite premises. For Camus and the existentialists, the individual was an integer whose meaning was defined through responsible action, and the world, however alien and indifferent, was formidably real. "I continue to believe this earth has no superior meaning," Camus states in *Lettres à un ami allemand*, "but I know that something in it makes sense, and that is man, because he is the only being who insists upon it. The world has at least the truth of man, and our task is to give man his justification against fate itself." In contrast, the so-called "absurdists" have stressed the gratuitousness in the relationships between man and act and the illusoriness of reality. Instead of adumbrating the world view inherent in the contemporary novel (and drama), Camus was actually among the last voices enunciating a tragic sense of life conceived in Europe in the nineteenth century and adopted, in the United States, by Heming-way and his contemporaries in the wake of World War I.

The vestigial Calvinism in Updike and his disinclination toward ideological constructs disqualify him for the existentialist label some critics have tried to pin on him, yet the influence of Kierkegaard, Camus, and Sartre during his intellectually formative years was significant. Reading their works in his youth, he says in the inter-view, "enabled me to become involved in life as an average, enter-prising, organized person." What he especially admired in them was the moral potential they assigned to revolt which is heroic even if doomed, particularly a revolt against death.

Updike's first novel, *The Poorhouse Fair* (1959), most clearly shows the effect of his enthusiasm for the existentialists. A new adminis-trator has ensconced himself in the poorhouse office, a conning tower-like cupola (hence his name, Conner) from which life appears to arrange itself into crystalline patterns. He would preside over his aged charges like a part-Skinnerian, part-Benthamite God, dedicated to their comfort and to the eradication of all waste. But the old people recognize that what he thinks of as a humanitarian anaesthe-tizing of their lives destroys their human dignity and they rebel. One of them articulates the case against the automatous content-ment Conner advocates: "Far from opposing the existence of virtue, suffering provides the opportunity for its exercise." In response to their physical deterioration and death's approach, they offer resis-tance, not because they expect ultimate victory but because, like Sisyphus, they know that the celebration of life requires that they scorn fate.

Although Updike obviously emphathizes with "the man of flesh, the man of passion [and] the man of thought" who oppose Conner, none, even remotely, could be called a persona. The protagonists of all but one of his subsequent novels, however, resemble Updike in one way or other; they are his contemporaries—or nearly so, and to follow the change in attitude they manifest is to trace a generation's shift of mood.

Rabbit Angstrom, the central character of Updike's second novel, *Rabbit, Run* (1960), repeatedly attempts to run from the *angst* that has suddenly filled his life. "Just yesterday [his wife] stopped being pretty," and he finds that what had passed for love has faded and no longer sustains his marriage; his work, selling kitchen gadgets, is thoroughly unfulfilling; the church, whose golf-playing minister is a secret non-believer, stands only as a shell over empty pieties. Like Nick Adams in "Big Two-Hearted River," aware that life has become the restricting swamp, he yearns for the illusion of freedom. Rabbit knows he is trapped, yet his instinct is to revert to the free existence of his youth. In the novel's brilliant opening scene, he almost ritualistically joins some schoolboys playing basketball and glories in the execution of his skill, his ease of movement on the court. Later, he enjoys momentary refuge at the home of Tothero ("tot hero"), his high school coach, who tells him that "better than the will to win . . . [is] the *sacredness* of achievement, in the form of giving our best;" but what to achieve or how to achieve it in the meaningless games of his adult world baffles Rabbit. Feeling deadness crowding in on him, he senses the importance of movement as an expression of still being alive, but unlike the poorhouse inmates, he never succeeds in attaining any symbolic triumphs. Just as his first attempt at flight, a frantic night-time drive, takes him in a circle, so his other escapes eventually return him to his problems. The novel's last words—"he runs. Ah; runs. Runs."—stress Rabbit's survival as a vital man and, at the same time, the inconclusiveness of his quest for something to affirm beyond mere existence.

In Updike's latest two novels, even the muted protest of *Rabbit, Run* is gone. Bech, the continuing character in the episodic *Bech: A Book* (1970), and the older Rabbit of *Rabbit Redux* (1971) seem to have conceded to the world's spiritual decay. Bech's memories of youth—the days of "classrooms smelling of eraser crumbs, and strolling evenings when the lights of New Jersey seemed strung gems, and male pals from whom to learn loyalty and stoicism, and the first dizzying drag on a cigarette, and the first girl to let his hands linger," —is all he has known of reality; the rest is as unreal an existence as "a coarse large doll" constructed of "the sticks and mud of his words." The young Rabbit Angstrom had felt terror at the thought of being "hung in the middle of nowhere;" Bech has reconciled himself to precisely this position: he does not run because he knows there is nothing to which or from which to run. For the young enthusiast who is interviewing him, Bech reflects on his middle position:

> he described his melancholy feelings in the go-go place last night, his intuition that self aggrandizement and entrepreneurial energy were what made the world go and that slogans and move-

ments to the contrary were evil dreams, evil in that they distracted people from the particular, concrete realities, whence all goodness and effectiveness derive. He was an Aristotelian and not a Platonist. Write him down, if you must write him down as something, as a disbeliever; he disbelieved in the Pope, in the Kremlin, in the Vietcong, in the American eagle, in astrology, Arthur Schlesinger, Eldridge Cleaver, Senator Eastland, and Eastman Kodak. Nor did he believe overmuch in his disbelief.

The portrayal of man in suspension seems even more trenchant in the second Angstrom novel, largely because it plays off our memory of its hero when he was "still fighting." In Rabbit's early middle age, the social system he had opposed—and through opposition, sought to redeem—is in disarray. Riots threaten the cities, Vietnam is a lingering national nightmare, the young have turned to drugs, marriage has been weakened by the acid of pleasure-seeking. The anarchy has invaded his private life—his wife is openly having an affair with a Greek car salesman, which he tolerates because he is spiritually powerless to condemn it. Thoroughly confounded, he mindlessly embraces traditional pieties. Patriotism looms as an especially important value because it fulfills his need to locate roots in something outside himself, and he goes to Orwellian lengths to justify his faith. "America is beyond power," he thinks, "it acts as in a dream, as a face of God. Wherever America is, there is freedom, and wherever America is not, madness rules with chains, darkness strangles millions. Beneath patient bombers, paradise is possible." One third of the way into the novel, however, Rabbit is bedding down with an anti-establishment, acid-dropping teeny-bopper in his house, and at the half-way point, a raving black militant has joined the menage. None of this implies Rabbit's conversion: rather, he has surrendered to the madness. At the end of the novel, the Angstroms tentatively pledge themselves to a reconciliation, not because they have resolved their differences but because they are tired. The final words—"sleeps. He. She. Sleeps. O.K.?"—return us to the closing five words of *Rabbit, Run*. They point up to contrast between the hero striving against his limits and the victim acquiescing in his fate.

Updike's gradual retreat from a 'fifties world-view which he then shared with his generation to a more problematical apperception of reality is related to the apparent uncertainty over aesthetic premises he intimates during the interview. The art of the realist depends upon the audience being able to participate in his assumptions about the values to be derived from the nature of the world. If this relationship lacks a firm basis in common belief, metaphor cannot operate. *Couples* (1968) illustrates the difficulty Updike has had in communicating his vision to his public. Written as "a loving portrait of life in America," it was read—and not just by Hollywood types—as a satire; "a romantic book" was received as an excoriating attack or as opportunistic pornography.

The problem is compounded when Updike, as a realist committed to the world as he finds it, tries to reconcile the "rottenness" he senses in it with his religious need to celebrate life. In a 1962 short story, he succinctly stated his creed as a writer: his rendering of a selected portion of reality should be like "a piece of turf torn from a meadow [which] becomes a *gloria* when drawn by Durer. Details. Details are the giant's fingers. He seizes the stick and strips the bark and shows, burning beneath, the moist white wood of joy." In the decade since the passage was written, the faith on which it was predicated has been severely strained as life, stripped of its bark, unremittingly shows Updike solipsism and self-centeredness.

As a result, his writing has become increasingly ironic in its underlying attitude. *The Centaur* (1963) is perhaps the most obvious example of this. Peter, its narrator, is "haunted . . . by the suspicion that a wholly different world, gaudy and momentous, has enacted its myths just around the corners of my eyes," and he constantly interprets his poignantly drab world in wondrous terms. The author's purpose is not to assert the coalscence of myth and life (as numerous critics have assumed) but to establish, through what Updike called "the counterpoint of ideality," the distance between them. The epilogue emphasizes this estrangement from the "longings in our minds":

> "Zeus has loved his old friend [Chiron, the mythic analogue to Caldwell, the novel's hero who is modeled on Updike's father], and lifted him up, and set him among the stars as the constellation Sagittarius. . . . though in this latter time few living mortals cast their eyes respectfully toward Heaven, and fewer still sit as students to the stars."

Updike has referred to the book as, in part, a "joke." Some commentators have mistakenly inferred that he intended it as lighthearted humor, but what he meant to suggest, I suspect, is the cosmic joke played on our aspirations. A similar dark laughter is heard in his more recent novels. *Bech*, particularly in its final section, ironically juxtaposes its writer-protagonist's pretensions as an artist and his exhaustion as a man, and *Rabbit Redux* reminds us of the woes Job endured because of a bit of raillery in Heaven.

Among the major writers of his generation, Updike is an anomaly: painfully aware of the unrealistic topography of contemporary experience, he remains devoted to the meticulous notation of the ordinary. In Richard Locke's phrase, he is our outstanding "reporter of the secular news." Yet in assuming that role, he has not turned his back on the philosophical concerns which trouble the contemporary literary imagination. Most serious fiction for the past decade has dealt in some way with the notion of an entropic universe—indeed, literature's turning back on itself in its penchant for design may reflect an attempt to derive from the artificial a vitality which the natural is no longer able to proffer. Updike's bedrooms in Olinger, Brewer, and Tarbox at first seem far removed from preoccupation with the behavior of the universal machine, but in fact, a sense of dissipating energies pervades all of his novels and many of his short stories. Norbert Wiener has observed that, as entropy increases, "there are local enclaves whose direction seems opposed to that of the universe at large."* The erotic agitation so often portrayed in Updike's fiction suggests just such an effort to counter inexorable and omnipresent decay.

John Barth

From the evanescence of certainty which has drained traditional fiction of its energy, Barth has drawn the primary conditions of his stories. "God wasn't too bad a novelist," he has puckishly observed, "except he was a Realist." Given the world as a grand fiction developed according to conventions which, in their very "realism," affront the modern imagination, Barth has preferred to "re-invent the world" in a fabulistic manner. No exponent of the new fiction has staked out greater ambitions for it or has better realized its possibilities.

Superficially, Barth's first two novels seem closer to the traditional novel of this century than to the exercises in fabulation of the 'sixties and 'seventies. Their Maryland settings are identifiable parts of our world, and the inhabitants of Cambridge and Wicomico do not differ in kind from our neighbors. On closer inspection, however, we begin to realize that his crucial redactions from the range of human experience serve to estrange us from the familiar world which the realist, in contrast, strives to invoke.

One has only to examine his use of the mirror—itself, since

---

*The relevance of Wiener's views of entropy to current fiction is developed at length in Tony Tanner's *City of Words* (New York, 1971).

Stendhal, a traditional metaphor for the novel—to gauge his differences with the realists. In *The Floating Opera* (1956), Todd Andrews happens to see a reflection of his sexual initiation; the disjunction between his amatory self-image and the animalistic fact causes an explosion of destructive, uncontrollable laughter, "for a mirror can reflect only what it sees, and what it sees is screamingly funny." A similar perception of absurdity lies at the center of *The End of the Road* (1958). Jack Horner tries to entice Rennie Morgan to eavesdrop on her husband Joe. She refuses at first, insisting, "*Real* people aren't any different when they're alone. No masks. What you see of them is authentic." (Rennie's trust in Joe's authenticity—mentioned some seven times on one page—has the quality of religious faith.) When curiosity finally lures her to the window, the stability of her world is shattered: Joe, after executing a series of military commands, gurgles like an idiot at the mirror; then, "his tongue gripped purposefully between his lips at the side of his mouth, [he began] masturbating and picking his nose at the same time." Jake's point— that "nobody is authentic"—is proved, and Rennie relapses into chaos and eventual destruction.

Neither book is quite a conventional novel. In *The Floating Opera*, the sailing back and forth in time goes far beyond the custom of flashback: Captain Adam's floating minstrel show too undisguisedly serves the author's symbolic purposes. *The End of the Road,* with its elaborations on Jake's "mythotherapy," makes even less concession to the probable. But each was far enough inside the established precincts for critics who were watching Barth's development to be startled in 1960 when he published *The Sot-Weed Factor*, a parodistic extravaganza evolved from a 1708 poem and inspired by Fielding's *Tom Jones*. Six years later, the appearance of *Giles Goat-Boy*, in which the Cold War is transmogrified into the setting for a fantasia blending archetypes from *Oedipus Rex* to *The Wizard of Oz*, confirmed that *Sot-Weed* had not been a temporary aberration. "Start [ing] with the premise of the 'end of literature,' " Barth had moved narrative fiction onto new ground by "turn[ing] it against itself."

The obvious difference between the "relatively realistic" early novels and the exploded vision presented in his subsequent works has prompted critics to concentrate on the metamorphosis the author apparently underwent after an initial, exploratory phase in his career. Behind the marked shift in strategy, however, lies the same aesthetic and philosophical problem. If all speculations on the nature of reality are perforce tentative, as Barth repeatedly implies through his characters, what is to be the basis for the pattern of action which orders and sustains the narrative?

The solution he hit on in *The Floating Opera* was to posit a certainty (the protagonist's decision to end his "voyage" by committing suicide) and then, after it has operated as a point of reference for the events of the novel, to destroy its basis at the conclusion. A similar conception governs *The End of the Road*. Jake Horner is sent out into the world by his doctor with an injunction to act according to arbitrary rules, to force life to conform to whatever "myth" he would impose upon it. But at the terminus of his journey, Jake discovers that no system can contain life's flux. Although the scenery along the paths of experience in Barth's later fiction changes dimension, his heroes arrive at conclusions which, like Todd's and Jake's, negate the premises that attended the launching of their adventures. As if pursuing the "mythotherapy" which had been prescribed for Jake, Ebenezer Cooke in *Sot-Weed* proclaims himself a virgin poet and, like Don Quixote, strides forth to redeem the universe; at the end, he acknowledges that the innocence he had worn as a badge of strength is paradoxically "the true Original Sin" and he awakes from his dream of subjecting life to a set of abstract precepts. The goatboy's quest closely parallels Cooke's. After consecrating himself to the attainment of his identity as "Grand Tutor," he tries to penetrate the contradictions of his own teachings, but every advance brings him back to his starting point; finally, he is "delivered" when he realizes that the way out of Zeno's paradox is to ignore it and act, not in conformity to an idealized code but in response to the exigencies of the moment.

The correlate of what Barth calls "cosmopsis," or paralysis, is the impossibility of certifying an identity in a universe in which neither Heraclitus nor the stream is fixed. As Henry Burlingame, Cooke's tutor, states, "'Tis but a grossness of perception, is't not, that lets us speak of *Thames* and *Tigris*, . . . but especially *me* and *thee,* as though what went by those names or others in time past hath some connection with the present object? I'faith, for that matter how is't we speak of *objects* if not that our coarse vision fails to note their change?" Yet, despite the evidence, Burlingame maintains, "One must *assert*, assert, assert, or go screaming mad." Virtually all of Barth's protagonists have provisional identities (e.g., "In a sense, I am Jacob Horner"), and we are constantly made aware that the interactions between characters are really the interactions of the guises they wear. This problem of shifting identities finds its proper myth-ological analogue in the "Menelaiad" section of *Lost in the Fun-house* (1968), where Proteus, in a carnival of stultifying confusion, assumes multiple personalities, including the narrator's own; the indeterminate Proteus perfectly suits fiction attempting to contend with a Quantum Theory cosmos.

As Barth has extended his terrain further beyond the "real," he has perhaps lost as many admirers by his virtuosity as he has won. Tony Tanner's discomfiture with the later Barth is typical. In writ-ing about *Lost in the Funhouse*, he laments the "impasse" Barth has apparently reached: "he can no longer get hold of any 'reality' at all; everything he touches turns into fictions and yet more fictions." Tanner is undoubtedly one of the most astute appraisers of con-temporary fiction, but here, like others who dismiss Barth's narrative ingenuity as "stunts," he misses the point. What he intends as an adverse judgment on an author "lost" in the funhouse of his craft actually describes the vision of the world which informs all of Barth's writing. *Lost in the Funhouse* represents no more an impasse than Barth's first novel, about being lost in life's floating opera, or any of the other novels which similarly deal with the futility of trusting to transcendent certainties.

Although an introduction is obviously not the place for a detailed discussion of a work, this remarkable gathering of stories deserves more scrutiny than it has received, for it may be the most indispens-able of Barth's books to an understanding of his artistic imagination.

All of the *Funhouse* stories are encased within "Frame-Tale," a Möbius strip on which the words "Once upon a time there was a story that began" join, head to tail, in an endless circle. The inner series of stories (and Barth properly insists that they be read serially) are related much as the words on the strip are related. The first story in a sense grows out of the last; and just as one must follow the coil of the strip, the stories proceed along a "turning [of] as many aspects of the fiction as possible—the structure, the narrative view-point, the means of presentation, in some instances the process of composition and/or recitation as well as of reading or listening—into dramatically relevant emblems of the theme." The circularity of the sentence on the strip undermines the linear convention on which sentence structure is predicated; similarly, each story, as it progresses, undermines the conventions which sustain it. The process is akin to what he does in his other books: working steadily against an initial premise or turning the literary tradition against itself.

Thematically, too, the series recapitulates the preceding Barth novels. The protagonist and setting of "Night-Sea Journey," the first item in the series, are never explicitly revealed. To the extent that a fictional voice must be embodied in something and exist somewhere, the "I" of the story, we slowly realize, is a sperm and his world is the womb; if this discovery were all that was to intrigue us, however, then the charge of preciosity which has been leveled at the story would be justified. But "I" is essentially a role, abstracted from specific being, and the sea the unplaced situation. The agent of the role could be many things—among them, sperm, author, and mankind, just as the environment might be womb, the readers' minds, history —but in essence, "I" is the quester, the typical Barth hero who unsuccessfully seeks the ultimate basis and purpose of his identity. The eleven following stories raise different aspects of the search until the last returns us to the propositions of the first. "Anonymiad" illustrates man's solipsism. A minstrel, tricked by his human desires onto a desolate island, creates fictions, "dreams more real that the itch that had marooned [him]." These products of his loneliness, which correspond to the stories Barth (or the initial "I") has given us in the preceding pages, are at once the stuff of life and fictions reflecting life's experience. "I," again the quester, "ejaculates" them into empty wine vessels and casts them into the sea with the fragile hope that, as the only proof of his existence, they will be read and his identity established.

ROBERT COOVER

The bibliography of Coover's books is shorter than that of any of the other writers in this volume; even so, it presents the greatest range of styles. His two novels—one an exercise in naturalism, the other a fantasy—seem written by different authors; the collections of short fictions and plays that he has more recently published are exuberant experiments formally unlike the novels. The spread of his subjects has been similarly broad: from the birth of a new religion to an awakened Rip Van Winkle's musings on the significance of his twenty-year sleep. Subtending this diversity, however, is a continuing attitude toward the role of the fiction maker in an age of depleted forms. In a dedicatory essay on Cervantes, Coover, keenly aware of living in a transitional period in history, claims as his tutelary spirit the Spanish master who also bridged two worlds.

What he says of Cervantes's stories indicates his intentions for his own fictions: "they struggled against the unconscious mythic residue in human life and sought to synthesize the unsynthesizable, sallied forth against adolescent thought-modes and exhausted art forms, and returned home with new complexities."

The Origin of the Brunists (1966) would seem an unlikely starting point for a disciple of Cervantes. Its setting is a small coal mining town whose inhabitants represent the ordinary run of stunted lives. When an explosion seals a section of the mine, all the trapped men die except one old man who should have had the least chance of survival. The community, responding to its latent spiritual needs, endows the event with supernatural significance, and soon an apocalyptic sect arises, taking the survivor, Giovanni Bruno, as its Messiah.

Although the events of *Brunists* are as bizarre as those of any absurdist novel, the narrative follows a classically naturalistic line. Coover intimates during the interview that his adherence to traditional practices resulted partly from commercial pressures and partly from a desire to test his ability to "handle the [novel] form as it now was in the world." Yet, finally, his commitment to the convention of naturalism serves an ironic purpose. Much as Cervantes combined the traditions of the earthy *picaro* adventure tale with the idealized sentimentality of the romance in *Don Quixote,* Coover plays the naturalistic surface of his story against the suggestion, at a deeper level, of the Johannine sections of the Bible. The intention, like Cervantes's, is serious, complex parody. At the same time that the account of the first days of the Brunist religion mocks the origins of Christianity and its commercialized "mythic residue," it dramatizes the compelling force and vital necessity of religious fictions for the human imagination.

Coover's best known work, *The Universal Baseball Association, Inc., J. Henry Waugh, Prop.* (1968), is only incidentally about baseball, or more precisely, about a parlor game based on the sport. Its true subject, like that of *Brunists,* is the relationship between life and the fictions which order it—in a sense, between man and his theological constructs.

The novel juxtaposes the tawdry existence of a marginal man, Henry Waugh, to the vibrant, imaginary world-as-baseball-league he animates by rolling dice. Invented to fill the emptiness of his time, the game becomes an obsession. So fascinated is he by the interplay between the necessity represented by the laws of probability on which the game is based and the modulations of those laws magically effected through the names and distinctive biographies he gives his players, that he neglects his work and even his creative needs. Like an author-God presiding over his creations, he meticulously records their activities in his ledgers, unaware that the Association history is taking on the quality of religious myth.

At the start of the novel, rookie Damon Rutherford pitches a perfect game. An ecstatic Waugh confidently predicts a new era of the U.B.A. as glorious as the Golden Age of the league's beginning years. His intuition proves perversely correct. While Damon is at bat, unusual combinations of the dice send Waugh to his Extraordinary Occurrences Chart, which decrees that the batter be killed. What Waugh has not realized is that Damon is a Christ-figure (just as the Golden Age is the Old Testament) and that the new era must therefore be inaugurated with the perfect rookie's death. The myth, now more powerful than its maker, has assumed a life of its own. Waugh grieves for his fallen star and thinks of abandoning the suddenly joyless Association, but he cannot: "Odd thing about an operation like this league," he reflects, "once you set it in motion, you were yourself launched into the same orbit." Many years later, Waugh either has departed from the scene or survives only as an umpire in the Association itself (Coover seems to insist on the ambiguity), but new generations of players ritually re-enact Damon's death. Fictions breed new fictions which, paradoxically, incorporate their generators. The world, God's own fiction, in turn re-invents God as it re-tells the story of itself.

In both *Pricksongs and Descants* (1969) and *A Theological Position* (1972), Coover, conscious that we are at once the makers and products of a new world-fiction, continues to use "familiar mythic or historical forms to combat the contents of those forms." Among the stories in the former and the plays in the latter are recastings of fairy tales and biblical material, of Billy the Kid and Rip Van Winkle. Coover's purpose is not to vary stock situations in search of new effects but to challenge a vision of the world trained by our traditional fictions. The same intention governs the volumes' "original" fictions, which shatter the pieties we expect our writers to observe. In "The Babysitter," for example, the author refuses to resolve a single story line for his characters: the sitter is/is not ravished by her employer/her charges/her friends/a mysterious stranger; she drowns/does not drown the baby; etc. As in solitaire, any number of games is possible, depending on which card the player turns over when confronted by a choice; Coover's strategy is to play all the games at once.

It is most unlikely that the irrational geometries of cerebral delight offered by the Coovers and Barths will ever command a public commensurate with that which read Hemingway and Fitzgerald, or even James and Hawthorne. Though we may never have had such profligacy of brilliant fictions as at this moment in history, the age of the dominance of written fiction has surely been swamped by the emanations of mass culture. The very inhospitality of social conditions, however, is cause for hope, for the writer, freed from the compromising demands of a mass audience, will be able as never before to explore the peculiar elements of his craft and to reinvigorate the art.

FRANK GADO

Schenectady, 1973

FIRST PERSON

Conversations on Writers & Writing

Glenway Wescott

You began publishing in Chicago at a time when Sherwood Anderson was a kind of godfather to young writers there. Was he much of an influence on you?

Very much, yes. Sherwood was very dear to me and I admired him immensely.

I strongly sensed Anderson when I read The Apple of the Eye *several years ago.*

Oh, I don't know that I would say I could see that direct a literary influence. We wrote differently. He had a knack for writing vernacular that I never had. I haven't got a very good ear for what I call baby talk.

I don't think Anderson's influence was as specific in *The Apple of the Eye* as Lawrence's. From my point of view, that book came smack out of *Sons and Lovers*. I was very much aware of it at the time. *Sons and Lovers* is a book I love, and I was conscious of doing the same kind of thing from my own family background.

The question of just how deeply Lawrence has affected my writing interests me. A few years ago, Frieda Lawrence sent a message to me saying that *The Pilgrim Hawk* was obviously very much indebted to Lawrence; she thought it rather amusing that I never acknowledged this. I was quite astonished because it hadn't occurred to me. It still doesn't seem to be very plausible, and yet there is that business of the symbolical animal which Lawrence did so well so many times. It's in *St. Mawr, The Fox,* and *The White Peacock,* as well as in the more symbolical things like *The Plumed Serpent.* Maybe I got it where Lawrence got it.

Han struck me as being quite Andersonian. She is very much like the old woman in "Death in the Woods" as well as like some of the

3

characters in Winesburg, Ohio. *Surely, there is no character in* Sons and Lovers *who corresponds to Han.*

No, that's true.

And isn't she, in a sense, the central character of The Apple of the Eye?

Yes—well, certainly to this extent: that book started with a story I wrote when I was seventeen years old about that woman, a woman I knew. She had lived adjacent to my mother when my mother was a girl. She was a bad woman—a bad-good woman, an earth mother person. My mother and her family, although they were pious and virtuous, were fond of her and appreciated her. She was very mysterious to me; I suppose that was why I wrote about her.

There are two parts to the book which represent levels of my own maturity. I began with the "Bad Han" part, which actually had been published before much of the rest was written. With the money that *Dial* magazine paid me for "Bad Han," I buckled down and wrote the rest. I think the "Bad Han" part is probably the best. I worked over it the most.

As a matter of fact, I am very interested in that book right now because I have at last managed to get a publisher's editor interested in it. I've been trying to get it back into print for years and years without success.

It was erroneously listed as being in paperback about three years ago. I looked for it, but it never did come out.

No, no one would ever touch it.

I looked at it just the other day. I'm going to have a little exhibition of manuscripts in connection with my election to the American Academy. I decided I would put in *The Apple of the Eye* manuscript because, for one thing, it was rather amusing: the first section in my handwriting had been torn in two by me and thrown on the floor—it still is in two pieces.

Anticipating its re-publication, I wanted to put back a lot of words that were cut out by my publisher's lawyer in the mealy-mouthed climate of those days. Then when I read it, I found to my great surprise that I myself had removed a good many sexy paragraphs, including one or two rather daring episodes of a bull and a cow in intercourse that I had described very voluptuously and a rather long erotic dream that went on for two or three pages. In fact, I found I had improved the text a good deal in the last version, taking out the lushness of the sensual adjectives and trimming the over-blown prose. My talent is supposed to be in a less romantic direction anyway, so I probably hadn't taken these things out just because I was timid, but because of taste.

I've decided now, however, that I'm going to have it all typed out as it originally stood—a maximum text—and then go over it again and publish as full a version as I can make. I'm not going to try to improve it, but just to put those things—or at least, some of those things—back.

Have you been emboldened by such things as Faulkner's treatment of the love affair between Ike Snopes and the cow?

That's one writer who hasn't influenced me. Not at all. He's one of my rather blind spots. I don't like Faulkner, although I respect him immensely. I'm aware of his greatness, his genius, and his merits, but he's not reading matter for me.

The 'twenties are now seen as a turning point in our literature. Were you conscious at that time of striving for a new aesthetic theory of fiction? For instance, did Eugene Jolas's "Revolution of the Word" have any impact on you at all, or was this just something else that was going on in Paris?

Just something else that was going on—Montparnasse stuff. What the painters—the Dadaists, the Surrealistes—were doing was so much more vigorous than what the writers were doing at that time. I think we were conscious of subject matter more than we were of experiments. All the writers, or most of us, were really—classicists isn't precisely the word—but conservatives as to the form.

In that you were aiming for a leanness of line and a simplicity of words?

More for narrative prose as an expressive instrument rather than as a display of art, or as a way of showing off, or as a way of changing anything. I think that's one thing that Hemingway, for example, had in common with me, though he was a vernacular writer and I wasn't. Above all, what he was striving for was effectiveness of expression in narrative.

It's interesting the way interest in experimentation has developed. Now, suddenly, there's a much more numerous school of people experimenting with writing than there was in the 'twenties. I don't quite know what it means, because the experimentation doesn't seem to be very new any more. But a great many people seem to be trying to pick up and practice the innovations of the 'twenties.

Isn't this part of what is called "camp?" Camp, after all, is titillating with dead things, things that have been done—a revival of the past in a rather uncreative way.

I hadn't thought of it, but that's a point very well taken. Have any of the theorists of camp—like Miss Sontag—made that point?

I got this from another professor on campus.

Well, it's new to me. Camp is fancy dress. It's making believe for one reason or another. Oddly, critics seem to have overlooked the homosexual element in the development of camp—camp talk and camp humor. I confess, despite all this recent fuss about it, I haven't been paying too much attention because I'm not very interested in those writers. I'm really getting rather too old for fun and games.

You were saying this morning that Gertrude Stein once referred to you as "syrup that does not pour." How relevant or accurate a description of your working style would you say this is?

Well, I'd have to talk an awfully long time about myself to make my own feeling about that clear because, of course, it strikes very deep into my psychology—into my life story. The main thing is that I never had a sense of vocation. I began to write for quite worldly and personal reasons, just experimentally, without any sense that I had any great ability or any vocation to be a writer. But then I had some success with it all along the line.

I got what I wanted by means of writing, but I have had an uneasy feeling of being a bluff, a fake. I've been insecure for that reason, and therefore I've worked, worked, worked, worked, worked in order to do the best I could. Having drawn this check with no funds in the bank, I had to work like fury to get some money there before the check came due, and this gave me an uneasy feeling. I don't think that I had very much talent, but I've always seemed to people around me very promising, very gifted. I've been given a good life for going along with the concept that I was an important writer who was going to get more and more important. I don't mean to say that, when I was a young man, I thought of this in any way as a swindle; only that, in the back of my mind, there has been an uneasiness and an anxiety.

The fact of the matter is that, if I'd been very much discouraged as a young writer, I would have stopped. I was talking to a young novelist the other day who is sort of a protegé of Albert Guerard. I was introduced to him, a nice friendly boy, and I read his book. I wasn't terribly impressed with the book—he'd written it far too large and then cut it down far too much, too fast—but it was a good, promising work. Harper's published it with Albert Guerard's foreword, and it wasn't even reviewed—at least it wasn't reviewed in any of the New York papers. Now, if that had happened to me with *The Apple of the Eye,* I would have quit. Instead, I was a young prince overnight.

Although *The Apple of the Eye* only sold about three thousand copies, my publisher was eager to go on. He wanted me to write another sexy, romantic novel to follow along the lines of the first. But I wanted to go abroad. I asked him for an advance of a certain sum. He wouldn't give it to me. He would only advance a thousand dollars because I wanted to write *The Grandmothers* and he didn't want me to write *The Grandmothers.* He thought this was going to be a stuffy old anti-macassar thing about my grandmother. (Well, actually, it might have been. I had promised my grandmother I would write that book—which is a not very fictitious account of my family traditions—and I thought I'd better hurry and write it before I forgot all the things that I knew.)

Anyway, there I was, twenty-three years old, with a published first novel. All my friends knew I was trying to get money from the publisher to go abroad and write *The Grandmothers.* One night I went to a studio party in Greenwich Village where I met a very typical aristocratic woman whose husband was a friend of the hostess. She said she had read *The Apple of the Eye* and had liked it. She had heard, not from me but from my friend, that I was trying to raise enough to go to Europe. The next morning I got in the mail a check for three thousand dollars. That was a lot of money in those days. With it was a note saying, "I don't wish to be a patroness of literature. I don't want to know you or be friends with you. Any experiences I have had along that line have been very distressing. I don't want to know you at all. Just take this—I happen to have this windfall of money that I don't need. Go abroad and write your book." I replied that I understood her not wanting to be my patroness, but that I wanted to call on her to say thank you as I'd been politely brought up by my mother to do. Needless to say, I befriended her; in due turn she got into trouble in her life and I meant a great deal to her. I knew her intimately until she died. It was a very close and responsible relationship.

Generally, that's a good climate for writers, but it was not good for me. All this was a part of my problem: I got into a situation where I couldn't back out. Everyone expected me to write novels, in spite of the fact that from my point of view, I was always late on everything. This has plagued me all my life.

I have aborted five novels. I've worked for two years at a time at a novel that wasn't worth anything. I just threw it away. People say, "Oh, that's just because you're a neurotic." Whereupon I say, "Well, read the goddamn stuff." Whereupon they do, and then they know I'm not making talk.

I know now that I'll never be a novelist. I'm never going to try it anymore. I know now what I can do, and I can do exactly what I want to do. If I take time enough, I can get to a point where I won't want to change more than a comma. Four or five years later, I'll look at the book and I'll be absolutely satisfied with it.

I'm now sixty-four and I haven't had to do anything else but write because a literature-loving family has supported me all these years. I've not been rich—in fact I've had a rather restrained and austere life—but I haven't had to write for a living. They provided me a living and absolute independence. It would be a pity to devote sixty-four years of your life, as hard as you could, just to being a writer. I've never done anything I didn't want to do, and I've never written anything just for money.

So you see what I mean about not pouring. I've never had the facile talent, and I've never had a great outgoing self-assurance and fluency.

Do you still think of The Grandmothers *as less than an important book?*

Oh, I think *The Grandmothers* is an important book. I've learned to think that. I'm very poor at giving opinions of my work because I don't read it very much. I think that *The Grandmothers* was my good luck. A lot of other people could have written that book, only they didn't. I had the idea of doing it and did it well enough. It was a book that needed to be done, but in a sense it isn't a very original book. It's everybody's book. It's a "collectivity."

So many writers at that time were concerned with America, with what America was, with what their relationship was to America, with the failed American dream. . . .

Well, I'm modest enough, as you have noticed, but every now and then I brag. Look at the dates. *The Grandmothers* was a very early book.

Pre-dates Wolfe.

Pre-dates all that stuff.

But it looks forward to real problems of America even after World War II. The election of John F. Kennedy . . .

No.

. . . is something of a manifestation of the ascendency of those descended from Catholic immigrants, . . .

No.

You don't see any of this?

No. No. I blush. I like to hear that, but I blush. I hope it's true.

Is Images of Truth *an example of what you've discovered you can do now?*

I'm writing one or two more portraits, biographical portraits. I don't think I'll be doing much more criticism, although I enjoy it and I'm in great demand as a critic now and very fashionable.

Mr. Gado flattered me before by saying that I don't repeat myself. I find it difficult to repeat myself, actually. Every time I've published a book, I've thought, "Well, at last, I've learned. Now I can do it. I'll be able to do a series of books like this." Then I try, and I can't do a damn thing until it's died down to nowhere. Then a few little shoots start up again. I just can't do the same thing over, but now I don't really want to.

I don't think that's been very good for my career though, because

I notice that people who like *The Grandmothers* loathe *The Pilgrim Hawk,* and people who like *The Apple of the Eye* loathe everything else, and people who like me as a critic or as an essayist think I never should have written anything else at all. My old friend Mr. Maugham thinks I'm the Madame de Sevigne of this century—the last of the living letter-writers.

How close were you to Somerset Maugham?

Oh, I knew him very well. He's one of my very dear friends.

Does he still communicate with people?

He's not supposed to except for about half an hour a day now and then. He's ninety-three. I had a letter from him, dictated two or three months ago, but he's in frightful shape, the poor creature. He's not only senile, he's mad; he has delusions and thinks people are persecuting him. Sometimes he curses in the middle of the night. Then it will clear up and he'll be fine for an hour or so. He has, fortunately, an admirable old secretary, a friend, who lives with him and looks after everything.

I wrote an obituary for Somerset Maugham six weeks ago. He was thought to be dying. He passed into a coma, and they took him to a hospital. Actually it was a very curious circumstance, because there had just been a very tragic death in my family. (As a matter of fact, it was the wife of the babe in "The Babe's Bed"; she died of a hideous cancer.) There had to be some kind of a funeral service for the family and they had asked me to read pantheist poetry. I couldn't find enough pantheist poems, so I was writing a little funeral sermon. While I was doing this on Friday—it had to be done by Sunday—*Life* called in the middle of the night and wanted an obituary of Maugham before Tuesday night because that was their deadline. I didn't dare say no. They offered me a very good fee, and besides, I didn't want them to do it themselves. I wanted to do it, because I feel very sorry for Maugham. He has had a tragic old age —partially his own fault, partially not—and I felt obliged to do it. So I said I would. Fortunately, he didn't die. When it was announced on Monday afternoon that he'd gone out of the hospital under his own steam, I laughed aloud because I thought I was probably the only person in the world who was glad. Including Willie. He was certainly not glad. I worked all the rest of the week and wrote a thing that I liked very much which they are now holding.

Which is the way they ought to do anyway. It's ludicrous to have to write these things on a deadline.

Sherwood Anderson once wrote a little piece about Gertrude Stein in which he described her as a New England farm woman working in her kitchen, making word cookies. It's the only thing I've read about her that makes some sense of the way she wrote.

I think that could be said of quite a lot of writers. It could be said of Marianne Moore, of that sort of eccentric, hardworking, independent writer who has an idea of something to do, who has a recipe. But there are curious other elements in Gertrude Stein's case. For one thing, she was a very brainy woman and a brilliant student at Yale. Studying under Munsterberg and William James, she had made a considerable research in word association psychology and did quite a lot of experimenting along this line. She found she had a passionate interest in the way words sounded, in the way words went together, and in the way people thought in groups of words, in clusters of words.

When she got to Paris and began to buy Picasso, she came very much under his influence. I think she might almost have been said to be in love with him; she was bewitched by him, as a great many people have been. She consciously and deliberately undertook to make modern literature—that is, to make a modernistic literature— the way the painters were making a modernistic art. She tried to write a kind of Cubism—a kind of Fauvist-Cubism—in which she'd break up the concept and the meaning of the sentence into non-meaning, non-intended, non-expressive but vital and real word patterns.

And a third thing is that she was so conceited, with all these flattering boys around, that she never would work over anything. She just scribbled. She really did just scribble. She never revised a single thing; consequently, her work is very loose and uneven.

There's some merit, experimental merit, in *Tender Buttons* and in the very early things that she did in which she worked with associative words. *The Making of Americans* is a wonderful idea which starts out beautifully. The first page of it is thrilling; then it just bogs down in its own verbosity. It cheats itself. A very boring book.

The first book that she ever took any trouble with was *The Autobiography of Alice B. Toklas,* which she wrote for practical reasons with an agent and a publisher advising her. That was sort of potboiling, from her point of view, but I think it and the other books that follow are her best.

She wrote several pieces for the theater, called landscapes, which have always seemed to me to reflect a good deal of Cubist influence.

Oh sure.

Are you familiar with any of her landscapes?

Yes, I've read all the masses of it, masses of it. I'm not sure that I remember them very well.

They don't seem to be scribbles. They seem to be very consciously structured, very odd as that sounds.

I wonder whether someone helped her with it. Were they ever put on?

Yes, some of them were.

Maurice Grosser made the *Four Saints in Three Acts.* He made that all up. He invented the scenario and fitted Gertrude's scribbles into the form that was eventually used in Virgil Thomson's opera.

I know that The Mother of Us All *has been produced.*

I think that also had other people working on it, giving it shape. I don't mean to say that they rewrote it, but that they put form in it.

Well, they're very interesting experiments in the theatrical form.

But then, again, I'm not awfully interested in Cubism, either in painting or things literary.

Did Thornton Wilder have much contact with Gertrude Stein?

Oh, my goodness, yes. He was one of her closest friends and greatest admirers. He would just be pained, profoundly pained and disgusted if he heard me say what I've said, because he reveres her.

Wilder is a very odd writer, a very classical writer, who is infatuated with everything that he isn't. He's one of the twelve greatest experts on *Finnegans Wake;* he's a member of the Joyce Society and explicates *Finnegan* by the hour with Kirkpatrick and all the rest of the scholars. He loves Kafka. And underneath all of his simple, or "classical," works there usually are inspirations of this kind from these wilder and more aesthetically creative men. And from Gertrude. I'm not sure he wasn't her closest friend. He's had a lot to do with the handling of her texts at Yale. I think she left him some money to do it with.

I've heard it said that, in Good-bye Wisconsin, *there is a leave-taking, a wrapping up of your dealings with the people who populate your stories. I was wondering if that's true, if that's why you said goodbye to Wisconsin.*

Well, the reason I said goodbye to Wisconsin is that I only lived in Wisconsin until I was sixteen years old. I went back for two or three summers for vacations; after that, I didn't return at all for a number of years. I went back in 1929; then, in 1934, my family moved away. I had used up my Wisconsin.

As for the title, as I explained to Mr. Gado earlier on, I don't think I even invented it. The account of my visit to Wisconsin, called "Good-bye Wisconsin," which begins that book was commissioned by Rita Van Doren's *Bookweek* magazine. She knew that I'd been living abroad and had written Wisconsin novels and stories there. Knowing that I was going home to see my mother, she asked me to write an account of how Wisconsin looked to me after life in Germany and France. I took this as an assignment and I think *she* put the title on it. I wasn't aware of saying goodbye to Wisconsin. I was aware of its meaning less and less to me because I had less and less connection with it.

At the close of that opening story—or essay as I suppose it might better be described—you say something which indicates an aesthetic change as well as a change of subject. Let's see if I can find the beginning of the sentence now. . . .

I think I remember.

Here it is: "The latter lies in a broken ring of dim olive-trees; and between the lemon-white quay and the battleships, sailors signal to each other with an alphabet of outstretched arms and small flags like handkerchiefs on sticks, their faces gone blank with concentration. For another book I should like to learn to write in a style like those gestures: without slang, with precise equivalents instead of idioms, a style of rapid grace for the eye rather than sonority for the ear, in accordance with the ebb and flow of sensation rather than with intellectual habits, and out of which myself, with my origins and my prejudices and my Wisconsins, will seem to have disappeared."

Lovely, lovely. The foreword to a book I never wrote.

Not The Pilgrim Hawk?

No, I don't think so. Maybe. No, I don't think so.

Well, in The Pilgrim Hawk *we have Alwyn without Wisconsin, without the frustrations of. . . .*

Yes, that's true—I'm not a very good critic of my own work. But I do remember what I was aware of at the end of that book: I wrote quite a lot of preparatory music having to do with a book called *The Dream of Mrs. Cleveland,* which I tried to write, which I worked on for two or three years, and which was to be without any of the Wisconsin background and without any of the problematic grief. I couldn't write it. It was the first of my abortions. It isn't any good. I looked at it the other day.

This is sort of a silly question, but did you know Zelda Fitzgerald at all?

Yes.

Did you ever read anything she wrote?

Yes, you know that novel of hers . . . what's it called?

Are you referring to Save Me the Waltz?

Yes, it's quite good, quite good. It was clever, clever, clever, although it didn't have the warmth of Fitzgerald.

Part of the problem of those Fitzgeralds is that she wanted to be a writer. She wanted to be creative. She felt creative ardor and urgency. She always did. Scotty wrote rings around her all the time and didn't, I think, believe that she had a very great deal of talent. Actually, when they got awfully poor, sometimes Zelda would write the stories for the magazines and Scott would sell them because he could get more money for them. Well, you can see how mortifying and unhappy that all was. They did themselves violence, those two, in their self-esteem and in their talent. Zelda was crazy. She was always crazy. I think we all knew that. Everyone knew that except Scott. Scott sensed it, but he liked it. He liked the poetical quality that she had. He liked poetry better than prose and, therefore, liked a crazy beloved better than an ordinary sane one.

Fitzgerald was an Irishman with an incredible gift of gab. He could flatter you in such a way that he could just lift you up into the heavens, and then, when he saw you'd got up there, he would come out with a little pin, stick a little hole in you, and pffsst, down you'd come, kerplunk! He did this to poor Zelda all the time, and I think it was very, very bad for her. I don't mean to say that it caused her to be mad. Hemingway—it's in the record—told Fitzgerald he thought she was insane. Fitzgerald had never even thought of such a thing at that point. No. There was trouble there, but I think that he worsened it by his manic depressive habits and his rhetoric and mischief and malice. And afterward, when she really was hopelessly mad, I think that Fitzgerald had a frightful feeling that he had driven her mad. He had a terrible bad conscience about it. It was one of the things that broke his heart.

I never knew the Fitzgeralds very well—I would have liked to, very much—and I'm not able to speak of all this as a personal observation, but I know all the letters and all the texts very well. I formed my opinion with what I knew at the time, plus all the things I've read.

That very touching letter to his daughter....

Oh, touching and terrible. I met her the other day for the first time. She's a most charming creature who is spooky to meet because she looks so like them both. She's got her mother's features, but she's a little more delicate, the way her father was. Her mother had a rather coarse nose, like a wooden Indian, but wonderful eyes, wonderful coloring. Their daughter has this same fierce look of the eagle, but with Scott's delicacy and Scott's blondness. She's marvelous looking.

This morning, you mentioned Simenon's interview in the Paris Review *briefly. What is your evaluation of Simenon as a novelist?*

Well, he's scarcely a novelist; he's a novella writer. Now I'm going to take a real flyer; he's probably the most gifted fiction writer now alive. You can throw away half of it, not because he doesn't do the best he can, but because he does so much that some of it doesn't come off. Sometimes he falls into an imitation of himself, or he tries things that don't work, but the rest of it is really extraordinarily good. It's narrow and intellectually not very admirable or very interesting, but as a rendering of life and as a rendering of reality, of people, in a continuous performance over a long period of years, his work is almost matchless.

My friends don't agree with me at all. He's not a writer whom I know, or ever care to know, but I've put him up for honorary membership in the American Academy—for foreign membership—and I'm determined I'm going to make a great fuss about it. It would be a lesson to all these professor-novelists we have, to face the merit of this man who has no pretentions. He writes for a living. He began writing for money as a pulp writer before he ever realized he had any talent. He's written two hundred novels—two hundred books of fiction!

In that interview he says—and he said this elsewhere, apparently quite seriously—that he writes because he has to, and only when he has to; that is, not for the money, but for psychological reasons. He claims indifference to the reaction to his works. Now, many people have characterized this idea as self-deception, as you seemed to, a few minutes ago, in your comments about the usefulness of your writing. Do you think he's serious?

I think he's serious, but I don't know him and I've never known anyone who's known him. I know him only through this interview, this brilliant interview. I thought it was a wonderful thing to read and I recommend it highly to you all. I can only guess at his psychology. My thought is that he's probably rather a stupid man with a simple life consisting of his wife and his little world. He probably goes fishing, or something like that, and putters around until a dream has accumulated; and then I think he has to purge his mind of these dreams. He may be much closer to the abnormal, to the psychopathological or sub-conscious creator, than most of us. There have been writers like that before, you know. Dostoevsky was like that: one of the stupidest men who ever lived, but he dreamed enormous visions of life.

*What are your views on why quite a few good writers go abroad?
Is it because one can write better over there and get away from the
distractions of America, or is it just for the cultural experience, or
what?*

Well I think that that depends. You see some people go for cultural
experience, fall in love with a French girl, and stay. You know,
there are odd things like that. I went, not wanting to go at all,
because a friend of mine [Monroe Wheeler] invited me to go with
him, believing I ought to go and meet great poets. I hated it, that
first round—that first stay abroad, I couldn't bear it. The next
time, although I didn't particularly want to go back, I went knowing I could live off the monetary exchanges. We all did that in
France. I've never really forgiven that silly, dear Malcolm Cowley in
Exile's Return all that stuff about how we were maladjusted in our
native land and we took refuge in the shadow of the Cathedral of
Chartres. What nonsense! In those days he was a Marxist, and you'd
have thought he'd have known about economic determinism. I
lived in Germany for a whole year on twenty-five dollars a month.
You could live on what you could beg, borrow, or steal, you see. For
me that was the whole story. (After this last war it was quite different. The currency was so very well managed that no sharp break in
the currency occurred to make living on exchange differences possible.) There's something else: it is very important for a writer to get
away from his family very often—to go away from home in some
sense; and Europe is a good place to go. It's probably not so good
now, but, in those days, you could get a servant to look after you very
inexpensively; you could set up a life which was not difficult or
expensive which would make it very easy to work.

Then, too, wandering around is very good for young writers. It's
a natural instinct to want to do it, and I think it's very good to obey
it. I'm worried a little bit, for example, about Updike, who's one of
the most fiendishly keen men I've ever known. I love his talents.
The New Yorker has been able to take enough of his work at a high
enough price (given to him in advance—by the year) so that he's been
able to live and do nothing else but write all day long. He has about
five children and lives, I think, in the country somewhere and does
nothing in a rush. Which is splendid, except that I sometimes wonder what he's going to use for material presently. Whom does he
know? What does he see? Where does he go? What happens to him?

Faulkner had a similar problem.

Well, Faulkner. . . . The South is funny. One of the things that's never been said, or at least not said often, is that the South is a stagnant culture with not a great deal of social mobility or migration. People stay in communities. Little boys and girls sitting on a porch hear their old relatives in rocking chairs telling the sagas of the cousins, and the uncles, and the aunts. They live where they can see whole stories develop. They see the plot germinate and the plot work out; they see a catastrophe happen and people get over it. They've got the whole subject—a kind of subject matter for fiction the rest of us haven't got. Does that make any sense? I think it's a natural kind of culture for fiction writing to come out of.

You remarked that there was a very close relationship, you thought, between the generations of writers preceding you and your generation. What association do you think a man, say, of Saul Bellow's generation has with literary . . .

I would say this ice is a little thin for me because I don't know that I understand or sympathize with Bellow's purposes. I respect his talents immensely; I admired his early works very much, and I pushed and fussed for him. But for me, he's a man formed by the university. He's a university man, a university writer. The relationship between his experience and the social milieu that he portrays isn't close enough; or, rather, it isn't as close as it ought to be.

Henderson the Rain King is his best, the one I admire. That's a very, very poetical and potent work, though not a perfect one. But *Augie March,* from my point of view, was an attempt of a rather brief, terse writer to write on a very much larger scale. It was overblown, over-elaborated, and over-extended, and it didn't seem to me to be intense or well-shaped. And *Herzog* . . . well, I simply don't believe in Herzog. That novel has too much intellectuality, too much willfulness and artfulness and artistry. It's as though that poor fool Herzog had hired a university person named Bellow to ghostwrite his book; there's no relation between the personality of the man and the way it's written. All these letters to Einstein and so on are absolutely too unconvincing to be written by the character to whom the events happen. It's very brilliant—page for page it's beautiful. He writes wonderfully in a style of great charm and color and power, but it just seems untrue.

18

Is this forced intellectuality a characteristic of Bellow alone, or do you think it is widespread among his generation of writers? May it have to do with the fact that he is a Jew writing about Jews?

There are very confusing issues involved. I don't really know whether Saul Bellow intends or is party to this, but Bernard Malamud, Philip Roth, and all those others who reviewed his last book seem now to be taking it into their heads that there is a Jewish school of writers, and that this is the dean, the Faulkner of the new school. To my mind, this is nonsense. I've spent a great deal of my life with Jews, and I've never known a Jew at all like Herzog. Never, never, never—and so I don't believe in him from my point of view. Bellow is no more a Jew than I am; he is an American, just as I am. I'm interested in reading about Jews, but then I read Isaac Bashevis Singer. Singer seems to me one of the authentic geniuses of this era. He tells me something that I never knew about a culture entirely different from mine.

Isn't there something about the Jewish situation and the traditional position of the Jew which has suddenly become quite relevant to America after World War II? I think Malamud has said that, in post-war America, "every American is a Jew." The kind of thing you find in Friedman's Stern, *where the protagonist, the butt of humor, is trying to. . . .*

I don't even call it Jewish; I call it German—this business of saying black is white and that the guilt is universal and the situation is eternal and every man represents all men. I don't get it myself. I just don't get it at all. It's Central European Monism. It's too deep for me, you know; I don't want it.

Do you believe that foundation support, by throwing young writers among themselves rather than among any of their preceding generations, might have deleterious effects?

I think so. It's all a part of that thing I called, roughly speaking, university influence—which, not being a university man in any sense, I don't know very well. But I do know that the university has now become the patron of a great many of our most gifted men, and I do know that I feel disappointment with their development, with the evolution of their work as they stay on in the university to teach and write. This situation encourages a self-conscious aestheticism, an over-development of the intellectual aspects, a deliberately intellectual attitude toward what they're doing. What prevents this influence from carrying as far as it might is the mundane portion of most existences. The poor blokes have wives and children, and, perhaps feeling that they're not having a good life, they want to sell a book to the movies.

Is All the King's Men *a typical product of university influence?*

No, that was a good book. *All the King's Men* is, of course, a popular novel; it isn't of any great interest or distinction as a work of art, either in style or in form. It's an ordinary novel, but a very, very good one. It's the best of Warren's works.

Your remarks about the novel betray a certain distress about its future. Would you agree that movies have made certain demands upon fiction which, perhaps, fiction cannot realize?

The relation between the movies and the novel is purely economic. Publishers are crazy about novels because, every now and then, they sell one to the movies and make a great deal of money. Now, even the first advertisements of a novel sold to Hollywood in advance of publication are geared to the film—you know, "Otto Preminger is going to make a movie out of this." That's all rather dangerous; it's hard enough to write a good novel without thinking you're writing two or three other things at the same time.

In another way, the movies are bound to affect the novel. The motion picture, as a narrative form, has become very important and very interesting. I really don't think that, except perhaps for Simenon, there's a narrator of that generation in the world who is as able to tell a series of extraordinary stories as Ingmar Bergman.

I wasn't thinking so much of the way in which a novel is sold or of the market a writer envisions while he is writing the novel, but of cinematic effects on his technique.

Perhaps more interesting than the movies' influence on the novel is that the novel form is wrecking a great many short story writers— they attempt to be novelists, or they succeed in being novelists (succeed financially, but not artistically). Then, too, a great many of those who practically devote their lives to writing have such difficulty in writing their novels it damn near kills them. They end up wasting an awful lot of time trying to produce novels.

Would you say, then, that the genius of American literature is in the short story?

I think so, yes. Americans have always had a great talent for the short forms—and Americans like to read them. The people, the common people, want to read *The Reader's Digest*—something very, very short and with a short focus. (I don't regard *The Reader's Digest* as itself important; it is symptomatic of the situation.)

Would you nominate Katherine Anne Porter as your number one example of a short story writer wrecked by the novel?

I certainly would not, because I think that *Ship of Fools* is probably the best modern novel. It's not a novel with an arbitrary form (which won't always work), but a superb novel. I didn't want her to do it, and, at one time or another, I would have encouraged her to throw it away. She perhaps destroyed herself getting it done— she had such a horrible time—but she pulled it off. Of course, you may feel she devoted more of her life to it than she could afford. She worked on it, off and on, over twenty years. She's now seventy-five, you know, so it was the last part of her life that she gave to it.

Both you and Porter have also found great success in another form which usually falls between two stools—the novella. Do you think there is any special aesthetic for this genre?

Well, I think you should state the aesthetic in such a way as to define the differences between the form of the novel and the form of the novella. Size, of course, to begin with. But there's something more than size. A novella is a novel in which you have, in some degree, the unities of time and place, and in which you find a relatively small cast of characters. You look deeply into their current lives, you look back in their lives, or you go into their psychology. In contrast, a novel is an organization, a form of fiction, that bears a relation to society at large, that usually wants to be set up in a chronology covering a period of time in which cause and effect work out. Usually, there are the dimensions of time and the strata of society which need to be organized.

That, at least, was the old form of the novel. But there are a great many reasons why it has become difficult to practice. One is a profound transition in morals, only loosely understood. Another is the much broader circulation of books than ever before outside the given society, so that your readers are scattered all over and you don't quite know who they are, what they are, or what they know.

Most writers nowadays, if they have interesting lives, have cosmopolitan lives. The best stories I know, the ones people are always urging me to write, are scattered all over the world. I couldn't write those things in terms of the old form of fiction in which you knew how your characters made their money and how they invested it, and about the law, the rents, and all the rest. Once, you could make everybody talk the way they really would talk. In these new stories, people are always hopping in from Long Island or Virginia; aristocrats in New York society end up in the hop fields in Oklahoma, or living in boarding houses in Chicago, or living in London for half a lifetime; you know—all that. The old novels weren't like that at all. People lived in a fairly small community and wrote for people who lived in the same community, more or less. Writers living in Paris or London wrote for their metropolitans. They lived pretty much the same lives their characters were living and they knew what their readers knew.

I think the form of fiction that will develop out of the good, big stories to be told will be much more like the Arabian Nights. It will be a question of tale-telling, because very few writers are able, except in their own autobiographical material, to manage such a broad range.

You mentioned Jurgen *this morning;* Jurgen, *besides the fact that it's fantastic, has something of the broken surface that I think you've been talking about. The time-space things—there's a lot of jumping around in it. There is a mystical, a magical aspect to it. There was a demise of that type of writing while Cabell was still writing, but recently there have been a few novels which, I believe, have the same kind of magical quality. Although they stick closer to common events and ordinary people in that men don't run around with swords or such, they seem basically fantasies. I'm thinking of books like Thomas Pynchon's* V. *or Heller's* Catch-22.

Yes, exactly, I followed. I knew you were coming to that, and it's very well observed. It's a cross. I don't remember *Jurgen* as well as I ought to, but it seems to me that what Cabell was up to was a cross between the historical novel and the surrealist novel. His kind of surrealist novel is certainly with us again, but stripped of the historical trappings. I don't like those books very much, though I have a great interest in them. They're too long for me; I haven't got that much sense of humor, and they're not that funny. *V.* isn't—I couldn't stand it at all—and, in *Catch-22*, though I do think it's brilliant, I just got tired of the joke about halfway through. Nevertheless, Heller certainly is one of the most promising, most interesting gentlemen.

Isn't there the same sort of thing in James Purdy and John Barth?

Barth? Who's Barth?

The author of The Floating Opera, *the* End of the Road. . . .

I never heard of him. Is he that good?

Oh, yes. Very good.

Purdy's work I know very well and like, though it's silly sometimes.

You're probably aware of the recent controversy about Tom Wolfe's attack on The New Yorker *in the* Herald-Tribune. *Do you agree that* The New Yorker *has been a pernicious influence?*

I certainly do not. There's always a great deal of talk, especially out in the Middle West, about cabals and "influencings"—all that sort of thing—in New York. They always think *The Partisan Review* runs the whole world. Well, to my knowledge, there are only two agencies in this country that are powerful enough to have any influence at all. One is the book clubs—the Book of the Month Club and, I suppose, the Literary Guild, now that it is back in the field; they really can do something. The other is *The New Yorker*. It is a most extraordinary success and a very, very rich magazine. They can do what they damn please; they don't have to pay any attention to anybody. They can spend as much money as they want, and they spend it very, very generously. They actually are so much in demand by advertisers that they have to turn down advertisements every week because they can't get enough prose to carry the advertisements over the pages. Being weekly, they have a bottomless pit; therefore, they have tried to back young writers. They've developed a whole string of them.

Updike, one of the most remarkable, has been supported by *The New Yorker* since he was a young, young writer. So has Salinger, so has Cheever (who is superb and one of my very favorite writers), so has Mavis Gallant, so have so many. You might say that it makes things too simple for them to have a ready market, but the fact remains that they are our most gifted writers. Nobody else has produced a little stable of writers as able as that.

I loathe that fellow Tom Wolfe, you know, and I shall be knifing him in the back for years and years and years. So will a great many other writers. The poor devil. We're all furious, mostly because Wolfe lied like a trooper about all sorts of things.

Suppose that you had submitted The Apple of the Eye *to* The New Yorker. *Wouldn't they have asked for at least as many changes as your publisher's lawyer?*

The New Yorker, yes. It is frightfully fussy about grammar and they feel that they have to have coherent texture. E. B. White's wife, who's been the literary editor for years and years, will take no nonsense at all about funny punctuation.

I'm talking about prudishness.

Well, it's a family magazine, as they say. They may be prudish—I really don't know. I've never heard of anybody challenging them on that.

Don't you think that, when you have a very rich magazine making it greatly to the advantage of writers to leave out some parts of life, it could be called a pernicious influence?

Well, that's a good question. But just as every writer can't write everything, every editor can't publish everything. The editors who like Updike and Cheever and all those *New Yorker* writers wouldn't like the sort of shocking stories you mean, would they? Neither would their readers. I don't think that a difference of taste can be called a bad influence. You're blaming them for the things they haven't done. I'm defending the things they have done.

A short time ago, Alan Duggan visited here. . . .

I think I've met him. He's the son-in-law of a friend of mine. [Ben Shahn, the noted American artist.]

We were talking to him one night about Cheever and Updike. He thinks they're rather phony because they write only about suburbia. He believes that they're not really getting at the meat of things.

24

What makes me squirm with both of you is this business of the "universal man." I believe that everybody represents just a little facet of the total experience of life. You have to have all these different writers.

You may not get all facets of life represented in literature. A very poor part of life may not lend itself to articulation, or it may be presented in such a boring or a crazy way that nobody will get the hang of it at all. It won't enter into literature because it isn't properly expressed. Then, too, you may get something for which there is no outlet, and new writers drawing their materials from that area will be discouraged (although I don't think there are very many writers who can be discouraged). Willie Maugham once said you must always discourage writers if you can, because if they're any good, they can't be discouraged. I don't think this is true of me, but I think it is generally true.

To get back to your career: do you harbor any grudges against the critics of the 'thirties who were responsible, at least in part, for the eclipse of Wescott, and certainly, for the temporary eclipse of Fitzgerald and even of Hemingway before he hopped on the proletarian bandwagon and became fashionable?

No. I don't have any grudges. I think the reason for my own "eclipse" is that I let my career lapse for personal reasons, because of inner crises. I know that in America you have to be fast in life. You have to keep in front of the public, keep in the public eye.

Naturally, I think the writers who were here during the Depression, or who grew up during the Depression, must have felt that we, being out of it, were callous and indifferent and so on. In a sense, we were. It wasn't that I couldn't or didn't want to return, and it wasn't that I was being introspective either. I feel truly, absolutely ridiculous when I look back upon the Depression. I lived in Europe during the whole farce; I cannot tell you how little I appreciated it, how little impression I got of it.

Should you have been criticized, as an artist, for turning your back?

Well, we shouldn't have been, and perhaps we wouldn't have been if we had stayed.

The interesting thing about the 'thirties was that you had two or three writers of the 'twenties who dominated the 'thirties by just hanging on. Steinbeck and Faulkner are both as old as I am, but they were late starters, so they got to be writers of the 'thirties. They really weren't.

The most interesting writer of the whole batch is poor Jim Farrell, whom I know very well. He was a great man in the 'thirties, and hasn't been able to keep body and soul together since; he's had the most miserable time of it. He's a very sincere man.

The same thing is true, to some degree, of Dos Passos, who claims he still has all the sincerity, all the drive he once had. And yet look at the sorrowful thing he did in The Great Days—*horrible self-castigation and feelings of failure poured out on the page.*

He's a funny man. I think his camera is out of focus now. He relied on a device. I don't wish to speak scornfully of it, but it was a gimmick, making a novel in flashbacks and so on. He was very successful, but I don't think that he has had a very profound influence.

He's a sort of journalistic type altogether because he is always changing. I don't mean to say that he's insincere, but I remember how angry I got with him during the 'forties when we were having great trouble in the Authors' League with a more or less Communist splinter group. There was a middle group, a splinter group on the right, and a splinter group on the left. By this time, Dos Passos, of course, was in the splinter group on the right. He wrote me a letter, accusing me of being a Communist fellow traveller. I was angry; I have never changed my politics from the time I was born till now, whereas he's been on every bandwagon that was going by. He wrote a book when he was about to be a Communist, then he wrote a book when he was being a Communist, then he wrote a book while he was ceasing to be a Communist, and then he wrote a book going on to other directions. Each time he was prepared to lead the country: "I am the one, I'm always right about politics." Well, from my point of view, if I'd made a gaffe as terrific as he'd made, I would just have said, "Well, I'm a fine, well-meaning fellow, but I'm no leader." But not Dos. He claims he's never changed, but I'll bet you nobody agrees with him about that. He's been rather like Malraux, you know. If the Communists should ever take over in France, Malraux would reappear and say "They've changed, I haven't changed."

We've not discussed your poetry at all, but you began your career as a poet. The anthologies which include some of your poems de-

scribe you as an Imagist. Would you accept the description? Also, there's been a lot of controversy as to what Imagism was. What did Imagism mean to you?

I think it meant to me that I was very much influenced by and imitative of poets who called themselves Imagists. I felt my poetry was indistinguishable from that of H. D., whose work I knew by heart when I was a boy. As I remember their aesthetic, it was an attempt to convey emotion and the personal situation without personal references, without dramatic expression of the emotion, and without any hint of plot. You conveyed emotion in terms of what was seen and heard and sensed. It's a wonderful idea—and one reason why I think myself a very second rate poet. I first began to realize that when, after a few years had passed, I would read some of the poems I had worked on for months which expressed my passions and turmoils and sorrows at the moment, and I would not be able to remember what they were about. It's all very well to write a secretive poetry in which you convey emotion devoid of narrative and dramatic development, but when you can't even remember it afterward, I think it's gone too far. It's uninteresting then. I don't know how poets now feel about that. Imagism was a rather short-lived movement. They soon stopped it, you know; the only person who went on to the end was dear H. D. herself.

Wasn't there a counterpart to this in fiction? I'm thinking particularly of Kay Boyle's "Wedding Day." Do you know the short story?

Yes. I don't remember it very well, but I remember I liked it.

There's no plot at all, and you have the Steinian repetitions—"The sun was an imposition, an imposition"—this sort of thing. Nothing really of any importance happens in the plot. It's simply a matter of reactions.

Yes, but you see, we tried it and then we gave it up. Kay gave it up, certainly. We were so close to our elders and admired them so much and loved them so much, and they were so helpful and so flattering —but the amazing thing is that we weren't influenced by them very much. We couldn't carry on; we couldn't go on from where they left off, any of us, very far. I can't think of an exception.

The influence of Pound and Eliot both—but especially Eliot—has been very much greater. The poetry of Eliot—the early poetry, that is—led into a lot of ordinary fiction.

27

I was reading one of the prefaces, I think it was to The Grandmothers, *in which you were quoted as saying that you couldn't write
an epic or a long poem until Pound had taught you how to write
the line.*

Yes, I said that, but I was very young. I think we all felt that you
had to start with the line. That they did teach us. Pound and Eliot
and Ford, more than Gertrude and Joyce, taught us a lesson we
could more easily have learned from the French, from Flaubert and
Maupassant and Apollinaire. But, of course, we didn't get to them
in time.

*Was the working with the poetry, with the Imagism, a way leading
into the prose?*

I sometimes think that, if I'd never been a poet at all, I might have
gone on better with my prose. The habit of writing poetry starts
you writing in a more minute way. You never learn, or you don't
learn soon enough, to write on and on. You should really see my
manuscript. It's absolutely ridiculous. The numbers of little pieces
of paper and the numbers of lines drawn out and the numbers of
revisions and then the retyping and the cutting of the paper with a
pair of scissors and the pasting. And gradually, as in a mosaic, I
pound it and hammer it together. Well, that's normal for poetry
writing, but it shouldn't be for composing novels.

One of the things that's the matter with the novel as a creative
form, I think, is due to the influence of Flaubert. Flaubert presented
a hypothesis in literature, a historic hypothesis, that a novel could be
as perfectly wrought and as entirely controlled and organized as a
poem. But any novel is many, many times longer than any epic. A
lyric poem is like an easel painting: you can do it in a day or a
week. But a novel is like the Sistine Chapel; it's an enormous thing
in area. Then Flaubert came along with the idea that you should do
the Sistine Chapel in egg tempera, stippling every single line with a
little dot of egg yolk. People since then have gone mad trying to do
this; they have broken their health, and their children's health, like
Virginia Woolf—and failed. All of which goes back to the "syrup"
thesis. I never intended to be a syrup or to pour, one way or another.
I intended to make a mosaic of perfect pieces organized in an orderly
overall structure.

The only people who made anything out of the Flaubert method
are the people who were his literary great-grandchildren and the

grandchildren of Maupassant. Maupassant was Flaubert's principal protege and pupil, but he approached writing in a somewhat different way. He made a very small, specific formula for the kind of writing he was going to do, perfected it, and then repeated it. By narrowing the thing down, the disciples get a kind of perfect performance that they can control.

But in general, that formulaic approach is too self-conscious, too limiting. Novels have to be written more simply somehow.

You mentioned earlier that you were very fond of Thornton Wilder's novel The Ides of March, *which has a unique approach to the novel.*

That was an invention, a real invention, because it derived from the drama more than from the tradition of the novel. It was an attempt to make all of his characters express themselves by their own utterance—not in their own speech, but in their own writing: in their own journals and their own letters and communications to one another. Oh, how I love that book! I've read it five times, twice aloud.

There's a mosaic pattern under that too. . . .

Yes, of course.

. . . but of a much different type from Flaubert's.

Well, that's a different sense of the word "mosaic." It's been arranged. It's more like a collage—cut-up bits—than a mosaic.

I work like that almost entirely. The next book I'm doing—although I'm not going to talk about it—I'm composing in chapters that long; I've got it all organized now—a new card, and a new page for each one, on and on—all constructed. I know just where they come. I know where there's a hole. I'm not having to write from the start because I find that that way I repeat myself.

Does this method go back at all to A Calendar of Saints?

No. No. The form of that I took from the old church calendars. I wrote it in six weeks, and it was a job!

In the first essay of Good-bye Wisconsin, *you said you were glad that you never wrote a word that was of any use to anyone. Then why do you write? What do you think your books do?*

I certainly wouldn't say that now, you know. Remember when that was written?

Yes.

In 1928. That's easily nonsense. I would hope that everything I wrote would be helpful, useful to somebody. Although I don't know that I always write with a view to making helpful suggestions, or to teaching a lesson, or anything of that sort, I'm a real believer in truth-telling and truth-hearing as an exercise for the mind. It's the most difficult thing in the world to tell the truth, and it's very difficult to recognize the truth—but very important that people do. One of the things that literature does is to sharpen one's sense of the truth, one's ear for the truth—to get the mind to be like a tuning fork so that it has a kind of perfect pitch. Then you can tell whether your politicians are lying. Our politics would go a great deal better if there were fewer books about politics and fewer classes about politics and people read literature more. Then, when they would go and listen to these blokes make their speeches, they could tell whether they were true men or whether they were engaging in the politics of false promises.

This runs counter to the whole tenor of American life.

It certainly does.

MAY 11, 1965

John Dos Passos

Mr. Dos Passos, you've long been known as a chronicler of the disturbances of the twentieth century. May I begin by reading from an article written by a twenty-year-old student before going off to war? I would be most interested in your comment.

Has not the world today somehow got itself enslaved by this immense machine, the Industrial system. Millions of men perform labor narrowing and stultifying even under the best conditions, bound in the traces of mechanical industry, without ever a chance of self-expression, except in the hectic pleasures of suffocating life in cities. They grind their lives away on the wheels, producing, producing, producing. And of all the results of this degrading, never-ending labor, how little is really necessary to anyone; how much is actually destructive of the capacity of men for living, for the fathoming of life, for the expression of life.

. . . Are we so certain of the benefits of all this that the last hundred years has given us that there must be no discussion of the question? Most people are very certain; but most people are always certain. . . .

Still, there is discontent among us. In the light of the flames of burning . . . towns civilized men look at each other with a strange new horror. Is this what men have been striving for through the ages? Is this ponderous suicidal machine civilization?

Where was that? I haven't seen it.

It appeared in a college literary magazine. The author is John R. Dos Passos, Jr. and the date is June 1916.

Why that's amazing. I didn't recognize it at all. It's really pretty good.

The essay is entitled "A Humble Protest." Although you were quite young when you wrote it, to me it has always seemed the most semi-

31

*nal of your early works—in fact, the key to understanding the fun-
damental attitude underlying all your subsequent work.*

It's one I forgot. . . . A monthly editorial. . . .

Back in the days of the Harvard Monthly. *Having sprung my one
trap, I'll go on to ask whether you see similarities between the feelings of your college generation and those being expressed so volubly
on campuses all over this country and, indeed, the world.*

Oh, yes, I see a great many. With one important difference, however: it seems to me that our ideas were really more constructive
than those of the current generation. Naturally, we were reacting
against the same thing, but now the reaction is on a larger scale
and more virulent. What we are witnessing now is a tantrum of
spoiled children who really have had too much done for them.

One of the most tragic things about the student revolution is its
negativism, and here I'm not speaking about the Americans particularly. I did read quite a lot about the French students' revolt;
despite all their cooking around, not one came out with a useful
program. This is not to say that I can't understand what led to their
rising up. The French universities are much more in need of reform
than ours are—and I think that difference should be borne in mind.
There has never been a society where education was finer or conducted on such a lavish scale than in ours, although of course a lot
of it is rather mistaken in conception, I think, and the results are
not always the best.

Initially, my generation was worried about matters similar to
those which concern yours. We were strongly hit because we were
brought up in a period when there hadn't been any wars for a long
while. We believed that nineteenth century civilization had pro-
gressed to a point where wars were no longer needed. Then, suddenly, this fantastic series of massacres broke out in Europe. I was
horrified by it all. The academic community became sold on the
war. This was my first experience with the fantastic way people's
minds became imprinted with slogans. Overnight, almost, men I'd
known at Harvard who were quite respected—I won't mention their
names—turned from extremely reasonable beings into fanatical Hun
haters. (I'm afraid I was very much in the minority at that time, as
I usually am.)

Today, we are seeing a similar turning away from reason. The
whole operation of the SDS presents a great potential danger. It

seems to me it is leading people to something very much like the Nazi Youth. By itself, I don't think it has the power to get very far, particularly should their funds be removed, as I hope they will be.

Who among you has ideas on this subject? After all, it's all much closer to you than to me right now.

Last year, I was at Columbia visiting a friend who is very active in SDS. We had a long discussion one night and, in the light of your remarks about SDS, it's odd that he was saying almost exactly, in fact practically verbatim, what you said in "A Humble Protest." Really, the similarity is incredible.

Except that they offer no solutions. So many things need attention in the modern world. Anybody with enthusiasm and a proclivity for self-sacrifice could dedicate himself to remedying a couple of dozen, seriatim. Our entire administration of justice in regard to criminals has become horribly misconceived, particularly the whole prison system. We started out in this country with a remarkably good system—that, after all, is what de Tocqueville came over to study: the excellence of American penal institutions. In that area alone, we need an immense amount of intelligent, self-sacrificing, dedicated work. But instead of setting such specific goals, the people making all this clamor seem to want just general revolution. All this accomplishes is a playing into the hands of the Communist regime, which, having the biggest propaganda organization in the world, is happy to take advantage of the commotion.

What structure could be proposed which, being different from what we have now, you wouldn't see as, in some way, Communist-serving?

Well, you certainly wouldn't want the events in Czechoslovakia to be enacted in this country, would you?

In some ways, we have them.

We don't at all. To try to claim that the system in the United States is equal to a police state is just insane. Really, it is just not true. Go live in a police state if you want to see. Look. There are plenty of them around. You can go to Cuba. . . .

. . . and hope they'll let you out again. . . .

. . . or in again.

We have gotten some distorted views of what happens in America. There is entirely too much encouragement by television, by the media of completely unregulated fuss and fury—although just why, I don't understand—looking for the sensational moment. They have lashed up the Negro thing to a point where we almost have a state of race war.

Do you attribute this all to T.V.?

It has a lot to do with it. Without television, the more moderate, sensible people would have retained control; it wouldn't have gotten out of their hands. We tend to forget that there are a lot of very sensible Negroes who are willing to live and let live and who realize that you don't get anywhere by rioting and by some of the tactics now being used.

Hasn't moderation just meant passing over the problems? One wonders whether, at this late date, we can afford to think in terms of moderation.

Now you've got me because, I must confess, I was pretty immoderate when I was your age. Part of my lack of sympathy with the intentions of some of today's young people is due to my just having lived long enough to discover the results of our own immoderation. We were very hopeful about the Communist revolution, and then, of course, it turned out to be the most flagrant despotism ever imposed upon mankind.

Had the media been, during the Communist revolution or the early stages of World War I, what they are today, do you think that there would have been greater popular support in America. . . .

No, because the establishment was so much against these events that it would have worked the other way.

The whole question of the effects of television needs a great deal of thought. Instead of giving the viewer the impression that he is part of the real world, it somehow transforms him into a spectator. Television feeds the spectator mentality. I am not all that satisfied with McLuhan, but he does open up all sorts of things. I can't read much of him at one time because his writing is so repetitious, but occasionally he flashes out and throws light on some paradox that's stimulating to consider.

Many of us are in that same bag. I don't advocate McLuhan's thesis —in many ways his theory is riddled with holes and inconsistencies —yet I often find myself coming back to observations he has made. He is certainly not the first man to note the emergence of the "world village" or to foresee the awesome effects of electronic communication; nevertheless, he has brought such matters to public attention by dramatizing them.

The trouble is, he jumbles his statements together—rather like a bag of eels in which you can't exactly see which are the heads and which are the tails.

Of course, with someone who has fired off in as many directions as he has, probability dictates that, just at random, a few shots have to hit the target.

Why, yes. In general, his books add up to much nonsense, but the phenomena he is dealing with are fascinating and demand careful scrutiny.

In your day, such public questions as entry into the World War, the early strikes, and the formation of the IWW were pretty much cut and dried issues. Obviously, people were getting a bad deal and something had to be done. But today, with problems as ambiguous as the Viet Nam struggle, things are no longer cut and dry.

Precisely. That's why these questions don't lend themselves to cut and dried solutions. The dynamics of a society are never simple matters. The IWW was a preparation for the CIO, and that, on the whole, was a good thing. The package of progress, though, does not just contain benefits. The problem with all social engineering is that when good accrues to one side, it is paid for with injury on the other. We have to be careful because sometimes the cure is worse than the disease.

When you were in Russia in 1927-28, what was it you saw that disenchanted you?

I had gotten a view of the revolution earlier in 'twenty-one and 'twenty-two in the Trans-Caucasus when the Red regime was just moving in. I got quite a feeling of the atmosphere of the Russian civil war. It wasn't pleasant, but I discounted it somewhat because all civil wars are pretty bloody and innocent people necessarily suffer. Then, when I was in Russia in 1928, that country was experiencing a moment of calm. Trotsky was in exile, but Stalin was not yet strong enough to persecute the Trotskyites.

What I wrote about Russia was rather careful. I did write a report of the Kronstadt massacre, which has always horrified me. But I didn't want to play up to the people who were all against the Russian Revolution because I thought that, at worst, it was an experiment—one which might produce interesting results and was therefore worth watching.

Along that line: the most fantastic thing about the Soviet Union today is that the results of their experiment are proving that a despotic hierarchical society fits the industrial picture better than does democracy. Practically. That's something that can't and shouldn't be laughed off. If democracy is to survive in this increasingly technical age, the challenge must be met in some way, and I don't think it is met by walking around with placards and attacking a harmless figurehead like President Kirk of Columbia. Although I've always had something of an allergy towards college presidents, that poor fellow didn't deserve all that abuse. It was so overdone, and in the long run such actions invite worse than what they are attacking. The Wallace movement is backlash against all this sort of stuff.

In one of the passages in The Prospect Before Us, *you spoke of college presidents being the most accurate mirror of society.*

Did I say that seriously?

Yes. In fact, you repeated those comments in The Theme is Freedom. *I have the passage here:*

Institutions of learning eternally form the sacred ark in which the ruling dogmas of any particular era are protected from the criticisms of the profane. Remember the Sorbonne in the great days of the canon law. A historian today could make out a very good case for sampling the opinions of college presidents as a way of uncovering the mentality of whatever ruling class is emerging. Since the business of a college president is to raise money, he has to be the type of man who will appeal to those who control the available funds. Forty years ago he had to be congenial with the individual capitalists of the day. Now the money, even when it has the names of individual fortunes still attached to it, is in the hands of institutions. So the college presidents of our day have to have the institutional mentality. How can they help feeling tender toward socialized institutions, whatever form these may take?

Oh, yes, I will endorse that thoroughly.

What has struck me so during years of reading your many books is how accurate many of your observations are. They have an essential —dare I say poetic—rightness. Much of the current cant about alienation and anomie is vividly prefigured in such characters as Mac, G. H. Barrow, and Janey Williams of U.S.A. Two years ago, over BBC, I heard Galbraith delivering the lectures which became The New Industrial State. *At one point, it hit me that he was saying something you had touched on in* The Prospect Before Us—*that at most levels there wasn't much difference between being employed by G.M. or by the soviet state.*

Except, of course, that you have much greater freedom of movement in G.M. and there isn't the risk of being killed or imprisoned.*

---

* Cf. This passage from *The Theme is Freedom:*

The corporation is the top part of the pyramid. The working people in the factory or office or store do their work under its orders. Wherever you find it the pattern is uniform. In the United States we call it capitalism. If you go over to England you'll find people behaving in much the same way but calling it socialism. In the Soviet Union and its satellite states you'll find a remarkably similar social structure going under the name of dictatorship of the proletariat, or by the oddest reversal of the meaning of terms, people's democracy. Other factors account for the greater well being that results from the pattern in some countries than in others. The same plant will yield differently in different soils. You can be sure that if an eighteenth-century libertarian like Tom Paine were resurrected today he would find more similarities than differences in the three systems.

People have been pointing out for years that the government of the Soviet Union, leaving aside the police power—the power to kill is a very different thing from the power to fire—resembles more than anything else the government of a great American corporation. It makes you wonder whether the bogyman we in America see in the menace of socialism and that so many Europeans see in the menace of capitalism doesn't lie somewhere in the structure of industrial society itself.

We have proof by experience that when you change from capitalism to socialism the corporations which administer industry or banks or railroads or chain laundries retain their structure. What happens is that under socialism the men who reach places of power tend to do so through their political rather than their financial influence. Both systems suffer from bureaucratic intrigue and internal

37

To return to your answer in which you spoke of student agitation being counter-productive, you wrote something in The Theme is Freedom *which is very apropos. I'm referring to earlier impressions of Russia which you reprinted in that book along with numerous glosses. Your report of a conversation with a cab driver. . . .*

Yes, I remember that fellow quite well—an old fashioned cab driver with a big beard. My Russian was extremely bad at that time—it remains extremely bad—and we had to struggle to understand each other.

He had thought you were German; then you corrected him.

"Americans are civilized but Germans are more civilized," he said. "Here in Russia what we need is more Germans. Now we have too much liberty. Every barefoot no-account in the village thinks he's as good as the next man. There is no discipline, too much liberty. With liberty everything goes to hell. Hindenburg, he's what we need. He's a great man. But the young men now they do nothing but talk about liberty. That will not make a great nation. To become a great nation Russia should have a great man to put every man in his place, a man like Hindenburg."

Then, to the reprinted passage, you appended, " 'Now Stalin, Stalin is our man,' the cab driver added. To this day, I can't imagine why I left that out of the account." The parallel to our own situation is very strong and ominous, isn't it? This great liberalization, this great opening up of society, this turmoil, has in a sense permitted destructive men like Wallace, disguised as conservatives, to surface. We are nearing a polarization not unlike that found in the early stages of Communist countries.

Yes. The destructiveness of the Wallaces has been bred by the thorough destructiveness of forces like those in SDS.

---

politics. Only occasionally does a man find himself in a job through plain ability. The fascinating thing to a dispassionate observer about the structure of life in the Soviet Union is that in their efforts to produce socialism the communist dictators have produced a brutal approximation of monopoly capitalism. Their system has all the disadvantages of our own, without any of the alleviations which come to us through competition and through the division between economic and political power which has so far made it possible for the humane traditions of the Western world to continue.

If you want to find out what is happening to a society the thing to study is the behavior of the people in it and not what they say about their behavior. But most of the writing and arguing about social systems is about ideologies and not about behavior.

Your views about social change bring Blake to mind. I've been writing a thesis on Blake and I've been intrigued by his idea that in a revolution, one form of tyranny replaces another. Can change occur effectively on a large scale without one form of tyranny replacing another?

I have never read Blake very carefully. He is exciting, full of sparks which he throws off in every direction. I'm glad you are working on him. Masses of words have been written about Blake, but there is certainly room for more: the whole thing hasn't been quite uncovered yet. I once had thought that someday I might try to do something with Blake, but I got involved in other problems.

In regard to what Professor Gado said about your insight into certain institutions and the American scene: you were talking about your art during a speech made in accepting an award in Rome last January. . . .

I'll be reading that same paper again tonight. I think its point—that an artist has to be both engagé and dégagé—is still valid.

You obviously believe that it is this which enables you to gain your insights.

I wasn't talking particularly about me. I was describing what I think is a way writers advance on phenomena. As the experiences of life pour past, there has to be some method for using them. Personally, I am sort of a naturalist. In that paper, I was just describing the old naturalist method so wonderfully demonstrated in Darwin's *Journey of the Beagle*. All the good early naturalists—Bates' *Journey up the Amazon* is a good example—are full of this type of observation which to me is so important.

In that same speech, I said that the great advantage youth has over age is undamaged senses which produce extraordinarily good perceptivity: the hearing, the eyes, keen smell, and the whole associative operation to the brain haven't lost the freshness of childhood. (I often think that the human brain is at its best at about eight or nine. It's amazing to watch how things come into the minds of children at that age.) How tragic for young men and women if they allow their minds to be stamped by one of these slogan factories! It will take them years to recover. The minute a slogan is imbedded in part of the brain and becomes an automatic response to any given stimulus, the perceptivity of that part of the brain is lost and you no longer can have a genuine reaction to that stimulus. Slogans, of course, should be examined, but they certainly have to be kept at arm's length. That, I guess, is what I was really trying to say in that address.

Wasn't this rejection of hollow words one of the quickening factors among the writers right after the First World War?

Yes, I think so. All of the fellows about my age suddenly felt that we just had to examine life directly. But of course, all we had to combat was the comparatively mild slogan-forming operation of the daily newspapers. We didn't have to contend against the new peculiar types. Most of you kids were probably brought up watching T.V. The medium is much more indefinite in form, and for that reason, the slogans may be harder to fight against. I just don't know what the real effects of that influence will be.

When Professor Gado mentioned the writers' attitudes just after the first war, it set me to wondering whether this reaction to the hollow-ness of words might not have been tied up with their wanting to leave this country. Didn't they consider "patriotism" to be one of the hollow words?

Among the people I knew, the pattern of the period was not at all one of anti-patriotism, though of course we were accused of it. It was actually a desire to get the ship of state back on its rails. Every ship of state has to be reorganized and gotten back on its rails every so often. —Now there's a mixed metaphor if there ever was one!

You once said that the only excuse for a novelist is that he serves as a second-rate historian of the age in which he lives; he digs up the raw material which a scientist, an anthropologist, or an historian can later use to advantage.

Having since talked to a good many contemporary historians in the universities, I no longer am as well disposed toward them as I was when I wrote that. They've come to think of history as a science, and as a result, it's become a pseudo-science. In the real sciences, a man can perform an experiment and gain certain results; another man at the other end of the world can repeat the experiment and get the same results. Does that hold in history or sociology? History isn't a social science; it's an art—a great one. (Remember, Clio was one of the muses.) I would go so far as to say that history is the greatest of the literary arts. They run pretty close together, but I would rate a good historian higher than a novelist.

At the time you wrote U.S.A., *you seemed quite pessimistic about the future in this country because of the construction of American society and the influence of technology. Are you still of that opinion?*

It seems to me that the nature of the problem has changed. A wholly new, strange world has come into being. We see a good example of this in the space program—and I'm talking not primarily about the astronauts but about the army of technicians involved in all the tentacles of the operation. Many of these people, soon out of college, make $25,000 a year and live in luxurious surroundings. They lead a curious country club life. Now this, of course, has some advantages, but it also tends to keep them away from the ordinary problems experienced by the great mass of the population. They constitute an odd salaried class: they go to their jobs every day, but it's all on a very plush level. Except for some few G.M. engineers, that kind of world didn't exist in the 'twenties.

Other changes, too, have been remarkable. New institutions which were then just becoming popular are now losing their power. Like labor unions. The working class has become so prosperous that we have a new layer of bourgeoisie forming. The old notions about the proletariat really don't fit the picture we have now.

After you wrote your social novels, Steinbeck started writing novels like The Grapes of Wrath. *Do you think he picked some things up from you?*

No, no, I wouldn't accuse him of that.

He wrote one very good novel about a strike, something called *In Dubious Battle,* . . .

. . . . *the best he ever wrote.*

That's what I've always felt. It's truly excellent. But for some reason, it's never mentioned.

We've taught it for years at Union.

It's really a little classic.

I haven't much taste for most of Steinbeck. So much meretricious sentimentalism. . . .

I liked his *Sea of Cortez,* an account of his trip down the Gulf of California with his biologist friend. It's a good travel account.

One of the most remarkable features of U.S.A. is the Biographies. It's a form I think you originated and I don't know of anyone who has been able to copy you successfully. (In fact, for a writer acclaimed as one of the most experimental of our century, you have had incommensurately little influence, technically, on younger writers; I think this is due to your having so fully developed the innovation that its possibilities for others have been exhausted.) You had started advancing toward the multi-centered novel from the beginning. Certain elements of it were in One Man's Initiation *and* Three Soldiers; *more were added in* Manhattan Transfer; *but it wasn't until* U.S.A. *that all the components of the formula found their place. Although there were small hints of the Biography device earlier, it was essentially a new element, and contributed mightily to the overall effect of the trilogy. What impelled you toward the Biography? What aesthetic concept was involved?*

It's rather hard to remember how one happens to hit on these things. The Newsreels were intended to give the clamor, the sound of daily life. In the Biographies, I tried to produce the pictures.

I have always paid a good deal of attention to painting. The period of art I was very much interested in at that time was the thirteenth and fourteenth centuries. Its tableaux with large figures of saints surrounded by a lot of little people just fascinated me. I tried to capture the same effect in words.

That was one of the ideas, but then a lot of things appear in books without the author knowing exactly how they got there. Also, I always had an interest in contrast, in the sort of montage Griffith and Eisenstein used in films. I was trying to put across a complex state of mind, an atmosphere, and I brought in these things partly for contrast and partly for getting a different dimension.

It has always seemed to me that the trilogy was very carefully thought out before it was ever begun. As I believe others have noted, in trying to achieve an amalgam, you were working on four levels: first, the Camera Eye, the personal experience of life in the twentieth century of the author himself; second, the narratives, mirroring the growth of this century, the emergence of this new beast U.S.A. following the Spanish-American War through which we became an imperial power —in fact, if not in name, an empire; third, the Newsreels, the Greek chorus in this heroic, hubristic, tragic drama; fourth, the Biographies, the men who influenced or typified that age. All these various levels kept moving toward a point of union which occurs in the final novel. As in Three Soldiers, *was it your conscious plan to go from stress on the commonly human experiences of youth to the rusting away of machinelike life at the end of the trilogy?*

Yes, I think it was. I started out to do it as one book. Then it became obvious the thing was going to be so long that it would be better to publish it in sections. But I did have a plan about the end particularly. Poe, you know, gives a very good maxim in one of his critical pieces: an author should always know what the end of a story is going to be before he starts the beginning.

Did any of these characters change in your own mind?

Yes. They always do. They change enormously. If the character is going to come to life, he is going to have to take things into his own hands.

Did you intend at any point to have one character or set of characters somehow typify each of the volumes? It seemed to me that Mac was the central character in the first novel, Joe Williams and Dick Savage the twin stars of the middle novel, Charlie Anderson the central character in the last, and J. Ward Morehouse perhaps the key figure of the whole trilogy.

Yes, that's about right. I think I did have that in mind, although I'm not sure how much I knew when I *started* about who was going to turn out most important in the various novels.

In 1919 you had a Biography on a man named Jack Reed. I was reading some critical material which discussed the emergence of "parajournalism"—writing which is half newspaper reporting, half personal reactions. It said that Mr. Reed had influenced such reporting. . . .

Jack Reed was a great character and, in addition, he wrote very well. His book on Mexico was excellent. And although it was not the most accurate, he gave us the most vivid account of the Bolshevik Revolution.

. . . in the newspaper vein . . .

Oh, it was better than that. It was the tops of American reportorial writing, in the same line as Stephen Crane and that fellow from San Francisco—what was his name? He wrote short stories.

Bierce?

Yes, of course, Ambrose Bierce. That was a great period in American journalism. We had awfully good writing in newspapers—which, unfortunately, you can hardly find today. Reporters then had much more freedom and there were a great many more newspapers. If writing according to your own tastes and standards lost you your job on one paper, you'd go on to another. Now we have journalistic monopolies and the business-like attitudes of the management are to some extent reflected in the reporters. The colorful styles, the flamboyance are largely gone.

What influence did the expatriate movement have on your work during that period?

Not very much. I was always opposed to it; I thought the whole idea was nonsense and I didn't spend very much time with any of those people. Hemingway was quite a good friend of mine and much of what I saw of all that was through him, although even he was not that much a part of that scene. Malcolm Cowley, whom I'd known ever since he turned up at Harvard, was more typical. He went on to popularize the expatriate thing, but he always had a genius for getting things wrong—just a little bit wrong, wrong enough to be not quite true.

In A Moveable Feast, *Hemingway struck out at lot of people who had been friends. You were close to him, have you any ideas why he did that?*

The poor fellow was going into a psychotic state. There are still traces of talent in *A Moveable Feast,* but it certainly doesn't rank among his best books. He was in rather good shape the last time I saw him, in 1948. The last two chapters in Hotchner's book contain a marvelous description of his decline; I've been trying to get psychiatrist friends of mine to read that book. It gives an excellent picture of a man entering—I don't know—you might call it schizophrenia or . . . well, the name doesn't matter. It seems to have been hereditary with him. His father apparently went into a similar state; he also killed himself—and at about the same age.

Could Hemingway's animosity have been due to his thinking he had been solely responsible for his success in writing and resenting others who tried to take some of the credit? That may have been the chief reason he turned on Gertrude Stein.

To an extent. He was a very competitive man. He would try to ride a bicycle as fast as the professionals could. . . .

. . . part of his fascination with the six day bicycle races. He seemed to love the endurance they call for and the itinerant, hedonist way of life of the racers.

Yes. He certainly made the six day races for me. Oh, he was a wonderful fellow to go around with—so enthusiastic and excited! He would point out all sorts of things you wouldn't have seen otherwise.

How would you rank your contemporaries, the men whom you are competing with?

I don't know. I've never had much of a sense of competition. It may be a weakness in me.

Do you think of yourself as being above the battle?

Outside of it—at least a little bit. I have always felt that way. Even in the period of the 'twenties, I always pretended that I wasn't going to be a writer, so I didn't feel as though I had to jockey for position. I had wanted to study architecture; I am a spoiled, frustrated architect.

How much did you and Hemingway influence each other?

Not at all, I think, although there were times when we were trying for the same things.

Didn't you ever have discussions about style?

He always used to bawl me out for including so much topical stuff. He always claimed that was a great mistake, that in fifty years nobody would understand. He may have been right; it's getting to be true.

At a certain moment, Hemingway produced some of the best short stories ever written in English. They hold up very well. Just as a stylist, he was awfully good. I used to claim that his style was a combination of cable-ese and the Holy Bible. He was a great reader of the Bible.

Did you really get into architecture?

No, not nearly as much as I once hoped to. I was always interested in objective painting, and I really did do more in painting than in architecture. By the time I got out of the war, I became involved in writing books about what I'd seen and felt over there. That changed my direction because I found that, having started writing books, I was always having to write one more to kind of make up for the deficiencies of the one I'd just completed.

Was it as good a time for writers then as it is now?

I think it was better. There were so many outlets. There must have been at least twenty, certainly fifteen, well-paying magazines in this country; if you couldn't sell something you'd written to one magazine, there was always the chance that another would buy it. Now the market has shrunk. Writers tend to fall back on teaching. Having the university as a patron may have advantages, but I think the disadvantages are greater.

I would agree. Most writers who find shelter in the university come to find that their work loses contact with the outside world. They begin to regard the university as an analogue to the universe. One sees this tendency magnified in the career of John Barth; to me it seems to have been injurious to the most dazzling of present talents.

Barth's first novel was awfully impressive, but I've gotten rather discouraged with him.

Getting back to your connecting the nature of the magazine market and the nature of fiction which is produced: the peculiar properties of the American novel are to some degree due to our writers having served an apprenticeship as short story writers; could your departures from the mainstream of American fiction be partly attributed to your never having followed this traditional route?

My "departures" were not due to my having rejected the short story, if that's what you mean. Rather you might say that the short story rejected me. I started a good many short stories, but they always got so involved, they turned into something else. Usually, they ended up as sections of some book. I never could write a short story.

So after "Honor of a Caliph" and the other juvenalia, you let the form go.

Yes. I found it just didn't work for me.

Having told us why you gave up on the short story, could you tell us why you gave up poetry?

My impulse for that sort of thing found an outlet in the novels, which do have poetic passages. That type of steam could be blown off in things like the Interludes in *Midcentury*. I got to a point where there was no particular reason for making separate little packages.

Did you ever feel impelled to be a poet?

Not exactly, no.

When Allen Ginsberg was here last spring, he listed you along with Whitman as an important influence on his poetry. I think he had in mind the similarity to Whitman in the beginning and end of U.S.A. *(the Vagabond part), but he might also have been referring to the relationship between the voice of the poet and the society he is commenting on.*

That's interesting. Some work I've been doing has sent me to my Whitman again; it's been a delight re-reading *Democratic Vistas*— I had forgotten how much insight there was there.

One of the things that strikes you about the great figures of that period is their ethics. At that time, people read the Bible and absorbed a body of tested wisdom about the conduct of life. Even when I was a boy, it was expected that children read the Bible; I remember my father seeing to it that I read chapters regularly. That's missing today and we're the poorer for it. No individual, no society can survive without ethics. I'm always very suspicious of the fellow who claims to have a personal morality; what he means is that he has no morality at all and feels free to do you dirt.

Do you see any relationship between the decline in constructive attitudes among college youth that you mentioned earlier and a decline in contemporary fiction?

I hesitate to say. I do think that the objective type of novel has now been run into the ground; it's become a means for exhibitionism in the technical sense, the psychiatric sense, of the word. It's become a bore for everybody.

Aside from Barth, are there any younger writers you have hopes for?

I don't read many novels—so many other things which give me so much more pleasure cry out to be read—but I might mention John Updike. I haven't read any of his things since *Rabbit, Run,* but that book was full of talent; he described his people remarkably well.

If I may, I'd like to move into another area. After the Civil War, there seemed to be self-conscious concern with writing an American epic, a Great American Novel. In the works of various writers, this was manifested as an attempt to encompass the whole of our society. We got this in Frank Norris's projected trilogy and later in a number of other works as well. Somewhat modified, it is reflected in Wescott's The Grandmothers, *in Sherwood Anderson's* Poor White, *in Gertrude Stein's* The Making of Americans, *even (to an extent) in the works of William Carlos Williams and the poetry of Vachel Lindsay. Certainly your own* U.S.A. *is a magnificent mural of a nation. How conscious was your generation of writers of striving for a panorama which would capture the essence of a nation?*

A good many people were pretty conscious of it. I think Scott Fitzgerald shows this in the one about the bootlegger—*The Great Gatsby.* It's his best work.

Perhaps the one Fitzgerald book which still stands up.

I was very much taken with the last also—the fragment of *The Last Tycoon.* Had the fellow lived long enough, it might have turned out to be a wonderful book.

You've said that in The Last Tycoon *Fitzgerald had created something new in the language. What was unique about it?*

48

It just struck me as being a well-rounded, Tolstoi-like picture of the things he was trying to describe. I mean Tolstoi at his best, not Tolstoi the propagandist.

Hemingway felt that Fitzgerald whined in public in The Crack-Up. *Didn't you upbraid Fitzgerald for the same thing?*

I didn't want him to publish *The Crack-Up*. I felt that he had so much more left to him and it wasn't the time to publish something like that. I think now that I was wrong. It really is a remarkable piece of work. He probably couldn't have done anything else.

Talking about The Crack-Up *brings to mind another writer who was involved in it—Glenway Wescott. When he was here in 1965, Wescott said he thought American writers went to Europe after the First World War, not so much because they wanted to flee from the artistic climate in America but because it was so much cheaper to live abroad. Would you agree?*

He gave a perfectly sound reason. Those were days when Americans had the advantage of a favorable currency exchange. But those writers did pay a price—after awhile, they tended to stew in their own juice. The world of the expatriate can become rather unreal, one in which the dégagé yet engagé thing I talked about earlier can disappear.

I'd like to ask you about a writer who is very engagé. Norman Mailer, especially in his The Naked and the Dead, *has frequently been compared to Hemingway, but I think the parallel to your work is closer. The similarity in the way you both broke up your narratives is obvious, but beyond that, there is a resemblance in your rhythms, in the way the words fit together. I was especially conscious of this in re-reading the Charley Anderson sections of* U.S.A. *I believe I once read that Mailer admitted having your rhythms in mind when he wrote about the members of his platoon.*

Maybe that's why I liked *The Naked and the Dead,* although to be perfectly frank, I'd have to say I wasn't conscious of the resemblance. His account of the platoon as it goes on reconnaisance is really marvelous—awfully good naturalism—but some of the early passages and the end seem phony and make me uneasy.

49

The Time Machine device, of course, was also derived from you. . . .

Strange, I hadn't noticed that. In fact, I don't even remember it.

There is also a parallel between Mailer's career and yours in that he has become increasingly involved in social issues and, in a way, writing contemporary history much as you did and do. Armies of the Night *bears some resemblance to the manner in which you reported the Harlan strike and the Sacco-Vanzetti case.*

That's an interesting parallel but a curious one because I've grown impatient with him. I don't think he makes for easy reading anymore.

In 1930, analyzing what was wrong with American drama, you said that the heart of Broadway was in Hollywood; do you still think that's true?

It was certainly true at the time I said it. Plays then were being written with an eye on Hollywood. I guess things haven't changed much. I keep getting encouraged about the new season when I read about it in the drama section of the newspapers, but when I actually go see the plays, I am very discouraged.

The situation in theater is tragic because we have such good producing organizations in this country—particularly in the small theaters—and a great many excellent actors. In all kinds of small theatres and in college theaters, I have occasionally seen first rate acting, first-rate production, and truly imaginative scenic effects. Yet, for some reason, nobody seems to be able to breathe any life into the theater.

Earlier, you stated that Eisenstein and Griffith influenced U.S.A.; *do you see any current relationship between cinema and fiction which might be producing something new?*

I haven't been following recent movies very much. I did see *2001* and was much taken with it. It's a very attractive, poetic piece of work—one of the few poetic things I've seen come out of Hollywood in a long while. It is, of course, reflective of a great mass of science fiction being written. I'm ashamed that I am not as up on science fiction as I might be, because that may be one form of writing where something quite good is being done. Some of Ray Bradbury's things, for instance, are really excellent.

The relationship between Eisenstein and Griffith and your work was one of technique. . . .

Entirely technique. It had nothing whatever to do with content.

Don't you see any connection between Godard, Truffaut, Polanski, and the rest of the cinematic avant-garde and the novel? Between the nouvelle vague and the mixture of comedy and tragedy, of farce and the real you get in writers like Barth and Vonnegut?

I don't think so. There is now probably less interest by writers in cinema because we have become so accustomed to this medium that it is less exciting than when it was very new.

Before our time runs out, might we talk a bit about the Sacco-Vanzetti case? Being of Italian extraction, I've always felt what happened to those two men to be part of my heritage. Because of your intimate ties to that agony, I was wondering whether you have read Francis Russell's Tragedy in Dedham?

Yes. It is very interesting, although I don't agree with it. I was very good friends with Carlo Tresca. . . .

That's why I brought this up. Russell bases his conclusion that Sacco was guilty on two things: the ballistics test he ran at the time of writing his book and Carlo Tresca's off hand statement just before he died that although Vanzetti was innocent, Sacco wasn't.

I wonder about his examination of the evidence because it was so long after the trial; and my report of what Tresca said would be different. As I remember it, Tresca was pointing out that there was no question but that Sacco and Vanzetti were both trying to protect members of the anarchist group. Carlo thought—and he knew more than he told about it—that his group had been involved with a professional criminal gang in some of these hold-ups.

You no longer think that Madeiros was involved in that crime?

It's very hard to tell. He might have been. Tresca's view doesn't necessarily rule out Madeiros. Madeiros's reasons for saying what he did were, I thought, perfectly honest and above board. The way he put things sounded as if he knew what he was talking about.

How much similarity do you perceive between the agitation over Sacco-Vanzetti, which was something of a watershed dividing the "two nations" in America, and current agitation over Viet Nam and the race issue, which is also dividing us into two nations?

To me, the Sacco-Vanzetti agitation was much more understandable. I had great sympathy for the anarchist movement at that time, even though it was obvious the solutions they were suggesting were non-sensical. But it seemed to me that those attitudes served to freshen people's minds. It was also interesting because it was the last expression of the great anarchist movement before it was finally crushed by the Soviet Union.

But now there is renewed interest in anarchist theories. . . .

We don't know exactly what these are. Incidentally, I think it will prove to be good for a lot of these kids to have this attitude for a while—as long as they don't get stuck in it.

We get back to your earlier question about one tyranny replacing another. With age, one discovers the way the human race works: in simple terms, top dog always gets to the top, no matter what the system is, and then top dog starts kicking bottom dog in the face. No change in ideology changes that basic fact. Fifty years of Soviet history magnificently exemplify it.

In reading your novels, one is hit by how often figures appear who are modeled in part on yourself. Very often you are quite unflattering to these people. Why do you expose yourself so? What makes you claw at such obvious personae *as Ro Lancaster and Jed?*

It's part of the search for objectivity. Any novelist gets a great deal of himself into all of his characters, although he usually starts by trying to describe something else and does get a great deal of other people mixed into these characters. Perhaps to say that he ends up describing himself would be an over-simplification. The blood and nerves of the characters have to come from the writer's emotions and frustrations. My system has always been to try to do it objectively. That's why I put the Camera Eye things in *U.S.A.*; it was a way of draining off the subjective by directly getting in little bits of my own experience.

For you, then, the author's relation to his novel is both that of the puppet master and puppet. You probably don't remember a chat we

*had seven years ago in which you mentioned the various influences
on your work. One you mentioned was Thackeray in* Vanity Fair. *I
took this to mean that you were intrigued by the tension between the
man standing above his theater (like the Camera's Eye) and the characters on his stage (like the narratives.)*

No. What influenced me in Thackeray was that he tried to give a
picture of society in *Vanity Fair* through primary and secondary figures. It's a marvelous job.

*Judging by that criterion, which of your books would you say are
best?*

I haven't the faintest idea. It's up to the critics to fight that out.

How do you begin to write a novel?

I get started somehow, and then one word just follows another. I have
a fairly definite notion of what I am trying to do. I try to do it, then
I rewrite. In the early stages particularly, I find things have to be re-
written a good many times. Then, later, I fall into the style I've
created and the writing falls together more easily.

*Someone reported, perhaps not accurately, that you were in the
habit of filing away newspaper headlines in a drawer until, eventually, a novel suddenly emerged.*

I did keep a lot of them. That's how the Newsreel thing started. I
kept cutting out little clippings that seemed amusing. I started doing
that quite early in my career. In *Manhattan Transfer,* I didn't use
them directly, but I introduced them to show that I knew more or
less what was going on in the world in which my characters lived. It
was important to know what these people were reading, seeing, thinking. Then some of these collections of bits started to look so good to
me that I put them in intact. Later, I started searching for apt headlines and collecting what would fit the story.

Did you ever make them up?

No. I didn't have to. It was a period in which the newspapers were
rather amusing.

Although you talked earlier about how U.S.A. *evolved, you've said
nothing about the D. C. trilogy and the way it grew. When you began*

Adventures of a Young Man, *Joyce seems to have been in the fore-front of your mind; you were apparently trying to do something different from your earlier writing. In* Number One, *however, you went in the direction of the more conventional novel. Then, in* The Grand Design, *you returned to the same technical attack you had used in* U.S.A.

I was anxious not to go on imitating *U.S.A.* I felt I had to get on different terrain.

The three were such different novels; have you any thoughts as to which was the most successful?

None. I haven't read them in such a long time.

This morning another Harvard man pointed out that many important literary figures from Eliot and Cummings in your day to Mailer and Updike among the younger generation went to Harvard. You burgeoned as an artist at Harvard: do you believe there is anything about the place, now or in 1916 . . .

For me, the main thing that was there was the afterglow of the great New Englanders. There were remnants of a kind of Emersonian Congregationalism that had turned out some awfully fine people. However, I fought against that quality all the time I was there. I stayed at Harvard only because my father wanted me to. He was getting quite old and I followed his wishes.

Wasn't there a lingering presence of Henry Adams?

Not very noticeable. Santayana was very noticeable, though he had just left. There was an aesthetic atmosphere filtering through the place.

I was thinking about Adams's concern with the dynamo, with entropy, and your reaction to the machine and industrialism.

Of those I knew, I was probably the only one interested in that.

Although you are now citing your respect for the influences of the great New Englanders, didn't you satirize puritan ethics in your early novel, Streets of Night?

Yes, I think so. But my encounter with that atmosphere, as I look back on it, now seems to have been much more valuable than I was aware at the time.

Paul brought up Streets of Night. *I have suspected that it, and not* One Man's Initiation, *was really your first novel, that you had begun it while an undergraduate.*

Strange, I don't remember. Yet, some notes I had made corroborate your impression. When I was writing *In Our Time* [sic], I started looking back into some old notebooks. I went back to them again even more recently because people at Cornell had found unexpurgated proofs of *One Man's Initiation,* which somebody must have bought in England and donated to the Cornell Library. They had been there I don't know how long before they were fished out. Cornell was bringing out an edition of this unexpurgated version and they asked me to do a sort of preface. In writing it, I looked up some of the diaries of that time that I still have. There was one for 1917 which referred back to *Streets of Night* as something already started. So I must have started it when I was at Harvard, laid it aside, and then tried to bring it back to life after the war.

Were you in the practice of taking many notes in preparation for your writing?

Yeah. A great bit. I wish I did as much of it now as I did then. Very useful to me. And it's wonderful to look back on these things because they sometimes contain most startling surprises.

Like "A Humble Protest." That brings us full circle. Thank you, Mr. Dos Passos.

OCTOBER 16, 1968

A Humble Protest

J. R. Dos Passos, Jr.

There is a tendency abroad to glorify, in sounding journalistic phrases, the age in which we live and the "wonders of science" which have brought it about. Man is pictured as enthroned on a girder-constructed pinnacle, calling the four winds to his service, enslaving the sea, annihilating time and space with the telegraph ticker. It all makes excellent material for the Sunday newspapers, and for the addresses of railroad presidents. A splendid thing it is, indeed, to contemplate the freeing of man from the elements, from the old base bondages of wind and tide. "He is ready," continue the clergymen and speechmakers, "mighty in blue overalls, to lay his hand to the task of constructing the new, the clean, the sanitary civilization." Meanwhile—so goes the peroration—our men of science sweep the universe with their telescopes, run into corners the most elusive of stars, taking their snapshots as it were, and feeling the pulse of their chemical composition by means of the spectroscope. Others, at the time, grow cells as our ancestors grew cabbages, and, through the agency of their powerful microscopes, walk in strange molecular gardens. Disease, with a capital D, is prostrate at the feet of medicine; even Death is receding, dejectedly dragging his scythe, before the incantations of Professor Metchnikoff.

There is a round of applause and the audience goes home to partake of its canned dinners—gathered from all the ends of the earth, economists tell us: raisins from Greece; bananas from Cuba; lamb from New Zealand; eggs from China, all reunited on one menu!—after which they read popular works of science, or, if they are enlightened, unpopular ones in German, before getting what sleep they

---

This essay was published in the Harvard Monthly *at the end of Mr. Dos Passos's senior year. The references to it in the text of the interview and its similarity to current sentiments argued for its being reprinted here. The original punctuation has been retained.*

may amid the roar of the traffic outside their windows. Such is the way we regard science, bowing down to it as abjectly as ever bigot bowed before the image of the Madonna, making it, in every sense but the literal, the object of our worship, the new god of our country.

Humanity has a strange fondness for following processions. Get four men following a banner down the street, and, if that banner is inscribed with rhymes of pleasant optimism, in an hour all the town will be afoot, ready to march to whatever tune the leaders care to play. Today the tune is science. Then, there is something very pathetic in the way the mob is now and again deprived of its idols and banners, and left to wander muddleheadedly through meaningless streets. You may be sure, however, that before the day is up a new temple will have opened its doors, where all the world will throng to do honor to the new god. Before long the priests will have distributed the words of the hymn, and all the crowd will be lustily singing, comfortable in companionship, the paeon of the new shibboleth. To this trick of the mind is added the tendency to believe, somehow, that what is, is right and must endure forever. Even in oneself it is hard to eradicate the idea, to realize that no state of society is inevitable or ultimate, and that, so far as the limitations of our perceptions go, its flux is eternal.

Once, long ago, it was faith in religion people thought eternal; then it was the tendency to liberty; now it is the scientific age.

Isn't it time, once more, to question; to try to discover where this steel-girded goddess, with her halo of factory smoke and her buzzing chariotwheels of industry, is leading the procession of human thought which follows so tamely in her trail? What, we should ask, is the result on the life of men of the spirit of science: the pursuit of facts for their own sake? What is the goal of this mechanical, splendidly inventive civilization of ours?

Before attempting to protest against the present attitude towards these questions, it is necessary to face the inevitable, unanswerable, question: what is the end of human life? So far no one has done much more than obscure the issue with glowing catch-words. All the Christs, all the philosophers, all the scientists have cloaked it under a sounding phrase and passed on. "Reason," "Conformity of Will," "Godliness," "Life, Liberty and the Pursuit of Happiness," "Virtue": any of them will do, since impotence before the ultimate ends does not preclude the assumption that some finite state or point of view is, so far as personal opinion goes, the highest. Of course, your mode of attack on the whole problem depends on the particular patch of tapestry you pick out with which to cover the hole in your thatched roof of dogma. It might be possible to divide life's aims, always under the limitations of opinion, into two half-opposed ideals; thought and art; Plato and Michael Angelo. To be sure, they overlap in great measure; but each has an outer fringe independent of the other. One is the desire to create; the other the desire to fathom. Intangibly mixed up with them is a sense of beauty, quick-silver-like, three times dangerous to argue about, to dogmatize on, by which, somehow, we veneer the crudeness of the world and make it bearable —far more than bearable.

It is here that the fundamental question comes. How do these two things fare under the rule of science and its attendant spirits, Industrialism, and Mechanical Civilization?

Perhaps it is only fair to inquire first what alternatives there are to these twin guide-posts for humanity, which I may call thought and art. Is there any other path to the fullness of life? Surely material comforts,—three meals a day, and machine-made shirts,—are merely a rung in the ladder, not the platform of attainment. Surely work is not an end in itself; labor, the mere wearing away of muscle, is not ennobling. Surely the investigation, the tabulation of all the component parts of the external world is not the summit of life.

And I do not mean the end of life for the few, for the initiate, for the specially prepared ones; far indeed from any ideal is the present human pyramid where the few at the top are in the sunlight while the rest sweat in the filthy darkness of meaningless labor. However much one may desire the supreme individual, the superman, he is not to be got by degrading the mass of men from whose loins he must spring.

With these two supreme desires in mind; to fathom and to create, this civilization of ours, prostrate before the popular gods of materialism, on the one hand, and the inner shrine of science, of divine fact, on the other, takes on a different aspect. If it accomplishes nothing else the present war will conduce to a less receptive attitude. The stodgy complacency of the nineteenth century can hardly stand such a shattering of beliefs. Men, at least those whose lives and souls are not sucked into the whirlpool, will be forced to bring their ideals before the bar of criticism, to sift them, to try them, to attempt to discover where they really lead. Indeed it is not very hard, at the present hour, to reach the sceptical frame of mind required for the breaking down of the modes of thought inherited from the last epoch. The war, the growing acuteness of labor problems, the state of contemporary art, the growing outward ugliness of life,—any of them can be used as an acid to sear away the old complacency.

It is then that you find the question before you: What are the results of our worship of this two-fold divinity: Science and Industrialism?

In the first place, positive knowledge has increased to an infinite degree. The method of knowledge too, the aggregation of facts into a systematic whole, has been firmly established. Then, through the omnipresent results of scientific invention, life has, in one sense, become far easier, more luxurious, more refined. The world has become very small, very united—(so we thought, until the war shattered, irredeemably perhaps, the cosmopolitan point of view). In short, man's dependence on natural phenomena has been enormously lessened. Whether that dependence, increased fourfold, has not been merely transferred to a force more subtle is another question.

It seems to me incontestable that since the Renaissance the greatest minds—with few exceptions—have been engaged in the building up of science. Their vigor and sheer intellect have affirmed in infinitely more striking terms the vague hypotheses of the Greek philosophers. The influence on all future thought of the mechanical view of the universe built up by Newton and his predecessors is impossible to estimate. Their activity in the period following the artistic Renaissance, the development of the atomic theory which succeeded, and the promulgation of the theory of evolution in the nineteenth century, are all gigantic milestones of human achievement. These, with their train of minor accomplishment, have stimulated all departments of thought and life. Most recently of all, the theories of probabilities and the laws of thermo-dynamics have entirely changed man's point of view towards the universe.

All this is an achievement not to be tarnished by the most fulsome praise from those people who run after every idea sufficiently old—or new, as the case may be,—with glad hallelujahs.

With minds strengthened, and channels of thought infinitely deepened, men of intellect would, one should have thought, have turned towards the problems of human life and social intercourse, or, what is of more importance, to the vivider living of life which lies in art and in abstract thought, with new vigor and keenness. Has this been the case?

The race, comparatively speaking, has lived a short time under a state of concentrated civilization. Even so, amid the surging triumph of certain phases of the intellect, it would have been reasonable for a man say of Shakespeare's day, sufficiently keen-sighted to have guessed at the importance of such a scientist as Harvey, to imagine that the next two centuries would see a nearer approach to the solution of the important problems of life. Can the most blatant optimist claim that this has been so?—outside, to be sure, of a number of purely superficial things like sanitation, which have genuinely changed for the better. Except for the single triumph of liberalism over superstition in all its forms, religious, political, moral, which was the French Revolution, can we honestly say that life is intenser, that art is greater, that thought is more profound in our age than in the reign of Elizabeth? Are we not still as aimlessly struggling as before, plunging merely from one bondage into another? You cannot honestly affirm that opportunity for producing great art,—and art is certainly one of the touchstones, if not *the* touchstone of a civilization,—or even the opportunity for a general interest in the forms of beauty, is greater than it was three centuries and a half ago. Most thoughtful people will say it is less; and some will go so far as to insist that civilization has outlived art, has grown beyond the necessity for it, as it has grown beyond certain forms of religion, and black magic. In that case, would it not be that civilization had outlived life? There must be causes for all this, causes which can be rooted out; for it cannot be that man has gained the whole world only to lose his own soul.

May not some of the fault—if we admit there is a fault—come from the unreasoning acceptance of this new superstition: science? May not something be traced to the tendency this new superstition has, I believe, fostered, to slight the part man plays in the universe as man sees it? It is possible that, from over-preoccupation with what is at the other end of our telescopes and microscopes, we have lost our true sense of proportion. In learning the habits of the cells of a man's epidermis, it is easy to forget his body as a unit. In the last analysis, the universe is but as we see it: all is relative to the sense perceptions of the body. In this consuming interest in science, in knowledge of the exterior, in the tabulation of fact, haven't we forgotten the *Know thyself* of the Greeks? Not that we lack self-consciousness. Heaven knows, we tabulate our emotions as eagerly as our observations of the spectrum of Uranus! It is not that which we need.

In succession, Roman stoicism, Pauline Christianity, and the Ages of Faith have kept prisoner under varying bonds that humanism, that realization of the fullness of man, which was the heritage of the Greeks, and in another form, of Jesus. The French Revolution, to my mind, was a manifestation of it, a re-birth more important than the limited Italian Renaissance. The most tragic part of modern history lies in the fact that the glorious movement of liberation has in turn been conquered by that bastard of science, the Industrial Revolution.

Thus it is that the minor, but the infinitely more numerous part of the energies of the scientific spirit have been turned to building about us a silly claptrap of unnecessary luxuries, a clutter of inessentials which has been the great force to smother the arts of life and the arts of creation.

Under industrialism the major part of human kind runs in a vicious circle. Three-fourths of the world are bound in economic slavery that the other fourth may in turn be enslaved by the tentacular inessentials of civilization, for the production of which the lower classes have ground out their lives. Half the occupations of men today are utterly demoralizing to body and soul, and to what end?

In Samuel Butler's satire on humanity in general and on the English in particular, *Erewhon,* describing a fictitious nation rather after the manner of Swift, is a chapter called "The Book of the Machines." It tells fantastically how all complicated machinery was abolished in this country of Erewhon because the inhabitants feared lest it should eventually find itself consciousness and enslave the race of men. There is a flash of profound thought in the idea.

Has not the world today somehow got itself enslaved by this immense machine, the Industrial system. Millions of men perform labor narrowing and stultifying even under the best conditions, bound in the traces of mechanical industry, without ever a chance of self-expression, except in the hectic pleasures of suffocating life in cities. They grind their lives away on the wheels, producing, producing, producing. And of all the results of this degrading, never-ending labor, how little is really necessary to anyone; how much is actually destructive of the capacity of men for living, for the fathoming of life, for the expression of life.

How long will the squirrel contentedly turn his wheel and imagine he is progressing? Are we so certain of the benefits of all this that the last hundred years has given us that there must be no discussion of the question? Most people are very certain; but most people are always certain. In the Middle Ages most people had no qualms as to the doctrine of intolerance or the institution of serfdom.

Still, there is discontent among us. In the light of the flames of burning Belgium towns civilized men look at each other with a strange new horror. Is this what men have been striving for through the ages? Is this ponderous suicidal machine civilization? The rabies of Germany has been a fearful disillusionment. The one modern nation which, as well as having developed the industrial system to its highest degree, has a really great living art has suddenly slipped back into barbarism. The same civilization has produced Wagner and Von Tirpitz, the Eroica Symphony and the ruins of Rheims.

This is the time of all others for casting up the balance sheet of Industrialism, of our scientific civilization. Shall we not find that man's material power has far outgrown his ability to put it to constructive use? Are we not like men crouching on a runaway engine? And at the same time we insensately shovel in the fuel with no thought as to where we are being taken.

Even if you deny entirely that Science and Industrialism, two forces at present bound up together, not inseparably I hope, have tended for evil, have they tended for good? Is life any broader, more intense, truly freer from material hindrances because of them? Can it be that we have abandoned our old benevolent gods only to immolate ourselves before a new Moloch—in futile sacrifice?

Cambridge, Mass., 1916

Robert Penn Warren

Mr. Warren, what led you to a literary career? That seems an appropriate place to start.

I had always liked to read, poetry especially, but when I started college at Vanderbilt, I wanted to be a scientist. That didn't last long. My chemistry course was rather dull; my English course was exciting. That course, to be short about it, led to my deciding to write poetry. It's not really as simple as that, but teaching provided the sparks. As for writing fiction, that started almost by accident. A friend, Paul Rosenfeld, who, with Van Wyck Brooks and Lewis Mumford, was editing a literary annual called *The American Caravan* and who had heard me tell some stories of the world of my boyhood, asked me to write a novelette based on them. I decided to try and discovered that it was fun. The novelette was published and a publisher asked me for a novel.

Thomas Hardy was happy when he could put aside his novels and write poetry. Do you prefer working in one genre more than the others?

Depends on what I'm working on at the time. I've thought about this some, and I think that writing poetry is more fun for me. It's so much more personal. I don't mean the material is necessarily more personal, but that it's a closer, more private activity. And technically it's a more exciting challenge: getting the words into the arc of the line and co-ordinating the meaning with the rhythm. I write poetry until it runs dry and the lines stop coming. Then I'll switch to a novel and ride along with that, sometimes for six or seven years or maybe more. I don't have any theories about this beyond riding with the impulse.

The key impulse, the germinal feeling, is rather alike whether it's fiction you're working on or poetry. Short stories, especially, are close to poems in their manner of conception. I didn't write a great many short stories because I kept liking the form less and less until I quit the form altogether. Long ago. As soon as I quit, I knew I wanted to write poems again. From 1944, I guess it was, until ten years after, I hadn't finished one short poem. I had started many, but could never complete a single one. Then the poems began again.

In mentioning how you change from one kind of writing to another, you've left out criticism.

That's a different kind of activity. It's an extension of teaching— even conversation. There's something about a poem or a novel that you've perceived, and you try to explain it, to bring it to clarity. That's what the critical act basically is, I suppose. I don't mean to depreciate it—we certainly should value good literary criticism— but writing criticism is less fun, at one level, than writing fiction or poems where you're in a dialogue with what you're creating, try- ing to find the implicit meaning. In criticism, you may have prob- lems organizing what you know, but you pretty much know as much when you finish the piece as when you start.

Does the fact that an idea can be realized in more than one genre account for the confusion of genres in something like Brother to Dragons?

Not in fact, but as an idea, it started out as a novel; then as a play; then, I think, I turned back to the novel idea. Then the thing as published. Then there was a dramatic version, produced in several places: American Place Theater and Adrian Hall's Trinity Players in Providence.

It seems historical events have a special hold on you. At Heaven's Gate, All the King's Men, World Enough and Time, *and* The Cave *—there may be others—all contain recognizable historical figures or occurrences. Why is this?*

Recognizable figures? I don't think they are recognizable from my treatment of them. I'm not being facetious. Writing a story about an actual person and using him as a kind of model are really not the same. I don't pretend that Willie Stark is Huey Long. I know Stark, but I have no idea what Long was really like. I heard him speak once at an enormous official luncheon celebrating the 75th anniversary of the founding of Louisiana State University—he had not been invited but walked in anyway and took over, and he was very funny. Then on another occasion I saw him—or I think it was he—in a passing car.

I knew stories about Long, but that's quite different. What happened with the real Long and what his motives were is between him, his God, and his conscience. There's no way in the world for me, or you, to know that. But I know water runs downhill; and if a bomb explodes, I know that someone lit the fuse. Events don't cause themselves. I saw the end-products of Long and I know that men's motives and actions are triggered and operate in certain ways.

Ducking the question . . . .

I'm not ducking it . . . .

No, I mean, let me ask the question in another way. What was it about the Kentucky tragedy that caught your eye?

That came right out of an historical situation. Sure, there is a relationship in almost all of my novels with something that was a germ of fact. Individual personalities become mirrors of their times, or the times become a mirror of the personalities. Social tensions have a parallel in the personal world. The individual is an embodiment of external circumstances so that a personal story is a social story. The mirror business has always struck me as being pretty interesting. I didn't frame this concept early in the process of writing novels, but I have discovered it works as a principle over a long time.

As for my use of history: I was raised in a world where people talked about the past a lot and read history. Formal history and the informal, local kind. So this sense of the relationship of past to present was a natural one for me. As a child, I remember reading and being read to—and it was primarily history. The history of the Romans, the history of the Greeks. The only history I ever took in my college life was English—and that was a required course.

My choosing the "Kentucky tragedy" tale was an accident. I was at the Library of Congress—I had the chair of Poetry—and Katherine Anne Porter, an old friend, who was a Library Fellow in American letters, had an office near mine. One day she said, "Look here's something for you," and handed me the *Confession of Jeroboam Beauchamp* and I read it. I had vaguely heard of this before, I guess through the two novels by William Gilmore Simms. It has been treated by others, too. Poe wrote a play about it, in Renaissance disguise. Then there was a book called *Greyslaer: A Romance of the Mohawk* by a fellow named [Charles Fenno] Hoffman—from this neighborhood [i.e. New York State] as a matter of fact. He changed the scene from Kentucky to the Mohawk Valley. He had earlier reported the trial in a book called *A Winter in the West,* a travel book published in 1826. This story, you see, has had a lot of literary adaptations, but I didn't know that before I got interested in it and began to look around. Without realizing the story had played such a role in American letters, I was caught right off by the character and by the situation, the conflict between what was called the "New Court" party and the "Old Court" party in Kentucky, between new and old, and by the "mirror" thing I mentioned before. Then, too, I shouldn't underplay the importance of the fact that it had happened around my home section. Beauchamp got into trouble in my home country, and I had some sense of what that world had been like. I could bring to my surmises a certain body of feeling.

When you write novels based on history, do you think of your reader as knowing the stories in the way that Greek audiences knew the stories on which the tragedies were based?

Well, no. You can't really. You have to carry a context. Oh, at a certain level, yes, you expect some familiarity with the period, but hardly anybody would know about the Old versus the New Court party in Kentucky in 1820.

Incidentally, the New Court party reminded me of the New Deal. The issues were somewhat the same: adjustments of debts, economic crises. You can sometimes see one political era in terms of another.

I hadn't realized that your use of history also involved a dialogue between the real and the ideal.

If I understand you, this would mean adjusting historical "fact" to fictional need. I can give you an instance in which such a change was deliberate. I found that my historical man, Jeroboam Beauchamp, who killed his ex-sponsor and benefactor, Colonel Sharp, had belonged to the Old Court party and that Sharp belonged to the New Court. Now that didn't suit my scheme. The older man should be with the Old Court, the young man with the New—the "idealistic." In terms of my theme, that was the wrong lay-out, so I shifted them around. I had no compunction about doing this, because the historical Beauchamp was merely a prototype of my hero, and besides was of no historical importance.

Your comments about a dialogue with history remind me of Faulkner. Faulkner said somewhere that there were only two nations in the United States—the South and New England. At least in part, he seemed to have meant that this sense of nationhood, of a people united by common body of myth, was tied in with the region's closeness to its history.

Americans in general have a more highly developed sense of history than the Europeans because our history is so short. A man my age has known, right in his own family, people whose memories go back farther than the mid-point of our history as an independent nation. Now that's bound to have an effect on our thinking about the past.

The South is a special case. It lost the war and suffered hardship. That kind of defeat gives the past great importance. There is a need somehow to keep it alive, to justify it, and this works to transform the record of fact into legend. In the process, pain, dreariness, the particulars of the individual experience become absorbed in the romantic fable. The romance, you see, becomes stronger than the fact of any one story and changes it; even if you are only one or two generations removed from the event, it's hard to see through the romantic haze. Maybe that's one of the reasons Southern writers are so concerned with history. They've heard the stories since they were kids and later on they try to understand them in terms of their own range of experience as human beings. And in terms of scholarly history.

All the King's Men was first written as a play. What virtues did it gain in its re-casting in novel form?

My approach to the question would not be abstract. The changes had to do with how the re-casting happened. As you said, I wrote the play version first. I showed it to a friend who knew about drama, Francis Fergusson, who worked on it quite seriously and gave me a brief concentrated course in drama based on my play. But then I laid the story aside and wrote another book. It kept nagging at me, however, and I decided to revise it and make it a novel.

It was a tight little play. When I read it over, I missed part of my feelings involved in the original idea. The significant context for the action, the world in which these things could happen, was not there. Formulation of the context grew in the process of writing a novel. It was this instinct for a context that drove me on. Besides, I knew more about novels than I did about plays. The notion—or *a* notion—behind the play was that a man gains power because he is drawn into a vacuum of power. In one sense, is a creation of history. There was the germ of this in the first version, but in the novel this became more and more important—as "context." The narrator, Burden, has a "vacuum"—purposelessness—that Stark can fill. The bodyguard stutters, and Stark "talks so good." And so on with the mistress and others. For each individual, the "strong man" is a fulfillment. Here the individuals are the mirrors to society, in a sense.

But to return to the narrator, as an aside. He was the key in this respect. But he originally came into existence as a kind of accident. As a matter of fact, technical requirements often dictate character and meaning. It may be an aside here, but I'll tell how this particular character came about. In the play there is, of course, the assassination scene, in which the young doctor waits in the lobby of the capitol for the political boss to appear. You know he's outraged and that he has a gun in his pocket, and so you know he's going to shoot this guy. Now what happens? Let's take the play. A man comes out on stage, hand in pocket, hat dripping rain. He stands there. Stop. Let's pretend we're in the audience; we have all the information—couldn't have missed it—and as we sit there watching we say, "Go ahead and shoot him." Well, he hasn't come out yet. To which we say, "Come out and get shot, coward." Of course, you see the problem. The author has to satisfy the demand to get on with the play, yet he can't go too fast or it would kill the play. It can't happen rapidly—automatically according to the expectations. A barrel, rolling down a hill, hits a tree, breaks up. That's action, but it's not drama. You've got to find some way to make the barrel bounce off here and bounce off there. Will it hit? Will it not? In short: distract attention. Throw something across the path of the driving object. A competing interest which serves as a "hold" to make the inevitable, when it happens, come as unforeseen.

This principle of a "hold" and distraction is rudimentary to dramatic art, to any form of telling which is not pure lyric poetry. It's as natural as breathing, but still it's very difficult to devise. You are not working out a syllogism or adding a bridge score; you are trying to fool people. You work towards something which is *expected* and at the same time *not expected;* you want a double take on it. You want shock or surprise, and yet a sense of its being logical. You want variety, and you want the obvious line of a simple plot.

So here we are in this scene: "Come on out!" If he comes out and it's bang-bang, then there's nothing to it, nothing but a blank spot. If you wind up this way, the play is dead. So I had to find something to fall across this moment when the assassin is waiting. Something both natural and distracting. So I brought in someone and tried to get a conversation underway. "How are things going?" "All right, I guess." "We had a lot of good times when we were kids, didn't we?" "Sure had good times." And the assassin says, "We certainly did."

That's the sort of thing you build on. Now, even at the moment before the act which means his own death too, he takes a backward look on life—boyhood, innocence, and all of that. "Yes, we had nice times,"—and in that little moment of speech there's retrospect to a lost world. Then out comes the victim. Bang! Bang! But you've gotten something across there, some current of feeling running counter to the other drive.

So when I first began to think of starting over with a novel, I had to decide on the "voice." The idea of an all-knowing author felt all wrong; no principle for dramatizing development, no internal dramatization of the "vacuum." So out of the air I pulled the name-less newspaper man, an old friend. Give him a role—"vacuum." Why not make it complicated? Make it an employee of the victim: his hatchet man. I've known men from the newspaper world and their theatrical stances. So, O.K., put him in and let him start talk-ing. You're on your way.

So, you see, the play got switched over to a novel because of a defect of meaning, because it didn't have a context, and because of a technical consideration. But told this way, things sound a bit too deliberate. They are arrived at by trial and error usually. You rule out one possibility and then grope around for something else. You follow some hunch rather than a line of abstract reasoning.

Did you recognize the problem with the play before or after it was first produced at the University of Minnesota?

That production took place after the novel had been out six months or so. A friend of mine, Eric Bentley, who is now an eminent critic of drama, was one of my colleagues there. He asked me, "Didn't you write this as a play once?" I said, "Yes." "Let me see it," he said. So I did and he took it around to the drama school where they decided to introduce it. It was a very splendid production.

Mr. Warren, in your talking about how the story developed in your mind, you said "an assassin," "a newspaper man," "a politican." At what point did these characters acquire an identity? When did "a politician" become Willie Stark?

The name was there at the start, but it was Willie Talos, not Stark. And the name was a little secret indicator buried in the play—back to the nature of the "strong man." Talos was the iron groom of *The Faerie Queen,* Book Five—the mindless, aimless groom of justice who wields the iron flail; he doesn't decide whether something is just or unjust, he simply attacks. This way my seminal notion; such a man as this Talos being somehow the "groom" of history or the "groom" of forces he cannot quite understand. He's not handing out justice or deciding on justice; he's exacting justice in a very blind, brutal way. But I took the name Talos out later.

When the movie was made, was there any use of the play version?

No, but when I sold them the book, I had to sign the play over to them, too, to prevent any chance of my coming out later and claiming that they had taken something from the dramatic version.

Perhaps you could settle an old argument. When I was in graduate school, a girl was writing a thesis on All the King's Men *which maintained that Burden was the existentialist hero of an existentialist novel. To me, this was nonsense, and I was secretly delighted when our advisor, on returning from a colloquium with you at Yale, told her the underlying philosophical scheme was Hegelian. She almost assaulted him physically. Practically called him a liar.*

It's instructive for me. I wish I had known it.

Neither existential nor Hegelian?

I didn't know about it, either way.

Didn't using Burden as narrator change the novel's center of gravity? In one way, he's more important than Stark.

There is, of course, a vast difference between the two. Stark is the control point of the narrative, the first impulse so to speak. But I had to set him within the context of a world. I needed an efficient cause. Power moving into a vacuum. So I got my vacuum fellow, or as it were, my partial vacuum fellow, into the story. But the real center of gravity in the novel is the dynamics of power. The newspaperman helps illustrate it.

Burden is fundamentally a decent man. What leads him to be an agent of evil?

He is a man with a grave defect of character and personality—and he knows it. He's blind in certain ways and he's ready to be a tool, to enter someone else's magnetic field. Sounds awful, doesn't it? But it's a constant thing—power operates that way. Even nice people like Adlai Stevenson operated that way. All the people I knew wanted to do something for him in their spare time, even if they had to push door bells. They were in love with Adlai. He filled their "vacuum." I voted for him, too. In 1952, that is.

There is a natural need to build something, to be part of a cause, to gain meaning. This can get to be an evil thing when the great blankness of life is filled by terrible forces. Look at what happens when this sense of cause is stimulated by a Hitler or Mussolini. I was in Italy when I was writing the play—I finished it in Italy in the first year of the war—so I couldn't help but relate these things, being right in the middle of it. I was cut off from my own world and I suppose this made my senses more acute. I was bound to wonder what made these events, what blankness had made it all possible.

I'm still confused. Which theme struck you as most important: Burden's quest for self-knowledge or Willie's political corruption?

Well, it wasn't so back and forth, you know, in the process of composition. Things don't come as clear options—rather, as aspects of a single complex process.

Which one provided the forward movement?

Well, I wanted them to be related. I wanted to make a story, rather than have the story make the relationship. It never crossed my mind that Burden . . . no, that's not true—I guess it crossed my mind. Let me put it this way: Stark was the conscious focused image.

Maybe I didn't succeed very well. I remember going to see Bernard Berenson and being quite shocked when he said, "I want to tell you about your book. That fellow Stark is not very interesting." Well, I was taken aback because I thought I'd done my level best by Stark. He gave me a real lecture on this, a real lecture. The book, he said, was all Burden; for him Stark was an excuse for Burden's existence. He liked the book fine, but not for my reasons.

You were also criticized for doing too well by Stark, weren't you?

Well, I've been called a fascist off and on all my life. That's what happens to a Jeffersonian Democrat in this crazy world we live in.

Why did you choose Huey Long as a model? Was it because the events of his life made for an exciting novel, or was there a particular moral issue about Long himself?

What I say might sound rude, but I don't mean it to be. It's not at all a matter of choosing in most cases, but of being chosen. The natural thing is for the story to be about you—it's always about you. You don't really start off: It's time to write a novel, what shall I write about? Now there may be instances—Hollywood or some commercial writing—where the writer is that objective. But I don't think most writers, good or bad, work that way. They tend to have a lot of stories available to them just because they are human beings. Anybody here knows a lot of stories—whether he knows he knows them or not, he knows them. Now, when a writer decides on one of the many stories he has encountered, he doesn't just say: I'll take the third from the left. He sees his material in terms of a type of story that somehow catches hold of him, like a cockleburr in his hair. Why it's this story instead of that one that he picks to work on may be accidental but, waiving that consideration, it's really because it has a germ of meaning for him personally. An observation or an event snags on to an issue in your own mind, feelings, life— some probably unformulated concern that makes the exploration of the connection between that thing and the issue rewarding. This can happen without your being conscious of why some particular scene makes it happen. I don't for the life of me know why the Long cockleburr got hold of me, but the accidental reason is easy: I was living in Louisiana where there was a world that was very dramatic and about which I had very ambivalent feelings. One gang was saying, "Oh, this saviour!" and another was saying "Oh, this son of a bitch!" You couldn't help but speculate on what accounted for this social situation. But you could be certain of one thing: it didn't happen out of the blue. There had to be a context beforehand. When you have incompetent or bad government long enough, you get Willie Stark. Somebody had to move in to fill the vacuum. It doesn't have to be a vacuum of power: it can be thought of as a vacuum of social goods. A felt need will be satisfied, one way or other, and it doesn't matter whether Stark is just making promises or is actually trying to deliver on them.

Now this was going on in Louisiana in a very dramatic way. But it was happening everywhere in the world. The New Deal—same thing. You see, somebody has to provide the bread and circuses; if not, there's going to be real trouble. You won't just have bad government but maybe no government at all. And I don't mean to sneer at the democratic process. When the voters have a need they want immediately satisfied and somebody says, "I can do it for you," why it's natural for them to elect him. Of course, you can have a leader who is fulfilling justified needs merely as a means of seizing power, or who uses corrupt means to fulfill the legitimate needs, and that raises the question of what price tag you're willing to put on the fulfillment.

The situation in Louisiana prompted my amateurish speculation about history and morality. It feels strange talking about it now—it was all so long ago; it's like talking in your sleep.

You suggested before that the method of narration in All the King's Men *presented a problem. Did any of Conrad's works furnish a guide?*

I've known Conrad since I was a boy of fifteen or sixteen and I like him very much. He's a wonderful novelist. But I don't think he influenced me. Not so I was conscious of it, but that sort of thing enters the public domain—after Conrad, novels could never be quite the same; he was in the air.

Getting away from fiction for a moment, would you comment on your view of political power as something shaped by an existing vacuum as it relates to the desegregation of the South?

Sure. In 1954, if there had been any leadership out of Washington —that is, if Old Ike had been even half aware of his obligation to exert his authority and leadership—a great mess would have been avoided. But he retired from the issue, and instead of giving a rallying point for moderate and liberal opinions, he put his head under a blanket for almost a whole year. There was a vacuum in leadership from Washington and on the local level too, and this enabled a hard-nosed segregationist minority to charge right in.

I remember talking to the Secretary of Education in one of the Southern states at the time. He said, "Look. Shut that door and I'll tell you right now that sixty per cent of all my country superintendents would like nothing better than to be desegregated tomorrow. They're all bankrupt, and integrating the schools would save them no end of money. What they need is for somebody to get up the right legal suit so they can turn around and say, 'I didn't do it—they made me.' If they could save face, they'd be glad. We can't afford segregated schools. But if you print that I said this, I'll call you a liar."

I remember, too, going up into a little county in Arkansas that had desegregated voluntarily. It was 1955, late '55, and there had been a lot of violence there. The people were poor; I remember seeing people lining up in the streets for government beans. I spent a very long time with one of the officials—chairman of the school board, I think he was. I asked about the decision to desegregate and he said, "We didn't have any theories. We were broke. It cost $16,000 a year to move them niggers to a Negro school and we didn't even have $16,000, so we figured it we integrated, we'd save $16,000 a year. But then the speech-makers started stirring things up and soon my business was being boycotted. They were getting ready to bomb my house, my wife was threatened, and my kids were being chased by little ruffians. I reached the breaking point. One day I was coming out of the post office when some guy stopped me and called me a nigger-lover. Well I let him have it. Now I don't care—I'll take the consequences." This is an interesting story, you see. This man had a problem in responsibility. He worked it out logically and defended his position, even to standing up to the bomb throwers. In the end, he came out on the side of a principle. If there had been some real leadership in the land, his story might have been multiplied many times over.

But if a man is a convinced segregationist from the start, how much of a possibility is there for his conversion on the basis of principle?

Doesn't prejudice rule out logical deductions?

You can ask a man, "Are you for segregation?" and he may answer,

"Yes, suh, segregation forever." Well, what he's really saying is that he's for segregation—everything else being equal. Would he be for segregation if it cost him a considerable amount of money? If it meant not educating his kids? If he had to go to jail? When things get sorted out, segregation is probably not at the top of his list of priorities—and leadership should sort things out.

There's danger in looking at the white Southerners and writing them off as Negro-hating segregationists. People, you must remember, are awfully complex creatures, and you may be in for some surprises if you divide the cast into heroes and villains. History plays some pretty cruel jokes. Remember when all the liberals in England were wringing their hands over the plight of the poor Boers in South Africa? You should: it's in the history books. Not too long ago, the Boers were the persecuted people. Not much sympathy for the Boers nowadays. The same Boers are now the prime racist villains of the world. And remember that wonderful book *Let Us Now Praise Famous Men* with pictures by Walker Evans and James Agee's text. Everybody's heart bled for those poor people—the white sharecroppers of Alabama. The book exposed the poetry and pathos of their lives for us to weep over. Now those who then were doing the weeping go down to Tuscaloosa or to the march on Montgomery and see those same people and they become the hounds of hell in the public eye. They're no worse and no better than they ever were, but you change the question and you get a different perspective.

Getting back to novel writing: have you ever used actual persons in your writing and then been embarrassed when you met them again later and they told you they recognized themselves?

No, they don't know it at all and—I don't tell them about it.

Sure, you use things—you even use yourself and try not to tell yourself about it. You use whatever you can get your hands on, but you're not really using a person; you use something attached to a person—some suggestion, some episode, some quirk or trait of character. Take Jack Burden: I used a model, but he doesn't know it yet. I know him very well indeed. I even know that he doesn't know what I know about him. And that's knowing a man mighty well.

Why did you have Stark start out as an idealist? Was it because one of the stories you heard about Huey Long was that he began this way?

75

In a way, it seems there was a deep mixture of impulses in Huey, which is only a way of saying he was human and stuck with himself. But Huey aside, dramatic considerations would have dictated the "idealism." I remember a lawyer I was interviewing in Arkansas. He said something like, "I started out to make a little money—to study law and make a little money. Then I wanted to square things up and I got caught up in it, you see." This man simply stumbled into idealism. You encounter such things all the time.

If you draw on real people you know, doesn't your novel, when you re-read it, have a depth it doesn't have for us who aren't acquainted with the models?

Oh, I know where the materials come from and I could trace them down, but the people in the book aren't the people I drew on. Bits have been projected, whole aspects of character have been filled in, basic changes have been made.

I'd like to ask a question about criticism. People are always asking, "What does this mean?" And critics write all their articles trying to explain away the confusion. Now, I don't read a novel to get at any real meaning behind it. I read for enjoyment. Is that so wrong? Isn't there a danger that literary criticism will get to be like logical positivism in philosophy: a concern with meaning that winds up just being a study of words? Maybe a book should confuse you just to make you think.

Do you mean you're confused when you think?

No, I mean that confusion inspires new patterns of action.

I'm not trying to make a joke when I say I'm so confused that I would welcome some clarity, or some help towards clarity. What we want, I think, is not added confusion but a mental experience that gives a sense of moving from disorder to order, to a moment of poise. It isn't a matter of just getting to some resolution tagged on at the back of the book. What we basically get out of a novel or play is an imaginative involvement in experience. The novel, say, starts with "confusion"—that is, with a problematic situation; otherwise there would be no "story." But you must move through the "confusion" to the point when you can say, "Ah, now I see." This is an image of the possibility of meaning in life. It's a metaphor for meaning. To me this is a key notion. There is a satisfaction, a lift, a liberation in reading a good novel, seeing a good play, or reading a good poem. I feel, "Oh, things *do* work after all!" Most of life is a hodge-podge in which it's very hard to feel meaningful. Seeing life in some way reflected in a guise that implies order gives a heightening of energy, of relief. It's a liberation. *Not*, I should emphasize, because of particular "solutions" offered, but because the process is an image of the possibility of meaning growing from experience —an image, that is, of our continuous effort to make sense of our lives.

But I can't construct a philosophy in books. What they do is to make me seek more, to give me new ideas.

Not by confusing you though, do they?

Yes. If I'm complacent, I won't go anywhere.

Oh, but that's another matter. Every story, to be a story, must put you in trouble. The other day I read a remark attributed to—I think —Kathleen Norris. She said writing her novels was perfectly simple: put a good girl in bad trouble and then get her out. Well, she may not write the best novels, but she had the best idea. You want somebody in trouble and you want to wonder if he'll make it through or not. No trouble, no story.

Let me try to synthesize a bit. You maintain that significant fiction deals with trouble and that art represents an attempt to lead from confusion to understanding; would you be subscribing to the theory that great periods of art coincide with periods of stress in history? And might this help account for the Southern renaissance my colleague John Bradbury has been writing about?

I don't think there's much doubt about it. But let me try to say what I mean here. Certain kinds of stress do not permit immediate artistic manifestation. As the seventeenth century poet Abraham Cowley put it, troublous times are the best times to write of but the worst to write in. When the house is on fire, you don't sit down to write a sonnet. But a period of cultural and moral shock, short of the final cataclysm, does breed art. See New England of the great days, or Elizabethan England. Deep conflicts of values can release tremendous amounts of energy. When the pieties are shaken, you are

77

forced to re-examine the whole basis of life. A new present has to be brought in line with the past, and the other way around.

The rapid rate of industrialization of the agricultural South had profound and sweeping effects. Smokestacks were rising—right in the bosom of the Jeffersonian ideal, and, it should be added, in the bosom of a good deal of poverty, pellagra and illiteracy, not to mention the local variety of racism.

When you've written a book, do you feel you've surrendered it to its audience? Should a reader be at all concerned with what you meant when you wrote it? I guess I'm really asking: Do you believe the so-called intentional fallacy is a fallacy?

Stated that way, it's primarily a question of semantics. I would prefer to approach it from the other side. A writer doesn't know what his intentions are until he's done writing.

So, in a way, writer and reader are approaching the work on a similar footing?

If you look on a work as the writer's exploration of possibilities, then the question takes on a different complexion. A work represents a growth of meaning. You, the writer, are chiefly involved in finding, in growing toward meaning, but you haven't got a fully organized intended meaning when you start off. You have a certain body of feelings you are hoping to control, but not a specific intention. Intention is closer to result than to cause. A reader can infer an intention—that's well and good and part of the way we react to art—but that doesn't mean it was created according to the reader's impression of intention projected into form. I should add that this impression is exactly what the writer wants the reader to wind up with.

Guide us a little further. When you are writing, are you directing yourself to the work of art, or are you using it as a means to approach your audience and reveal something of yourself and your view of the world?

I don't think about my audience when I'm working. This doesn't mean that the audience isn't important. It is, but not right then when I'm concerned with trying "to make it right." I've heard many writers say the same thing. Now, making it right, of course, means making your vision available to somebody. But if you see it's not being made available, if it's going off the rails, it's not because it isn't grasped by an audience but because the thing isn't right itself. You are your own audience, but because the thing you've written doesn't conform to what you think you wanted to express during the process, then it's wrong and you had better start over. No, I'm not saying what I mean. The question is not whether the thing being done fails to conform to a preconceived notion. It is whether —and let me emphasize this—the thing being done is violating a logic implicit in the process of composing it. Or worse, because you have not discovered the internal logic.

FEBRUARY 8, 1966

John Updike

You are a young writer. In your mind, is there something that separates you from the previous generation of writers?

Yes, there certainly is and I used to be very aware of it when I was in fact a young writer. I don't believe that, being thirty-eight, I'm quite a young writer anymore, but I used to think about it. I really did.

What is it that differentiates you from the writers of the post-Second World War period or those of the post-1950's period?

Every generation's attitude is characterized to some extent by its historical experiences. I came to birth as a writer in the 'fifties, and insofar as we can be self-conscious about such matters, I suppose I have a "cold war" way of looking at things. I had an interest in delicate strategies, an interest in forestalling apocalypse—whereas now, I think, there's considerable interest in bringing it on. There was then a concern with maneuver; in my own case I even attempted to stake out and explore a quality that I somewhere called "middleness," or the quality of things at rest. We, the writers of my period, have tried to find the excitements of normal, everyday life. Yes, I believe that is a significant distinction: we focused our interest on investigation of the quotidian, whereas the generations older and younger than mine have been more economic and political in their orientation.

Who are your contemporaries in terms of this historical view of fiction?

I would say Salinger is—more or less—although I think of him as older by a good bit. It's in him that, as a college student in the early 'fifties, I first heard announced the tone that spoke to my condition. I had a writing teacher—now dead—who read aloud to

80

us some of Salinger's first *New Yorker* short stories. I remember especially one called "Just Before the War with the Eskimos." It seemed to me to say something about the energies of people and the kinds of ways they encounter each other that I did not find in the short stories of Hemingway, or John O'Hara, or Dorothy Parker, or any of that "wised-up" school of short story writing. Salinger's stories were not wised up. They were very open to the tender invasions. Also they possessed a refreshing formlessness which, of course, he came to push to an extreme, as real artists tend to do. However, in those early short stories there's a marvelous tension between rather random, "soft" little events which pulls the whole story together into the final image, e.g., a dead Easter chick in a waste basket. It had a quality of real magical truth for me.

Are there others you regard as contemporaries?

Some, about my age, are not very well known: Harold Brodkey, a writer who is a little more than a year older than I, is a contemporary. His writing seems to go deeper into certain kinds of emotional interplay than the things written by older writers. Were I to try to make all this into an essay, I'm sure that I could find more ways in which writers now in their thirties and forties resemble each other.

Would you look upon someone like John Barth as being "post-Updike?"

Mmmmm . . . no. In Barth—especially in the first novel, *The Floating Opera,* which is the one I liked best—there is an attempt at celebration. In some ways the book reminds me of my first novel, a book called *The Poorhouse Fair,* which also ends in a kind of . . . somehow the word "celebration" again leaps to mind, although it is a celebration not without shadows or severe doubts. Nevertheless, my own direction, in so far as there has been direction, has not really been the same as Barth's. The feat of *Sot-Weed Factor,* both as an extended piece of invention and as a piece of mimicry, is something I can only be in awe of. I find it really incredible.

Kerouac I would also claim as a contemporary. Clearly, he is not a man of Salinger's intelligence, but there is something benign, sentimentally benign, in his work. He attempted to grab it all; somehow, to grab it all. I like him.

That's strange. Kerouac and Updike! I couldn't propose two writers who I thought were more unalike in their approach to literary art. Kerouac, with his binges at the typewriter, dumping the words down onto a continuous roll of teletype paper and leaving the cutting of it into pages to a more somber moment. . . . That's not the picture I had of you at work at all.

No, I don't agree. I don't use teletype paper, but there isn't an awful lot of revision when I'm writing. Things either grind to a halt or they keep on moving. I think he was right. Kerouac was right in emphasizing a certain flow, a certain ease. Wasn't he saying, after all, what the surrealists said? That if you do it very fast without thinking, everything will get in that wouldn't ordinarily. I think one tends to spoil not only the thing at hand, but the whole art form, by taking too much thought, by trying to assert too much control.

I don't mean to imply, of course, that I resemble Kerouac in writing style. He and I don't have the same sense of a sentence. I think he just had a different grammar teacher from mine in high school. I had one, and for some reason I was able to get firmly into my mind what clauses and phrases you put commas around, and which ones you don't. I'm not so sure that this ability hasn't almost vanished. I'm the last writer around now who actually seems to enjoy using commas, not just placing them where they happen to fall.

The difference between Harvard and Columbia?

[*Laughing*] Yes.

If I may, I'd like to return to Barth again. Have you read Lost in the Funhouse?

Part of it, not all.

To me, it's a remarkable performance, especially the short story "Anonymiad." It makes capital out of the impossibility of writing, out of the utter solitude of the artist. I sense something of the same thing (or, at least, a different expression of the same thing) in your book Bech *which, in the title, you pointedly called not a novel but "a book." Am I drawing it out too fine?*

No, no. Obviously anybody writing now is bothered by an existential question: Why are you doing it? Is that the thing to do? The *Lost in the Funhouse* stories—and I speak as one who confesses to not having read the book through—savor a little of stunts. To be sure, they are stunts tried from a feeling of confidence and they display rigor; nevertheless, there is a terribly bookish feeling about them.

Now, as for the *Bech* stories. . . . For a writer, life becomes overmuch a writer's life. Things happen to you that wouldn't happen to anybody else, and a way of using this to a good advantage, of course, is to invent another writer. At first, he is very much an alter ego, but then, in the end, not so. At any rate, I have used the writer in *Bech* as a subject in order to confess sterility in a truthful way. It was an effort, but an effort you can't keep making. Once you've written a book saying how hard it is to write and to describe, in one way or another, the way the facts of fiction creep into your own self, it makes your self and the enterprise seem unreal. Once you've written a story or two that actually unravels in front of the reader's eyes, then you should either do something else or, as Salinger has done, retreat into silence. There's a kind of dignity in falling silent, but it's not very profitable. And it leaves you with a lot of the day to kill.

In my book, I tried to—and I believe I did—package and dispose of a certain set of anxieties and tensions which I have as a practicing writer. Barth's, in a sense, is from a much higher point of view. Mine is merely a kind of complaint about the curious position that the American writer now finds himself in; he is semi-obsolete, a curious fellow without any distinct sense of himself as a sensible professional.

Is this your dilemma, or is it rather general?

I think that this kind of notion in a writer's life is very much alive today. Behind Hemingway and Fitzgerald stood a number of men of letters for whom an authentic literary environment existed. Now that world—the world of New York publishing—has become something else. In part, the academic sphere has moved in, but the universities aren't really a substitute for an audience you can conjure up out of the masses. If a text is reduced to something to be incorporated into an anthology, if the author is to trust to being taken up by enough English courses, then there's been a fall from the grandeur of a lusty transaction with the ideal reader.

My book, morally, is about this situation: a little bit about the way in which it's hard to be an American writer. The Europeans, in contrast, have retained the professional sense. Over the years, they've had more opportunity than we. There, writing has been thought of as a respectable craft that could be learned, whereas in America, as soon as it becomes a craft, it's thought of as really uninteresting. Anything that can be boiled down to rules and hard work is obviously not worth anything.

Apropos of the contemporary writers in your book . . . where would you place the Jewish-American writers in the American literary scene and what influence do you think they had or have on American literature?

Their importance and influence are cardinal now and have been ever since World War II. I think that, even though creating a category "Jewish Writer" creates the impression of more conformity than there is. Salinger's Jewishness, which I think is actually half-Jewishness, is certainly not nearly as prominent or important as it is in most of Malamud's work. Mailer's Jewishness doesn't sit on him as comfortably as, again, Malamud's does on him. But definitely, they've been a force. Can you describe post-war American writing without including them? If they are not at the center of our literature, then who is?

Why has this contribution been so prominent in recent times? Were the earlier Jewish writers more "Jewish?"

At a time when the country's center of gravity shifted from the land to the city, they were right in the city, seeing the neighborhoods change, the Puerto Ricans emigrating there, and all the rest. As Jews have moved into the mainstream of American life, they have looked back, checking their course and trying to assess what no longer being a minority means. The pre-war ones, who are not often read, were, I think, more consciously writing minority literature. They had talent, but it didn't find a wide audience. Unfortunately. Daniel Fuchs is one Jewish writer I could name who might have been happier if he'd had his literary career after the war.

All the graces we think of as Jewish reflect a totality of embrace of the world. It's something you feel in the Jewish sensibility that isn't elsewhere—although you do find something like it in Southern writing. Conceivably, the war ruined our sense of the world being divided and charged in every particle, a sense of the world that I think the various Protestant writers have tended to view as part demonic. But it seems to me that the Jewish Americans kept up the belief a little longer—it is implied, at least, in their mental activities of all sorts. They arrived at the written page equipped with this belief in the instinctual importance of human events. If you don't have this belief, you aren't really going to sit down and write fiction in the first place—and they have had it in abundance.

However, I'm not sure there are going to be increasing waves of such writing from those with a Jewish background. Much as I admire aspects of Philip Roth, you don't really feel in his books the human qualities you get in Bernard Malamud. I think of Malamud as an almost fatherly writer whose concern for you and mankind is on every page, whereas Roth's concern is so very egocentric and he is given to wanton destructiveness. Shortly, I would think the process of assimilation will have done its work and the term "Jewish writer" will become as meaningless as the term "Jewish musician" is meaningless.

What about the victim psychology, which is supposedly part and parcel of the Jewish tradition? Has this made the Jewish artist privy to a special metaphor for an absurd world beyond one's control, for the defeatist's perception that he is forced to play with a stacked deck?

Yeah. Well . . . I'm trying to match my memories of books with the word "victim." What you do get in Jewish writing along with this sense of being a victim is an underlying tone that the world is somehow getting better under these awful conditions. There's a Yiddish word "vey"—isn't that how it's pronounced?—that in the context of Jewish expression connotes enduring through adversity. It means "What can we do?" doesn't it? A marvelous scene illustrating this attitude comes to mind from Malamud's first novel. (You see, Malamud again.) It's in the one about baseball. When the hero at last gets to fornicate with his girl, he has stomach trouble and diarrhea. This kind of thing occurs again and again to Jewish novel heroes, but then there's always available some other kind of triumph, or the thought that what has happened is in some way good for them, or, at least, the balm that it is inevitable.

But the Jewish writers don't, as far as I know, produce utter victims in the manner that a Protestant novelist like James Gould

Cozzens does. I recently reviewed Cozzens' last book, *Morning, Noon, and Night*. It is really a bad book, bad because the sense of defeat, or futility, is so total as to immobilize the novel. All of the things that make a novel move, or that make you want to read on, are not there. I think a writer can portray a victim without forgetting that there is a primitive star, or whatever, that keeps him moving, that keeps him running after something, however impossible it may be to achieve it.

Do you see the black writers in America eventually assuming the position now occupied by Jewish writers? They seem, in a sense, to have almost the same element of the victim that the Jewish writers have. Can you foresee anything literarily significant coming from this?

Yes, I can—somewhere—although it will certainly take a different form. (I wonder, however, whether I should be making predictions in this area; I speak, really, without much knowledge either of black writers or of black novels.) Despite the vogue-ish interest now in black writers—and it's quite understandable—it will be some time before they, as a group, will be making a literary contribution commensurate to that of the Jewish Americans. Anger so charges their writing now as to cut them off from novelistic invention or concern with the aesthetic niceties of novel writing. Even Baldwin. Look at what has happened to him. He lived in Harlem in the 'forties and, in the beginning, he was able to reproduce that world rather objectively. *Go Tell It on the Mountain* is, of course, deeply felt and obviously experienced; still, there is a perspective on those experiences, a detachment enabling the author to give them some sort of form. Of late, and for the time being at least, he has lost the ability to get enough away from what he is experiencing to contend with it in fiction.

It's very hard to picture a totally committed person writing novels at all. There's an element of play in writing fiction that a full emotional involvement with social issues does not permit. Although I may be overstating it, I think that while one man achieves some expression of art, it's also a product of his society. Therefore, it's difficult to separate the individual black writer's development from the black community as a whole. What his community feels, thinks, and does in a way composes his material. At this time, perhaps, the blacks' mood is too angry, the issues too serious to allow for the kind of playfulness I mentioned. But this is a generalization and there may well be some current black writers who disprove the proposition. I keep meaning to read somebody called Ishmael Reed. Is that his name?

I think so. He's a black poet, isn't he?

He's a black writer who has been recommended to me by a black man I know as being somebody well worth reading. His books are supposed to be very funny—wicked but funny. He might indeed be someone with these art-treating qualities of which I've spoken.

But—to get back for a moment to your question about the parallels between the situations of Jews and blacks—I'm not at all sure that it is correct to expect similar results from the coincidence of certain rather superficial factors. The traditions of a people, the cultural graces they have developed, are really more important in determining such things than where they live in a city or how they are treated by the rest of society. I don't think, for instance, that we have gotten or ever will get from black writers the same kind of immigrant joy you get in Jewish writing. Negroes are not new arrivals to America in the way that the East Side Jews were. They've been here as long as anybody, and in the course of all those years, they've had a very different historical experience. Certainly, they have contributed substantially to American culture—in music especially—but perhaps the written word is not the instrument whereby the Negro artistic genius tends to express itself. There are, of course, great black memoirs, great black autobiographies, and all sorts of good writing, but I'm not at all convinced that fiction is their "thing"—not at the moment at any rate.

To be sure, I'm using "they" as a kind of noise-maker. There are many, many people in the black community with all kinds of experience and I'm not ruling out the emergence of great black novelists, but I would be pleasantly surprised if a *body* of great, black novels appeared.

You point out that blacks are too angry, too caught up in what they're doing to be at the center of the current literary movement, and yet at the same time, haven't you indicated a similar involvement by our Jewish writers? Is there a difference in their distance from the problem? Or is it something else?

My impression, and it's only an impression, is that Jewish anger and despair never really arrived at a political doctrine. The classic ghetto Jew was a man grateful enough just to escape from his problems in the Old World. He had just left an aristocratic, feudal society and he was very willing to work in what the American system seemed to him to be. And he proved that he was able to succeed in it. Or, at least, so many did that now, in certain parts of the country—New York, for example—the American system is sensitive to the wishes of Jews. On the whole, the system is what Jews want it to be.

All this, if I'm correct, has implications for literature. Politically, socially, and financially, success could be and was secured by the individual. The Jews' struggle, their factional strife, the emotions generated within the group, found a focus in the personal unit and was expressed in terms of the individual life story. This ordering of experience naturally lends itself to novelistic treatment. Traditionally, the novel has been geared to life stories and practically, as a form of artistic expression, the novel is an individualistic art form (one can imagine, for instance, a team creating a mural; but it's hard to imagine a team of men producing a novel).

It may be that for minorities now coming into their own in American society, the dynamics called for by the way the system is operating have changed. Like it or not, we have all arrived at a moment when the single, personal unit seems inadequate, selfish, and solipsistic.

Mr. Updike, would you say that you subscribe to the existentialism of Camus, some other writer, your own brand, or none of the above?

You don't hear the word existential much any more but, again to be "generational" about it, it was used extensively to characterize my generation.

Though I've not kept up, there are some new writers, Europeans and Americans, who are really philosophically oriented persons and have continued to work within the framework of existential investigation, but right now, I don't feel it's terribly much in vogue.

I do resent the notion that the concept of being "a generation" was self-imposed. Surely, to see each generation as involved in some sort of common enterprise of wisdom is a nice way to view the human adventure, but not quite accurate. Essentially, it was my own upbringing, the kind of family and the church I was raised in, which disposed me to fall in love with Kierkegaard in my early twenties. I read him quite a lot. I read the works of other existentialists, but mostly of the Christian existentialists, from whom, funnily enough, it's not much of a jump to Camus and Sartre in whom I found the same gravity of moral concern persisting even though they had done away with the theism.

I'm least familiar with Camus as a European political philosopher, but I do admire him as a writer and I think he's solidly in the middle of the greater existentialist moral tradition. I'm an ignorant man; I've not put that much effort into pursuing such questions. I remember reading *The Plague* in college and it didn't seem to me then to solve any problems the way Kierkegaard's approach did. I have quite forgotten Kierkegaard's books or even his sentences, but somehow the whole idea I got from him of existence preceding essence was very liberating for me; it seemed to give me some kind of handle on my own life. As a young person, I felt that thinking of myself as being suspended quite pointlessly in an immense void of indifferent stars and mathematically operating atoms made it difficult to justify action. To act because, if you don't, you'll get hungry—to act simply because of animal reaction to stimuli— was not to act in a way that gave shape to life. Justification was not there and it was a problem for me. I read the existentialists seeking a handle for something it had been hard for me to grasp, and thinking about life in this way enabled me to become involved in life as an average, enterprising, and organized person.

Our horizons, the horizons of the American writer of the 'fifties, were not very broad. In a funny way, it then seemed enough to orient yourself within the world of the given things around you. The causes of fear and confusion that we thought were worthy of our combat are, viewed from the standpoint of an Asian peasant struggling for food, ridiculous aspects of an alien scheme. I think our lives really are solipsistic, self-centered. And perhaps, in part, because of a new sensibility about such things, the particular swing to life that we knew in the 'fifties is really not around anymore.

The difference between the heroes elevated by the early 'fifties and those of 1970 reflects this. We tended to make heroes of men who were more perky and defiant than the common lot. There's a baseball player called Williams who played for the Red Sox. I really admired him because he was defiant, and because he could concentrate so terribly on that one act of hitting the ball. His concentration at bat and his casual rudeness elsewhere seemed attributes of an admirable model. The literary people you admired were rather like that, too; somebody like Eliot. I once went to hear him speak at Saunders theater. He delivered a long paper, quite interesting if you read it, but I had been in line so long waiting to get into the theater that I fell asleep during the actual reading. I woke up in this great wave of applause. Here was this whole auditorium filled with shining faces and he, in the face of the applauding audience, nonchalantly put on his rubbers, carefully inserting first one shoe—tucking it around, seeing that it was unfolded here, there—then the other. The way that old man put on his rubbers on that stage seemed, in some uncommon way, heroic.

If I understood you correctly, you were talking earlier about the difficulty of a writer today having a sense of his audience, of who is reading his books. Am I right?

Yes.

Who do you think are the people that make your books, and other books, best-sellers? To put it another way, who are the people who buy books today, and why do they buy them?

I do have trouble picturing them. If you look at the best-seller lists, it is obvious that it is not the same audience which makes each book a best-seller, but mostly—nine out of ten—it's composed of books of the kind women would enjoy reading. People, even people who are not entirely uninformed, still show a Victorian taste for long novels. The reading public likes books with information in them, books telling how to do things: how airports are run, how Michelangelo actually did party with his models. They want something concrete. This is not unrelated to the fact that people are still interested in sex and love; these are things that they are interested in having explained. The erotic urge is an inexhaustible subject, though a good attempt to exhaust it has been made in the past four or five years.

To what extent have your audience's tastes affected the way you write?

I began my writing career with a fairly distinct set of principles which, one by one, have eroded into something approaching shapelessness. A writer doesn't begin to write well by worrying about his readership, let alone about a large readership. In practical terms you begin with yourself as your own "readership." You should attempt to write things that you would like to read. There are certain intrinsic qualities, both in language and in the merit of art, which you want to obtain and which challenge you. You try to get your vision of reality into the written symbol. Out of this, living art will come. It may be strange and unconventional, but one side of a really authentic artist is that his stuff, by and large, is puzzling to begin with. Then, slowly, comprehension grows. Paintings that are on everybody's walls took years to get there.

This seems to place an obligation on society to accept novelty. Do you believe the "great books" of the past are irrelevant to today's writer?

Not at all. Keep in mind that the sense of human strengths has not altered awfully much since Homer's day and that certain truths about writing well are more or less established. It's the reason for reading the classics.

When you write, is it for a particular magazine?

Well, here it gets all muddled. It's hard for me to write without actually picturing the words in print. I find that those stories I can't really see in *New Yorker* type cannot get into *New Yorker* type.

But there are dangers in such associations. For most of my literary life, I've managed not to tire of short stories geared for the *New Yorker,* a magazine I respect above all others. Nevertheless, it is a magazine, and magazines are governed by the tastes of the editors. You can get to know the editors too well, be with them too often, and hint at what you are trying to do with the story. I think it's a mistake for the writer to develop in this sort of way.

But you are not primarily a magazine writer, are you?

Circumstances have weaned me a little away from that into this awful thing of being a novelist, which is a funny word. They will call you a novelist even though you've written a million other things. Even one novel and I'm in *Time* magazine as a novelist.

The novel is problematic. I'm in the middle of quite an involved. . . . When I read my paper tonight, I want to show one of the features of the novel. It's a discussable subject because it is so vague and maybe because it deals with a nonexistent problem. The novel —what does reading it do for you, actually? Who and what is it? Negatively, I don't see the novel as appreciably creating any political reforms. I don't even see it as producing any cry for change.

Positively, I see each book as a picturing of actual tensions, conflicts, and awkward spots in our private and social lives. My books feed, I suppose, on some kind of perverse relish in the fact that there are insolvable problems. There is no reconciliation between the inner, intimate appetites and the external consolations of life. You want to live forever, you want to have endless wealth, you have an endless avarice for conquests, crave endless freedom really. And yet, despite the aggressive desires, something within us expects no menace. But there is no way to reconcile these individual wants to the very real need of any society to set strict limits and to confine its members. *Rabbit, Run,* which is a book much on my mind lately, I wrote just to say that there is no solution. It is a novel about the bouncing, the oscillating back and forth between these two kinds of urgencies until, eventually, one just gets tired and wears out and dies, and that's the end of the problem.

Has the rise of film had an artistic effect on the novel?

Of course, the cinema, as it arose, was a whole new way of telling a story, wasn't it? It was really revolutionary, and its grasp upon novelists shows that almost immediately. *Ulysses* is to some extent a consciously cinematic book; it is haunted by the cinema's electricity. Cinema gave a new sense of space to the novel. The technique of cutting, in effect, eliminated, except in a kind of tongue-in-cheek way, the authorial voice which had dominated nineteenth century fiction. You've always been aware that it is Count Tolstoy telling you this, or even more aware that it's Dickens telling you that. There was always the author behind you to usher you through the tedious parts or to clarify and explain. Then suddenly, in an uncanny way—and it may have something to do with what novelists learned from movies—this voice is gone. In movies, something makes its entrance onto the screen and the viewer doesn't know how it came in, nor does he feel he needs to have it explained. The movie has the strangeness of a natural landscape. Nothing seems to have been created; it just happens to be there.

It seems like fewer people are reading and more people are viewing than ever before. As a writer, does this disturb you?

I find that fewer people are viewing than used to, too. If it's true that fewer people are reading fiction, it's also true that the great standard audience Hollywood packed in from the 'thirties to the early 'fifties is gone as well.

Sure, people rush to the movies who, in the nineteenth century, were enclosed at home and read. But then, who were the great novel audience of the nineteenth century? It certainly wasn't the people down in the slums—and there were lots of them. It was the upper middle class, which was not numerically as great an audience as the novelist ostensibly has now.

Nevertheless, I do feel, maybe wrongly, that a sense of assurance has left the novel form. I think you begin to see it die after the generation of Hemingway and Fitzgerald. They did have that sense, but after them it really begins fading fast.

But before we consign print to the museum, we should remember that a book has certain advantages. It is portable, for one thing. Also, it is readily retrievable. And you can enter it anywhere. Unlike a computer, a book can be gotten into from the edges. It has all sorts of physical qualities that film does not have. I see an irreducible place for the book in human society as long as people are produced on recognizably the same model that we have now. Maybe the model will change, but today we all read more than ever. If not books, magazines and newspapers and billboards.

There remain things which can be done better on the printed page than in the films: for instance, certain kinds of introspection and the process of how people adjust. Also, books can handle ambiguity in a way that movies almost never can. If you encounter something really ridiculous in a movie, you're really mad about it, essentially because you're not used to ambiguity. Movies, I think, are tied to simplistic story-telling, even after all the experimenting film makers have done. There is something crude, I think, about the attempts to find cinematic equivalents for literary devices.

You spoke of the cinematic influence on Joyce in the early days of film. Has cinema affected your development?

In my tiny corner, movies have been exciting and they really affected me as a young person more than books. They gave me my idea of what a full story was. Without having sat through all these 'thirties and 'forties movies, I don't think I would have come to narration as easily as I did.

How do you react to the idea of a film being made of one of your books?

I had the eerie experience the other day of sitting in an empty theater looking at a movie made from *Rabbit, Run*. The movie fails in a number of ways, but one of the ways was in trying to be faithful to the book. They'd been faithful to it in a literal-minded way, but by not being so to the underlying spirit, they produced an enigmatic version of what is very clear in the book.

And yet certain things, like the furniture in the people's apartments, had been done with a richness that I had never even approached. I couldn't have imagined all these things they found to put in those sets: these identifying kinds of calendars, the style of furniture—all just for a few seconds on the screen. How incomparably more solid and entertaining the physical environment became, and yet, curiously, the inner story of the book became thin and even nonsensical.

How people are going to spend their time is a riddle, but, finally, film and books occupy realms that aren't necessarily competitive. Writers could survive on a rather small market. Even if people only read in airplanes, it would still be a sizable market of bookbuyers. A friend of mine has a theory that books are sold primarily to people visiting friends in hospitals. And some books do seem oriented toward the hospital patient.

How diabolical if your friend's theory is right, given all the sexy books in the stalls. Imagine a guy laid out on his back, immobilized in traction, getting to a particularly erotic passage and unable to do anything about it. Sounds like torture.

I thought *Airport* was in large part successful because people are more or less compelled to sit when they fly. The only things they can do are sleep or read.

But if that's so, then a novel should be designed to be finished on one flight. Airport *is much too long a novel to finish in one sitting.*

Well, I find length very intimidating in books, but I'm apparently in the minority. Most people would as soon read a thousand–page book as a two-hundred page book, not realizing it takes five times as long. There is definitely a school of readers that believes the longer, the better. The writer, for them, just can't write enough.

I have wondered about the physical qualities of a best-seller. They seem to run about eight hundred pages, big pages. They tend to be books that you really can't hold in one hand. The whole industry is geared toward physically big books. When they last had something of mine that they thought might sell well, they took it out of my normal format, which is smallish, and set it in the so-called best-seller format, which is about an inch bigger all around. Apparently it works; the book did sell.

You mentioned that Joyce consciously used cinematic technique in Ulysses. *I got almost the same impression from reading* Rabbit, Run. *Maybe it was because of the use of the present tense, and also, perhaps, because of the way it employed action.*

It was conceived of as a movie. Originally, I had a short introductory section in italics talking about entering a theater; having entered the theater, the reader was presumably sitting down and watching the opening in which the kids are tossing the basketball around while the super-imposed title and credits rolled. And my use of the present tense was in some way to correspond to the continuous present of a movie. As the book went on, I think it lost some of its cinematic quality; and yet, picking it up again recently, I was struck by how speedily it moves—like a film. I used few time-bridging paragraphs, the kind of thing where I'd say: The weeks rolled on and the leaves turned yellow and meanwhile, back at thirty-five Oakhurst Drive, Janice was still drying the dishes.

Funnily enough, when they made a movie out of this book, they didn't see that it was written as a film in my mind. They didn't put the titles over the opening with the kids playing basketball. Instead they made a little box out of it and surrounded it with the titles. The big hands, the ball bouncing on the ground—it would have been a natural thing for an overlay. Which goes to show. . . .

Were you consulted on the film adaptation of Rabbit, Run?

I was invited to try to write the *Rabbit, Run* script, but I was not willing. Then I was invited to read the script they'd written, but I wasn't even able to do that. I remember this big, bulky thing arriving; I opened it up in the middle and one of the characters was saying something like, "It always feels so good in a cemetery." The line was not in the book and I couldn't imagine this person saying it. The irony of seeing *my* characters saying things that they wouldn't have said was really disagreeable. So I closed it up again and told them, "I can't read it, just do the best you can. Good luck."

I didn't hear anything more for a while. Apparently the outfit had folded, or it went underground, or something. The *Rabbit, Run* people were a shoe-string operation of the kind that will go into a project trying to get a package together. They gather a script and a star or two, and then they attempt to peddle this package to a producer. It's all very chancey. The movie scene isn't really anything like it used to be when it was settled in stable studios. It has gotten to be very weird. The original outfits change and become other things, come up with different names. It's not unlike microscopic water-life eating each other.

I never really thought they were going to make a movie of it, but in this case they stuck with it, or somebody stuck with it, and finally Warner Brothers put up the rather little money needed to buy me off. The man who took it over was in love with it. He would call me on the telephone to talk about the book. He was always quoting passages to me—obviously, he is in love with the book. In the movie, the words "by John Updike" are very prominently displayed and it ends with my last sentence being super-imposed on the screen.

I collaborated only to the extent that I went to see the screening and then wrote him a few impressions. But then he said, "Actually, I'm cutting all of this." By the way, it's fascinating to have a glimpse of how movies are made. I complained about one actress especially who I didn't think really fit the part at all. He said, "Yes, you know we did a lot of scenes with her, but they were all mortifying footage." How interesting to think of it as "mortifying footage!" I discovered that, to make a movie, you are constantly shooting around things. You tell crews to do this and that, and then they don't do it. Instead, they go off and get drunk. There are constant fights. As a result of a union dispute, nobody takes any pictures of the car being driven at night in the running away scene. And so they have to use stock shots which consist of fannies and headlights in alternation. The director kept one set "hot"—i.e., he kept a set intact and roped off—for six months in the hope of going back to shoot some scenes he hadn't been able to solve. But despite all these problems, he made a movie. Out of what? Out of those little scraps he had left at the end. That's how you do it. You literally piece it together.

Haven't the director and screen writer of Rabbit, Run *both requested that their names be taken off the film? Apparently, the studio got hold of it and cut it up terribly so that it didn't end up as what its creators wanted.*

Wild scissors, yes. You could hear the snip-snip as you watched it. It's a shame because it shouldn't have been all that bad. They used parts of my home city of Reading, Pennsylvania. It's quite a striking city—a strange looking place—and they used the streets very well. Also, the girl who plays his wife Janice—and it's not a sympathetic part—does a very good job.

I was rather sorry about how my images of the characters were changed. Janice was meant to be a dumpy, nasty-looking little brunette, but in the film she's a very soft, nice-looking blonde. The charmingly plump red-head became a rather skinny brunette. And Rabbit is too fat.

Haven't I read that someone is making a movie from Couples?

I doubt if he'll ever do anything with it. An enterprising fellow called Wolper, who made a good thing of various television documentaries, got hold of *Couples*. He had quite ambitious plans for it. In talking to me, he kept using the word "important" all the time. "Most important book," and then, "Make an important movie."

At one point, I intended to say to him, "Would you like me to come out to Hollywood and write the movie for you?" I can see it as a film and I know I could do it. I understand the book; I understand that it is a romantic book, a book written by a guy who went to a lot of movies. It has a happy ending. It's about a guy meeting a girl and the guy getting the girl. But I know that they don't see it that way. You know, they were talking about it as satire! Satire—this wonderful story. It's a loving portrait of life in America. It doesn't have a dirty sentence, not a dirty word in it. No, I don't think I will write the screenplay, even if they were to ask me out there. What happens is that you just wind up breaking your heart. Really.

One of the advantages of the kind of writing I do is that you are your own boss. You shoot your own stock, choose all the scenes, cast all the characters. You're your own everything, really—and the product, then, is yours. If it plays, great—and if it doesn't, there are no alibis. You know all about it. You did it. Working in a co-operative art like the movies would just scare me.

I realize that strong-willed men, especially in European countries, are able to get hold of enough capital to use film as an independent artistic medium. I think Bergman has done this, and I think Fellini used to do it. Even in the heyday of Hollywood, a movie like this would sneak through once in a while. They were making so many then that occasionally an authentic product of one mind in motion would sneak through. But I don't feel that about films now. They all seem a hodge-podge, the result of tussles to show how far you can go. The questions that lay behind them are so transparent. Questions like: "Can we really show pubic hair?" And then there's this sort of ghoulish desire to get young people in, to exploit a market so cynically. In my view, this is a bad time to try to make movies. Anyway, the movie business isn't the place for the shy writer used to a very low investment operation.

Your mentioning this introduction of sex into films—how far to go and so on—brings to mind my reading of Rabbit, Run *quite a while ago. It seemed to me at the time—and I heard other people make the same comment—that your sex scene was too graphic, even crude. But it seems rather tame in comparison to what comes out and is generally accepted today.*

Yeah, I meant it to be . . . I think the word is "courageous," although there was nothing more at stake than whether or not a book would be published. I thought then, and I still feel, that if you're going to have sex in a book, you really ought to have it. You should go into it enough to try to show what happens, to make it a human transaction. The convention of closing the bedroom's doors that worked so well for the Victorians doesn't seem honest applied to today's world. Yet, despite the freedom the contemporary writer enjoys, in a way we are comparatively bloodless. Certainly, the reader has no doubt that Tolstoy's people are sexually alive: every page is full of an animal solidity. All those novels seem to me to float on the assumption that sex is just enormously interesting. At any rate, in writing *Rabbit, Run,* I thought the time and conditions were right for candor about the way people do indeed behave.

For a writer writing about sex the first time, there are possibilities of new visions. But as you are dealing with one specific physical act, don't you tend to exhaust the situation? How many variations are there before you can only copy what has been done before?

After the particular scene in *Rabbit, Run* that was referred to earlier, it hasn't been quite as easy for me to write about normal heterosexual love-making. The interest I brought to that one because it was a first for me is difficult to regenerate.

In writing *Rabbit, Run* I was aware of predecessors and of what had been done with the language in this area before. The model I really had most in mind was *Ulysses*. In that one famous scene, Joyce went as far as you can go with naturalistic sex. At the same time, it was completely justified and convincing: the sex is there because it's part of his big picture and not because he made a point of picking on it, or because he was trying to sell the book, or because of any consideration other than the artistic one. I'm quite convinced of its absolute rightness. As far as one can know, this is how those characters would have thought and acted.

And of course the topic of sex in literature prompts thoughts of Lawrence and *Lady Chatterley's Lover*. I am not one of those who find *Lady Chatterley* in any way funny. Those love scenes reach for what is tender in people and they *are* touching. And yet, I don't feel about Lawrence the way I do about Joyce. Lawrence was advertising sex: I sense a pushing of the product. I was also affected by Nabokov's *Lolita*. Beneath the constant coruscations, the stylistic hijinks, there is a very serious attempt to show the actualities.

Those are about the only models I really have had. The sex in Henry Miller, to me, is quite strident and very anti-female. He can't get over the notion that there is something monstrous in the female genitals, that there is really an unspeakable quality about them as objects. But then Miller is not a very good writer, for many reasons.

Once, I was trying to fall asleep in my bedroom when a friend—it wasn't even my roommate—walked in with his date and crawled into the other bed. They assumed that I was asleep, and I didn't want to embarrass them by letting them know I wasn't, so I was trapped there for the duration. For a nonparticipant, the clichés of seduction, the thrusts and ripostes, and the fact that they were taking the whole thing very seriously were all extremely comic. Does an obligation to realism ever present a problem of unintended comedy to you as a writer when you draw a sex scene?

I don't worry much about producing unintentional comedy. If it makes somebody laugh . . . well, that's just his reaction, isn't it? The writer's concern should be a more private one—writing the right sentence. All of which, of course, does not mean that, in describing sexual behavior, you cannot try to write funny sentences; I wouldn't be afraid to show sex as funny. Have you all seen *M*A*S*H*? In that movie, they broadcast noises people are making during intercourse and it does become very funny indeed, perhaps even unbearable.

In a cover story a couple of years ago, Time *either stated or implied that your writing, stylistically and linguistically, was more attuned to the Victorian novel than to the novels of any of your contemporaries. Do you think that's true?*

Gee, I hope it's not true, although the book they were referring to is, I suppose, an old-fashioned book—a big roomy book with a lot of little chambers and many characters—and in that respect it could be called Victorian. And, yes, it is kind of a cozy, close book. But I don't feel "Victorian" and I don't much enjoy reading Victorian novels. That's one chore I'm glad I'd gotten behind me in college.

Frankly, I'm chary of arguments about literary traditions. I distrust traditions of any sort except in so far as they are derived from the sum of human experience and do testify to certain probabilities of behavior manifested by the human animal. I'm all for seeing new things done in fiction. No, I don't feel that I am old-fashioned.

[*To the students.*] Who is writing appropriately now? Who speaks to you?

The one "big" novel for my college generation is probably Catch-22. *Everybody seems to read and relate to this book. It captures the seemingly illogical nature of life. Illogical, not existential, as events just don't seem to have any foundations at all. Everything is just all messed up. Our world view no longer has a moral basis. If I were to cite something that I think appeals to most people my age, it would have to be that.*

I remember getting the galleys of *Catch-22*. One of the joys of being a writer is that you are sent galleys of books that other people's editors are trying to push. After opening it and reading a few pages, I was so offended that I put it in the trashcan. It was messy to me: it didn't have the qualities of refraction and interplay of wit that, at that point in my life, I was very strong on. I've never tried to read it since.

Maybe you should have. You might have gotten a different impression of Heller's intentions.

Perhaps you're right. Perhaps it foretold, in its self-professed absurdity, the way the novel was going.

But what you gave as the reason for a feeling of kinship with this book puzzles me. Is it really true that you feel there is no basis for anything? Obviously, you were able this morning to get your right shoe on your right foot, for example, and all the mechanics of your life were operating today, as people's generally do. At the technological level of people getting food and getting to places on time, I've no sense of any real breakdown. Aren't you perhaps indicating something else? Aren't you making the assumption that, at some point, things were less in doubt and more predictable?

Yes. In a sense things were more categorized before. You knew what to do from the very beginning; you could follow a plan. Now, basically, there are so many opportunities open that people get confused. That's my personal view.

I think your perception of the dilemma is accurate.

Wouldn't you say that, in a sense, Rabbit was a victim of the absurdity of life and that that is why he's still running?

Actually he's a victim, I guess, of the kind of the dreadful freedom that was just described, but dreadful freedom 1959 style. The problem of having too many possibilities open to him is not *quite* his, for he knows enough about the possibilities to see that they lead to dead-ends. We have been liberated from the elementary need to work in order to eat; and strangely enough, with the lifting of this grinding pressure has fled a certain dignity of vocation.

I think what's happened to the American middle class is that it is trying to prove that they have open to it almost the whole range of freedom that had hitherto been enjoyed solely by the aristocracies of Europe and Asia. But the capacities of past and present societies to bear, psychologically, the consequences of this freedom are rather different. The aristocrats were never very numerous and their diversions or confusions were either tolerated as eccentricities, or hemmed in by threat of assassination, or simply explained away as the spasms of a dying class. But in America today, you have millions of people trying to live aristocratically. Inevitably this produces disjunctions. Indeed, a number of my heroes feel very keenly the lack of dignified vocation. There is in man a sense of the need for doing useful work; this value will remain quite important till we grow more adjusted to having been picked completely out of the elementary patterns of the struggle for life. So closely is the notion of work linked to life that millions feel compelled to go through the motions of engaging in productive activity. The people in *Couples,* for example, play at their work. They do it grudgingly, as a kind of a joke; but their only real interest is in their personal lives. Essentially, this concern is expressed in seduction, which, as you know from eighteenth century French novels, is one of the ways the aristocracy filled its time.

What I'm saying, I realize, can be applied to the vocation of writing, too. Well, it can, can't it? If not, then where is its ultimate necessity? What is the ultimate blessing on it?

You are saying, then, that the problem is really one of boredom rather than of more fundamental disillusionment?

Yeah, I think so. There are a lot of problems in the lives of *Rabbit, Run* and in some of my other stories that some really severe crisis, such as a defensive war, would cure. I don't mean to say that these are not real problems. They certainly are—but they would not surface were it not for the drift of modern life. People need to feel a purpose underlying their actions. Divising such purposes will be a critical task for our society. War has served in the past: the number of suicides goes down in wartime and people in general feel happier because they can believe that they're all doing something useful and because they are being directed. But people will have to think of other ways to engage themselves, because war—which was never very attractive—is getting less so.

The lure of being transported from the routines of our circumscribed private lives to engagement in some movement toward a goal, of transcending our limited selves by partaking in a corporate will is what makes strong men—dictators—always so tempting. I think that much of the current impatience with the System and the criticism that it does not allow for freedom is really due to the fact that it does not enforce a direction for our lives. Rather than being too repressive, it is not repressive enough. It is not a rigid system at all. And the appeal of having somebody organize every corner of our lives is considerable. It's hard, really hard, to be a member of a democracy and it's hard to be an affluent youth.

If you see man's nature as this, can there be an alternative to war and dictatorship?

Well, the Silent Generation . . . (gee, I've almost forgotten that phrase. The label used to amuse me: we were really silent only on certain topics, don't you think?) The Silent Generation, I think, tried to find the alternatives in terms of personal gratifications. Some of them, admittedly, seem strange now. How much has changed in the last fifteen years. It comes as a shock to realize that almost all of us thought we should have large families. Most of my friends, and I, have four children—four somehow seemed the right number. Now it would be ecologically obscene for people, before they are twenty-five or twenty-six, to have that many children. But then there was a different sort of conscience about such things. There was some general agreement that the path to salvation lay in getting a woman, making a family, and, in doing your own thing, knowing that some things are better to do than others.

No, I don't think America is going to fall into political dictatorship. But there are dangers to individual independence. Maybe I'm wrong, but the increase in our options, in the questions we are called on to resolve, can be exceedingly fatiguing. The circuits can get overloaded and we jam, like a computer. When we sense this starting to happen, we are vulnerable to a deep instinct to surrender—or, at least, to minimize—the prerogatives of decision-making in our personal affairs.

Has a member of the Silent Generation special misgivings about living among the Aquarians?

Well, I confess that I haven't really felt at home since the Eisenhower years. I grew up accepting a certain decorum for behavior, and now that is gone and it is rather unsettling. Seeing long hair on men older than myself disturbs me; I have the feeling that they're out of uniform.

The difference between the decade in which I was in college and the one we're living through now is especially significant to a writer —or at least it is to me. For us, Eliot and Joyce lived the lives of gods; now, the gods are down off Olympus. The Beatles have been much more than fantastically successful entertainers—they were key figures in a cultural revolution. There's no question but that the living art for people under twenty-six is music; the passion for writing, among the young, is gone.

I consider myself very fortunate in that I've been allowed to do what I really wanted to do. Writing doesn't make great demands on my time, it's always an authentic challenge, and the work changes. For many men, work is always the same: you master it and then it's the same operation for thirty or forty years. That's cruel. But it's also the way most people have lived since the history of time began.

In Of the Farm *you speak of reality as nothing more than the jelling of illusion. One of the illusions that troubles your hero in that book concerns the past, the way of life, of which the emblem is the farm in the title. He is an uneasy contemporary who hasn't made peace with the kind of life he finds himself living, isn't he?*

It's another case, I suppose, of a man discovering that all the alternatives are unattractive.

It may be heresy to say that the frontier is gone, but really it is. Frontiers of all kinds have closed. And this makes for a difficult situation for America because we have been, and are, a frontier-oriented country. Part of the agony of the United States is that it was founded to be better than anywhere else on earth. It was a kind of heaven. This concept is still very much on the nation's mind. At the same time, Americans are placed in an invidious position by the European countries' feeling superior and smug. This country makes very severe demands upon itself in attempting to measure up to the mission which it conceives itself as having.

At the end of Bech, *you supplied the reader with bibliographical appendices. I tried to make some sense of them but couldn't. Is there a key? Or was it just the vestigial gagster in you wanting to play games with the magazines, critics, and writers?*

It was meant two ways: first, as a light-hearted attempt to give Bech a concrete bibliographical existence as a writer; second, as a means of re-establishing a distance between Bech and myself. He's nine years older than I, and partly for that reason, his career is quite different from mine. In this aspect, the bibliography was intended to be a specimen history of an American literary career of the period. He began as a kind of war correspondent, a soldier who wrote stories with gung-ho titles for magazines like *Liberty* and *Collier's*. He was intellectualized in New York in the post-war period. And now he has fallen into silence. There are a number of careers like this, but Salinger's best fits the pattern. He began as a writer of war stories for *Collier's* and *Esquire*—"For Esmé—with Love and Squalor" is a kind of war story.

To be candid, the bibliography was also a matter of scoring off various grudges, a way of purging my system. I've never been warmly treated by the *Commentary* crowd—insofar as it is a crowd—and so I made Bech its darling. Norman Podhoretz has always gone out of his way to slam me, and this was my way of having some fun with him.

And then, I don't know, it just seemed to help make it a book.

Bech has been strangely successful. I have never written a book that has received so few bad reviews as this one. Even some of the critics who haven't had much use for me in the past seemed not to be able to screw themselves up to write nasty things about it.

If, as you said, Bech is deliberately set some distance off from you, didn't you have a problem writing about him? How real could he be to you if you tried to steer clear of points of identification?

As a writer, I made use of the capital I have acquired—the peculiar sensation of being a literary person. In that respect, I knew Bech intimately before I started. His background, of course, is not at all mine, but he became fairly real to me as, in story after story, he filled out a little more of his past.

"The Bulgarian Poetess" is the first written of the stories, and there I gave the titles of his main books, which was meant to represent the curve of his rise and fall. He rises with *Travel Light,* which is his *On the Road,* then passes on to a book which, I suppose, is his *Barbary Shore,* and so on. Being specific in this way helped me to see him as a concrete character and, in addition, to make a joke.

How do you react to the kind of criticism John Aldridge offers in his long piece on Bech *in the* Saturday Review? *He talked about your myth and story failing to mesh, but basically, he was playing minor variations on Alas, poor Updike with his arabesques on nothing again. Do you get tired of that?*

Oh quite, yes. But Aldridge did rather grudgingly concede that he liked *Bech,* although he devoted almost all his space to the book about me by a Canadian couple.

Aldridge's complaint was not about the recent book but about some of the earlier ones. The comment about the myth not meshing with the story was directed towards *The Centaur.* I think Aldridge is a man with quite coarse critical perception and he was quite crass about that book. Somehow, he missed the point. Now, there's a limit to which a writer can defend his own stuff: obviously, you do something and if people don't get it, there's no way you can make them get it. There are enough books written with submerged myths; I wrote one in which the myth was overt. It jangled—the way life sometimes does. It was about a man who sees myths everywhere—that was the point. I tried to create the effect of sense eroding away; that was something that felt right to me.

A much more kindly critic than Aldridge, Arthur Mizener, also complained that its Greek gods and goddesses didn't have the luminous power of, say, the gods in the *Cantos.* Well, I wasn't trying to do what Pound had done in the *Cantos.*

I was really quite pleased with that book. The chapters felt right while I was writing it. And it's one of the things that seem better to me now than when I wrote them. The prose is fresh and sharp. I had something I wanted to say, and I said it. There's no way a critic can get you to say what he might have wanted to say. That's one of the rubs between critics and authors. Critics really are often disappointed that the book they have to review is not the book they would have written if they had had the same topic.

You don't wish you'd written The Party at Cramden?

Don't wish. Don't wish. There are enough things around of which I'm envious, but I don't envy Aldridge that book. Gee, I thought it was terrible. But you've got to feel sorry for Aldridge. Any critic who writes a novel is going to get it. Inevitably, a critic makes too many enemies in trying to separate winners and losers.

He didn't pick many winners in After the Lost Generation, *did he?*

I haven't read that. What does he say?

He starts with yet another run-through of the 'twenties figures; then, shutting the door on that era, he tries to identify the new stars. He points out people like Vance Bourjailly, Truman Capote, Gore Vidal, and Norman Mailer. It's as though he had distilled his wisdom from the New York Times *book reviews, and of course in doing that he missed what was really germinating in post-war fiction. There is—let's face it—a crass opportunism about academe which I sensed in this book. It's as though he wanted above all to get into the territory first, and to my mind he was proclaiming a new generation in our literary history before the new generation had really coalesced. His treatment of the 'twenties writers is shallow in one way, of the post-war figures shallow in another.*

Although I grant that he's a pretty bad critic, in all fairness you must say it was a hard time in which to write that kind of book. My own sense of what was happening is that people who wrote the war novels essentially wrote 'thirties novels. There had been no advance in the art of fiction during the war—or not here at any rate—and they all wrote somewhat old-fashioned books which are interesting only because there was something worth saying. For example, I think *From Here to Eternity* is a good book despite the fact that James Jones is really quite a bad writer. It wasn't until 1950 that a change began, that there was a need to do something new in terms of fictional technique.

The writers you named—it's a funny, melancholy roll-call, isn't it? Mailer is the only exception. You'd have to say he has kept on top. He hasn't sunk from sight. He's kept alive. I thought those last two things of his were quite remarkable, really.

As reports, yes. Mailer is at his best when he himself—or his mind —is the protagonist. But when he needs to invent, he strains. Per-

haps he realizes this—he never has come out with the "blockbuster" novel he promised for so long. His biographical essays (I would hesitate to call them journalism) are superb, but his recent fiction seems the product of a different sensibility. I can't understand people like Frank Kermode's enthusiasm for it; they must have a deaf ear for language or no sense of what good characterization is.

But do you think all that stuff matters? I mean characterization and fine language. Does an ear matter if you live in a world that is, as he says, jangly? Why have an ear? Maybe the truth is only going to emerge in rotten books like Mailer's novel. In their rottenness, they are true to life.

That's like saying you could make quite a great film by rolling a camera along 42nd Street and cutting every once in a while to a bar in York, Pennsylvania. It would be unshaped, unpolished, maybe even unintelligible—but it would be life. I can't accept that appeal. Life is the material of art; it is not the equivalent to art.

The relationships between life and art are essentially unsolved in my mind, so it's nice to talk about them.

Isn't much of contemporary writing concerned directly with that question? Earlier, in referring to Barth, you spoke of stunts, but isn't he really exploring something metaphysical? It strikes me as being a bit like pop art where the art object is imitative to the extent that it changes places with the reality it imitates; it's playing games across the line that separates reality and mimesis. Barth's enclosing the Lost in the Funhouse *stories with the frame tale that is a Möbius strip seems prompted by the same notion: the two dimensions of art and reality exist in a continuum. Your* Bech *seemed to play with a similar approach. So much of what is being done in writing and films today deals with the artist creating a work of art about an artist creating a work of art about an artist creating a work of art about . . . It reminds me of a Little Orphan Annie mug I had as a child on which there was a picture of Annie holding a mug on which Annie was holding a mug,* ad infinitum. *I used to feel that mug pulling me into it. I would get dizzy from it.*

Well, enough of that.

You've been very patient with us. After more than an hour and a half, I'm sure you'd appreciate our stopping the inquisition. Have you, perhaps, something you'd like to add before we break up?

One thought, difficult to express. Not only is it difficult for me to picture my ideal reader, but there's also some confusion in my mind as to how he relates to what I write. Slowly, after years and years of writing, making a living at it and gaining whatever glories that go with it, I've begun to realize that there is a collaboration between you and this reader, that the reader more or less supplies out of his own friends a basis for your characters. This is a line between you and his reality. No amount of adjectives—and I've not been leery of using them—is really going to succeed in carving into that reader's mind the exact image I have in mind. Given the fact, then, that you are working in the dark in this foreign land, maybe the less said the better.

Tolstoy often creates an impression of great solidity with quite minimal descriptions. But I was early taken in by Proust and admired what I thought was his heroic effort to say it all, to carry sensation to its final little tendril root.

There is a contract between writer and reader about where the reality of the book exists. There has to be, because on the page there are just some symbols which need a mind of translate them. The phenomenon is worth a little thought, though it's hard to solve by thought. As it works out, the procedure by which an illusion is created comes from your own instinctive feeling of the problem.

NOVEMBER 4, 1970

John Barth

When asked what his criterion was for including a writer in his book The Southern Renaissance, *John Bradbury used to say that anyone born below the Mason-Dixon line was fair game. He admitted it was arbitrary, but he said he needed a definition which would not exclude John Barth.*

The Eastern Shore of Maryland actually is Deep Southern. The real Mason-Dixon Line which divides North and South isn't the east-west surveyors' line across the top of Maryland; it runs north and south down the Chesapeake Bay. The Western Shore, Baltimore and all that, resembles Pennsylvania in its geology and topography and in the character of its people, but the area where I grew up is rather different. During the Civil War, when Maryland was a border state, all the Eastern Shore uniformly supported the Confederacy.

Ambrose, the character in some of your Lost in the Funhouse *stories, spends his childhood in the same place. Do you and he have the same background?*

Not really. Ambrose's family is a kind of traumatic ideal, the sort of family I might have enjoyed having had. My own family was much more ordinary—less hung up on things and, therefore, maybe less interesting, though more serene. My father owned a lunchroom and restaurant in Cambridge, Maryland; none of my family had very much education, although they were intelligent people.

My grandfather, a stone-carver by trade, moonlighted as a ticket agent for North German Lloyd's and also dabbled in rural real estate in Dorchester County at the turn of the century. He sold marshy acreage to his fellow German immigrants who had gone out to the Middle West, found it too cold and unfamiliar, and come to the more temperate clime of Maryland. It was the only land they could afford, but they drained it and it became quite valuable farmland.

Was it your early education, then, that fed your ambitions?

Hardly. I came out of a rural Southern public school during the Second World War, and there were few books at home. Do you know—can you even imagine—what those three circumstances add up to? Perhaps you can't.

I had the disadvantages, and whatever perverse advantages there are, of going through the usual benighted Southern school system of those days which, in addition, suffered the particular deprivations that all schools experienced because of the war. All the male teachers were off in service and many of the younger, more vigorous female teachers were either following their husbands around from army post to army post, or had taken more lucrative jobs in the cities. What one was educated by, in short, were the leavings. Now some of these leavings during the 1940s period were of a noble sort, and I have affectionate memories of a few of the elderly ladies who were filling in until the war was over, but it *was* a peculiar kind of schooling. Everything was deprived. No sports or even sporting equipment; no band activities; no funds, it seemed, for anything. I got to the point where I would read anything and everything just for something to do. Most of it was garbage, but, looking back on it, I remember Faulkner and Dos Passos, and some Hemingway mixed in with all the Agatha Christies and the other mysteries in the stacks of paperbacks (they'd just been invented) I'd bring home from my father's store and return to be sold. The good things, however, were hit on just by accident. No one pointed the way. I remember reading a Dos Passos novel, for example, and being excited by his devices, by the realization that a novel could be written in this different way; you see, I hadn't encountered Joyce.

At that time, it was an eleven-year school system. You graduated after the eleventh grade, and nobody expected you to go to college. But I did, on some sort of scholarship. A sixteen-year-old, fresh from the background I've just described, I entered Johns Hopkins University right after the war: another world entirely.

It was at Hopkins that I discovered literature, in the happiest possible way. There, there were splendid professors—magnificent, noble professors. I didn't know what they were talking about, especially, but they gave me a new sense of human possibilities.

I have particular memories of a few. One was Pedro Salinas, a Spanish poet, dead now, a refugee from Franco. I read *Don Quixote* with him in Spanish. He was a famous poet, but I didn't know that;

for me, he was simply a splendid old gentleman who inspired by his style and manner. He taught the kinds of things teachers teach you without teaching you: for example, that devoting your life, your little mortal life, to the pursuit of literature—to the making of it and the understanding of it—could be not only a very passionate enterprise but a noble one. Passion, nobility, dignity—all very Spanish and calm and graceful—and to a country boy, very impressive indeed. As I speak I see his gold teeth, his long cigars, his unpressed suits. Many years later, during a chilly winter in Malaga, I translated some of his poems for my own pleasure. Love poems, stately and moving.

Back to Johns Hopkins. I was lucky to be poor. In order to make up the difference between my scholarship and the actual cost of going to school and living there, I filed books in the library for a large number of hours a week. I was assigned to the classics library, which, along with some other arcane categories, at that time included the stacks of the Oriental Seminary. The library had much more help than was needed, so you didn't have all that many books to file. In effect, you were told to take a pile of books, go back there in the library, get lost, and show up a few hours later. I did, and of course I read, at random, the stuff I was putting back on the shelves.

As it happened, that "stuff" proved to be marvelous for a person who ended up writing. Not just the Greek and Roman classics, but ancient narrative in general.

Much later, I learned that Thomas Wolfe decided when he got to the New York Public Library that he was going to read all the books in it. Something like that. Well, back at Hopkins, I started to read with that kind of German ambitiousness. Half seriously, I decided as a sophomore that, having come from a background where I had hardly read anything, I was going to read all the books in the classics stacks and all the books in the Oriental Seminary stacks and then move right on to the other things. If I was going to file them all, why shouldn't I read them as I filed them?

I remember going through the Harvard Classics, for example, by starting with Volume I, then going on to Volume II, then Volume III, and so on. System? That number two followed one and three followed two was enough for me. I did in fact read them left to right, first to last.

Some of the things I absorbed, not knowing at the time what I was really osmosing, were the great Oriental tale-cycles: the incredible *Ocean of Story,* that marvelous tenth-century Sanskrit classic in ten folio volumes; Burton's *Arabian Nights*—which I'm now in the middle of re-reading completely for the first time since, in filing the Oriental Seminary stuff, I read them Volume I through the terminal essay in Volume XVII; the *Panchatantra;* and later derivatives like the *Decameron,* the *Heptameron,* and the *Pentameron.*

Would you say that this was your apprenticeship as a writer?

I didn't realize it was an apprenticeship—I was just immersing myself—and for that reason, it was the happiest kind of apprenticeship in the world.

I was not an English major at Johns Hopkins and took few courses in that department. I never was taken through the classic American literature, for example, nor did I take a course in the history of the novel—subjects I've wished since that I'd received formal education in. But my informal education in literature was truly enormous in those two or three later undergraduate years, and most of it came from my piling into the ocean of ancient narrative, many hours a day. Some of it haunts me still and very directly affects the kinds of things I think of to write.

Was it this reading that made you decide to be a writer?

I backed into the decision, if it was a decision. That writing, writing works of fiction, really was the only thing I was interested in was something I discovered at about age nineteen by way of passionate default, of an inspired lack of alternatives.

I had gone to Hopkins as a disappointed musician. I had played jazz through high school and was interested in orchestration. But then I went to Juilliard, in the summer after my graduation, with money I had saved up from playing in local dance bands, and was for the first time thrown into the presence of people my age who really *had* talent, who were going to be the professional musicians of my generation. I saw that I didn't and, facing the painful fact, I came back from New York wondering what to do for a living. "Maybe I'll make sandwiches in my father's shop," I thought. It didn't seem like a bad idea. In that time and place nobody expected anything extraordinary of you. If you managed to hold your own in the hometown and make sandwiches as well as your father, you were doing O.K. Just finishing high school was something to celebrate. Whose father did? Whose mother? And if you went to college at all, even if you flunked out after your first year, you were away ahead—

the first in the history of your family who had gotten that far! Imagine what freedom this permitted you to enjoy, if you were also born with some imagination and stumbled onto enough books—as David Copperfield did living with the Murdstones—to give you a notion of an expansive life beyond the immediate, rather grim one! All those alternatives—and anything you did was bound to be tremendous! There was no way to lose. In retrospect I can appreciate now that I had one of the greatest luxuries a child can be afforded. It's a luxury I suppose I haven't been able to afford for my own children.

In those days one didn't have to make up one's mind to attend college in September until around August. So I came back from Juilliard, learned I'd won the Hopkins scholarship (I'd forgotten I'd even taken the exam), and went to college, simply by default. After the first couple of years, I found I was very interested in literature and, by that time, in not very much else. I'd had no particular flair for writing, but I tried it—and wrote a lot of very bad stuff.

Then I graduated, and the question was, what to do next? In summers, I had worked in factories around Baltimore. I had been a stone mason, and I had worked in offices. So I wasn't innocent of various kinds of work. Having seen what these jobs amount to, I went to graduate school. It was not at all because I thought I had a gift for scholarship; but I had acquired a great respect for scholarship—good scholarship—from my professors at Hopkins. Also, I thought graduate-assistanthood would give me more time to do what I wanted to do and at the same time earn a minimal support—and believe me, it was minimal—for the wife and children I had by that time picked up. It would have more to do with writing than anything else I could think of which would earn my daily bread and not cause me to hate what I had to do to earn it. And, meanwhile, I could be learning a few things too, if only by having to teach them. It worked out well. That's the life I've been leading ever since.

You said the first writing you did was not very good. When did you start hitting your stride?

After four or five years. Between my nineteenth and twenty-third year, I wrote reams and reams of things; it makes me sweat a little to remember. Luckily, I don't remember very much of it. Simply put, I was trying to make some elementary discoveries about my

limitations and my strengths (or what I supposed would be my potential strengths), about what kinds of things interested me as a writer,
what kinds of imaginative experience I could perhaps address myself
to with some confidence, what kinds of voices I could be eloquent
in—or, at least, more eloquent in than in others.

Even after finishing college, I was still very rooted, emotionally,
in the marsh-country, the swamps of the Eastern Shore of Maryland.
I began to write a novel about this milieu. At the same time, I was
also carrying in the back of my head—not too far back—the memory
of all those tale cycles in which stories framed other stories framing
other stories and so forth. Well, I thought, I'll write a series of tales
(children *are* ambitious)—a hundred tales (I had Boccaccio in mind),
all set in that tidewater Maryland area, at all periods of its history,
from the Indians (I was thinking of Faulkner, I'm sure) through the
Revolutionary War (perhaps—for it wasn't an especially interesting
war in Maryland), the War of 1812 (a very interesting one in Maryland—I'm still fascinated by that subject), the Civil War (which
split the state in half), down to the present (that being 1951 or 1952),
and perhaps even into some kind of imagined future.

I didn't write the hundred tales. I wrote fifty—and they didn't
get published. Justly so. It was the first volume I'd written, not
counting the novel, which . . . well, never mind that novel. It never
got out of the marshes. Somewhere it sulks and bubbles yet among
the primitive creatures of the swamp.

To look back at these stories now is to be embarrassed at the false
steps one takes en route to the true ones. But one has to find what
Bellow in *Augie March* calls "the axial lines."

*You didn't read just the oriental and classical prose, did you? Was
any modern writer at all suggestive—in terms of a way to approach
fiction, not specific subject matter?*

I *was* impressed by Faulkner as a young man. What I admired was
a particular kind of narrative dimension—a way of having stories
pick up from one another, of repeating characters—that, for better or
worse, I didn't see much in other modern literature (although one
sees it in Hemingway's early story collection, too). It's all through
older literature: in Boccacio, in the Greek drama. When Aeschylus
mentions Orestes after Clytemnestra has killed Agamemnon, the very
name conjures up, without any further explanation, whole tribu-
taries of narrative material which impinge ironically and with in-

tense economy on the narrative at hand. What an advantage that is: to be able to draw on a great reservoir of prior and subsequent story just by invoking certain names.

It's hard to do that, of course, in a culture where you can't presume a volume of shared acquaintance with specific narrative. But one way to imitate it, modernly, is the way Faulkner does it. If you're within the corpus of Faulkner's work, you have something like the Greek mythos on a local, on a personal scale. By giving a man in a story a certain family name, he conjures up in his readers' imagination all those generations of history that led up to that man and, often, what will happen to his descendants. It's a very Greek quality.

Someone, perhaps in a lecture here at Union, observed that The Floating Opera *has a lot of Wittgenstein in it, and almost all commentators regard it as a philosophical work. If this is so, it would make you quite unlike most American writers. To write a novel from a philosophical premise is generally a more European trait—or maybe it's just French.*

I was not a philosopher. But like many people in their early twenties of a certain cast of imagination, I was beginning to think hard about certain kinds of questions. I was possessed by the idea of suicide at that time, and the problem of nihilism gripped me.

At first I thought I'd write a minstrel show—a philosophical minstrel show. I remembered this showboat that came into Cambridge, Maryland; I'd seen it as a child and heard about Tambo and Bones, the black-face acts, and so forth. So I thought I might adapt the classical minstrel show form to contemporary narrative purposes. I wasn't thinking of a novel at all, but it turned into a novel—*The Floating Opera.*

The plan grew (I was twenty-three or-four); I decided to write three novels, all dealing with the problem of nihilism. My lack of philosophical training didn't bother me because I thought I knew what I was talking about artistically. And somehow, although I really knew much more about ancient literature than about twentieth century literature—I wasn't at all sophisticated about contemporary literature at that time—I sensed that these novels I was going to write weren't going to be conventional novels. Nothing at all like John O'Hara or who have you.

My notion was to take a man who commits suicide, or at least decides to commit suicide. (I hadn't read Camus's book about suicide then, but I read it shortly afterward; I felt a congenial spirit there.) His reasons for choosing to die are ostensibly logical: he can find no rational justification for living; he can't abide the idea of living irrationally; therefore, as a rational decision, he will terminate his life—blow up the Floating Opera. Then, one way or another (it's more a Humean than a Camusian thing, actually), he comes to the conclusion, by the same operation of reason, that there's no more reason to kill himself than not to kill himself; that, indeed, there's no reason to do anything. And with that very qualified, ironic *raison d'etre*—or, at least, *raison* not to not *d'etre,* he proceeds with his life. I wanted, not a happy but a wry ending, a shrug-shoulder ending.

The second novel, which was to follow the first immediately, would begin with the conclusion of the first as its premise but come to completely different conclusions—horrifying conclusions, where people who shouldn't die do die, where people are destroyed by their own and other people's ideas. I was aware, even in those days, that ideas aren't toys. Some people I have known—passionate, good, deep-thinking people—have torn their and their friends' lives apart with the seriousness of their thinking. The discrepancy between the ideal of the rational life and the kinds of facts of our non-rational or counter-rational nature with which we indeed live interests me. So the second novel, *The End of the Road,* was written as a deliberate counterpart to *The Floating Opera.* Both novels were written very fast, each in three months when I was twenty-four. I took the summer off in between.

The third was to explore the same general notion in a different way. It turned out to be much more different than I originally thought. It turned into an extravagant novel, an extravaganza from history—*The Sot-Weed Factor.*

Historical novels do well commercially, but the genre isn't treated with much respect by critics and it doesn't attract our better writers. What led to your choice of the subject?

I'd gotten immersed in the documents of Colonial history, particularly of Maryland's history. Joyce has Daedalus say, "History is a nightmare from which I am trying to awake." When you get away from the history books and into the documents of the times, there is indeed a dreamlike feeling that takes hold—certainly in investigating the Colonial period. It was in many ways nightmarish, but reading the documents, one laughs in one's sleep. The whole enter-

prise was so precarious! Pirates really did sail up the Chesapeake
Bay a few years after the Plantation was founded and captured the
legislature while it was in session (just as a few years ago they were
doing with university presidents). They would capture the legislature, pillage the town, steal the state seal because there was forty
poundsworth of silver in it, and sail down the Bay. Imagine being
a first settler, almost completely vulnerable to any depradation!
I love the notion of that fragility.

Though I was not a patriotic writer, I had feelings about America.
In the late 1950s, which means my late twenties, I had a feeling
comparable (but ironically) to the one Virgil must have had about
Rome in those sections of the *Aeneid* where he describes, lovingly,
the marsh that was originally there. I was deep into the idea of the
mythical America by that time.

I still shake my head when I think of the archives of Maryland,
of those painfully earnest documents. The people of the province
seriously believed (and with good cause, given the faulty communications of the time) that at any moment they could be pushed right
back into the ocean. In a sense, they *were* in the middle of the
bloody ocean, between Europe and China. There was every reason
to believe that cabals of the French and Indians, or of the Catholics
and somebody else, were simply going to exterminate the province
at any moment.

I love that phase of our history, and I remember it with pleasure
because of the apocalyptic feeling that we all have about America
at the moment.

There were two versions of The Floating Opera, *weren't there?*

The original version went through many editors, all of whom turned
it down. Then, finally, an editor liked it and wanted to publish it,
but he found the ending unbelievable.

The showboat in my novel, like the original, had two sets of footlights, an electric set used when it pulled into a landing that had
current and a set of acetylene footlights for the landings that didn't.
My thought was that Andrews, in the middle of the vaudeville act
on stage, would go under the stage of the floating opera, where there
was a galley. Then, this being an electric landing, he'd turn on all
those acetylene footlights and floodlights—the houselights and everything else had a separate acetylene set—and go back into the audience and wait for the whole show to blow up. That was the image
that began the novel.

Of course, the attempt, because of practical physics, couldn't work, or was certainly bloody unlikely to work. Given that much cubic space and the fact that the windows would have been open to provide ventilation in the muggy southern Chesapeake Bay summertime, it was near impossible for it to blow up. So the show would continue to its end and my character would go out coming to the conclusion I told you about before.

This didn't ring true to the editor. No man who loved life as much as Todd Andrews seems to, he said, would be likely to commit suicide in any case, but if he did, the last thing he would do would be to kill his mistress, his possible daughter, and the townspeople, for whom he had genuine affection. This demonstrated to me that the man simply hadn't understood the story at all. I've never known anybody exactly like Andrews, but I've known people close enough to him, including myself in some moods and particularly what I was like in my twenties, to know that not only can one smile and smile and be a villain, as Shakespeare says, but that one can smile and smile and be a hell of a good guy and still decide, goddamn it, to take the whole theater with him if he has to go. I've known some people who were in combat and had the attitude "If I'm going to die, Western Civilization has no right to persist after me." So, to me, that kind of mental cast was by no means unrealistic.

Chekhov says that you should never change anything in your writing to suit the taste of an editor or critic. If you're going to hang, hang for your own sins and not for his. Well, I was twenty-four, had published nothing yet, and I was eager to get published. So I did change the ending, I'm ashamed to say, and the novel was published. And very properly, critics, even those who liked the novel, jumped on that altered ending as sentimental and unwarranted.

When the novel was re-issued, I exercised my right to change it back. Fortunately, fiction is different from painting. My first wife's grandfather was an amateur painter all his life; when he got old, he recalled all his paintings. (This was easy to do because the only people who had them were relatives.) His eyesight was failing and he painted them all over in brighter colors which he could see. That sort of revision is too bad because the original is destroyed, but literature is not that way. If a book of mine were going to be re-issued and were I to have the time and the inclination, I would never hesitate to look at it again and touch it up a little bit. The original is always somewhere still floating around the libraries, and if anyone is at all interested ten or twenty years later, some Ph.D. who needs something to do can make a comparison which can keep him employed for a year.

You must know yourselves that when you look at anything you wrote last semester—even something you are rather pleased with—infelicitous phrases and injudicious images jump out at you as if they were in red ink. "How in hell could I ever have said *that?*" you say. You look at the page and whang! You notice a metaphor which completely contradicts the point of one three pages back. As one gets older and more cunning, the sensitivity towards such things increases; I see nothing wrong with making little emendations.

One doesn't want to be a Soviet historian about one's own literary past, but in literature there is much honored precedent for an author's textual revision, and I'm conservative enough in some directions to be impressed by literary precedent. It's a rule of thumb, among critical editors of a text, always to use the last corrected edition printed in the author's lifetime. In many cases, as you know, this means choosing from lots of variations.

On the other hand, I would not change the plot or anything substantive. *(The Floating Opera* revision was a special case—I had the chance to stick the proper ending back in and I took it.) The ideas you had when you wrote a book at twenty or twenty-four should not be tinkered with no matter how far you've come from them since. That was the man you were. I would never think of repudiating a story I wrote or materially altering its substance or thrust.

So much of your early reading was in short tales but your publication, at least until recent years, was of novels. Didn't you write any short stories after The Floating Opera?

No short stories. I found the short story form simply uncongenial until I was nearly forty, when I rediscovered it for other reasons.

The novels, superficially at least, are very unlike the oriental tales that fascinated you. Did that reading teach you anything practical that you could use in writing fiction?

You do re-imagine your history retrospectively when you're older, but what I think now that I was learning at that time was certain values I would still very much affirm if I were crude enough to try to write a writer's manifesto—things having to do with narrative pace, with a sense of timing.

For the last fifteen or twenty years, I've had the chance of working with apprentice writers in universities, and I've learned that what was true of myself is true, in many more cases than not, of those I've worked with. Their initial gifts are for language, for a way of handling words, for observing things in a certain refreshing way—in other words, for images. Now these are essentially the gifts that lyric poets have to have, and this is one of the reasons why there is so much splendid poetry in the corpus written by very young people, and very little splendid fiction in the corpus written by people your age. The last things that are learned in a literary apprenticeship are (1) a sense of genuine narrative shape—that business of the whole dramatic action as Aristotle called it, (2) a sense of pacing the progress (the disclosures and wrap-ups within this shape) towards the revelation which makes the work an integer, and (3) a sense of the characterization that is necessary for all kinds of writing, whether it be fantastical, parodistic, irrealistic, or realistic. These things we seem to learn later, both from the accumulated experience of our own writing and, in the case of most writers, from the enormous absorption of a great many narratives read.

Is this late fruition of literary ambitions a recent characteristic?

Very few American writers decide at an early time in their lives that writing is what they are going to do. I suppose this was less true of the nineteenth century men of letters, but most of our twentieth-century American writers, it seems to me, stumble into literature, and this has had its bad effects.

In continental Europe, in England, and in South America among the educated class, children are brought up to think of literature as at least as honorable an undertaking as law or medicine, I gather. A Flaubert decides at age twelve or thirteen that he's going to be a novelist, in the way a kid might decide to be a doctor or a scientist. He chooses models, tries to understand his tradition and accepts or rejects it, and eventually enters into some sort of literary circle. He sets himself an apprenticeship and works towards the perfection of his craft. To be sure, we do have our Updikes who, as young men, make a literary career their star and chart their route deliberately via Harvard and *The New Yorker,* for example, but this is not a typical American pattern. Not by any means.

It amazes me to watch students come into the vocation of writing comparatively late and do rather well. I'm very interested in the process of their discovery of their literary voice, and of their finding out about the corpus of this curious art to which they've committed themselves, perhaps innocently, for one reason or another. There's a lot of crap they have to get done with before they develop even the faintest notion of who they are in the medium, of what their voice is, of what their radical subject matter will be. As a rule, one doesn't discover these things easily. In my own case, it took some years to learn even whether my basic inclinations in the medium were toward the comic or the non-comic.

There are, of course, startling examples to the contrary. Kafka seems to have been Kafka from the first time he wrote anything. There is in fact some early Kafka, but the difference between it and the later Kafka is not very sharp at all. With Kafka there is a consummate vision, most extraordinary and felt to the bone, from the first works to the last.

Most of the giants, however, show us another kind of career, in which growth and change are quite striking. And the European sense of the profession, apparently, is best suited to this evolution. American careers tend to be more meteoric. Where are our Manns and Nabokovs, doing first-rate work in their latter decades?

The short story has provided a training ground for American writers, wouldn't you say?

Traditionally, yes. I can think of two reasons why this has been so. The first may have something to do with our writers coming to the profession well on in their education; they have a lot of catching up to do, a lot of discovery to be accomplished in a concentrated period, and the short story form offers that opportunity. I advise my own students, for example, not to embark on lengthy projects until they're along in their apprenticeships. For the year or so they'll be working with me or some other captive critic, they are better off completing several projects and getting a response. Also, there is a benefit in conjuring up different sets of characters and different conceits, in working in different voices and from different points of view. Generally, they'll learn more from trying a variety of things than from making that enormous emotional and imaginative investment that goes into conceiving one novel and sticking with it for years. Writing eight hundred or so pages of sentences will teach a young writer a great deal about English prose, but if it's all towards one novel, he will learn considerably less about making characters, managing narrative pace, working subplots against mainplots —that sort of thing—than he will by attempting a number of narrative pieces.

The second reason is practical. It makes good sense to have published a few things here and there in magazines just to have some credentials with which to approach a book publisher.

Then, because the novel is more lucrative, they stay with it?

That's obviously true with people like Joe Heller, who wrote a few short stories, then abandoned them after the success of his novel. Ralph Ellison, I believe, has done the same thing; so have William Styron and Philip Roth and J.D. Salinger, and many others. I don't mean to say that the reason is simply economic.

Yet the big money—and the making of reputations—is in novels. Film rights, for example, pay much more handsomely than producing any number of short stories, especially in a shrinking fiction market. But doesn't this pose the danger that a writer will prematurely abandon his schooling in the short story?

Discussing this subject becomes complicated because we are speaking in general terms. There's a difference between the stuff written as an apprentice as a testing of self and the first fruits of a professional career. And "novel" and "short story" are not constant, tightly defined qualities.

The pattern of working in the short story, building a reputation, and advancing to the novel—the Hemingway pattern—is something I associate with the end of the nineteenth century and the first half of the twentieth century. It's characteristic of the modernist tradition which gave us the kinds of fiction written for sixty or seventy years up through the Second World War, let's say. There are still writers who follow that pattern and write those kinds of fiction, but, with some exceptions, they are writers who continue to think in terms of the audiences of the 1940s and 1950s. But the general change in our audience makes working with that sort of address rather anachronistic, and the writers I admire recognize this. It's not simply because they're more aware of what your generation is like—that would be mere trendiness—but because they themselves have followed out certain currents in their own thinking; they are not only alive to the ideas in the air, but responsible for those ideas being in the air.

Obviously, it is still more lucrative to write a novel, insofar as writing fiction is lucrative at all today (and it just isn't, not compared to the way it used to be). The economics of publishing place a premium on the novel. But the *living* contemporary writers are finding the kind of novel we usually associate with the term much less congenial a form artistically than shorter, different kinds of things.

Some of the earlier 20th-century writers have foreshadowed this development. Kafka's novels don't hold up for me as well as the shorter pieces; it seems he was always uncomfortable in the longer form; the novels themselves are fragmentary. Borges, you know, has never written a novel. Samuel Beckett's career goes from the substantial novels of the 'thirties and 'forties into briefer, deliberate fragments. Among my contemporaries Barthelme, whom I admire a good deal, sticks to relatively short and definitely non-traditional things. Jack Hawkes, who may be the most important American writer among us all, never worked in long novels. In this connection, I might also mention Italo Calvino, a contemporary Italian I find terribly exciting. He wrote some novel-length things in his past, but what he's been doing in the last ten years or so, that which has been translated recently, have been short pieces related to one another in such a way as to make a volume which isn't a novel in the usual sense. They really are pretty much discrete pieces, and they don't resemble—and here I'm coming back to what I started to say—the anthology story of the modernist tradition.

I, myself, as a student and as an apprentice, found writing that kind of short story simply uncongenial, hostile, anti-pathetic to my own temperament. I wrote those tales I told you about, but that was another kind of thing entirely. I did write novels after that, even long novels like *Sot-Weed Factor* and *Giles Goat-Boy*, but when I'd written those two gigantic novels (not only gigantic but gigantistic—deliberately bloated—novels), I realized I would probably never want to do that again. It was not just because I decided that I had sinned enough against civilized attention, but for aesthetic reasons.

Mr. Barth, doesn't having a university affiliation disturb you? To some degree, it has to isolate you from society in general and thus limit the world reflected in your books.

We used to have a great deal of that sort of criticism: the professor-writer, it was popular to say, was a tweedy recluse from life. But you haven't heard much of that in the last few years, because the campuses are right in the center of what's happening in our society. Some of my friends who are rather removed from the university scene almost seem to envy my being involved in it—at least so it appears from the way they question me about what's going on. And I fail to see why one ambiance is necessarily more limiting for a writer than any other. Certainly a university would be one of the least limiting.

That aside, there is a happy advantage about working in a university. I've never liked to live meanly. I've always liked a measure of physical comfort, and teaching has given me that, so that I've never had to think for one second whether the next thing I published was going to make a dollar or not. Of course, I always hope it will—it's not disagreeable to have money.

My definition of a commercially successful book is one that loses so little money for its publisher that he's willing to publish the next one. If that's the case, you're ahead of the game. It's a lovely state of affairs. I knew when the *Lost in the Funhouse* stories came out that the book could not possibly turn a profit for its publisher. The publisher knew it too, and neither of us cared unduly.

Has it?

No, it hasn't. Oh, I don't think it lost money. It did in the hardcover, but the paperback is doing all right because it's used in the colleges.

It's used in my course. In fact, it's being used in three courses here.

My first novels were financial losers. Being responsible for others beside myself, I would have felt less free to explore as a writer if I had not had a separate income from teaching. But all I need from the books is to break even. I'm certainly not getting rich off writing, but I enjoy the freedom to follow purely aesthetic leanings, just as a poet will, and not have to worry about other considerations. A friend of mine used to say, "When you're writing, never think of what you are doing as a commodity." In fact, I don't. Obviously, I'd like a large distribution and as large a readership as possible, but such thoughts don't begin to enter until I've finished a book. Then it properly *is* a commodity; I'm finished with it.

The big-name professional North American novelist need only turn out a book every two or three years to live comfortably, but that book *must* be a good seller. To be merely a critical success wouldn't be enough. Most of these people live at a relatively high level of affluence—they don't live on the margins of society as Kafka did—so they've got to hit the best seller list consistently if they're going to maintain the life style they have by that time committed themselves to maintaining. I don't have that kind of pressure bearing down on me, and I just love not having it.

Mightn't the Updikes, Styrons, and Mailers reply that it's worth the moral risk to have the time?

Worth the moral risk to have the time? I don't follow you.

I inferred that you were saying there was a moral or aesthetic risk in having to think of sales while writing. But couldn't they argue that you don't have to publish a jot. . . .

Oh, I see . . . yes, I agree. I understand that.

. . . the time you have to devote to teaching, they can spend writing.

Here and there in my academic career, I've had enough years off to know that I never get more work done when I'm not teaching than when I am teaching. I don't know how other temperaments are, but my own is such that I simply could not spend every day of every week at the writing desk.

I have very mixed feelings about this vocation of mine; as McLuhan and Norman O. Brown and nearly everybody else have told us, it's a peculiar way to spend your life. It's queer for a live human animal, endowed with intelligence, to spend most waking hours of a very mortal life cooped up in a room not talking to anybody, just scribbling words on a page. It's like being one of those guys in the Thruway toll booths, particularly the booths no one ever drives up to. They can't talk to their friends—all they can do is wave out the door every now and then. I think about them.

For most writers, weaving sentences together is a long, lonely, solitary process. I once asked Bob Creeley (he's one of our staff at Buffalo) how long it takes him to write a poem. He said, "Half an hour." Of course, he was pulling my leg, but there are some writers, by God, who can get things done in spurts. Their ability embarrasses me. Carlos Williams tells us in his autobiography that he used to write poems while practicing medicine. A patient would walk out of the room and Williams would turn to his typewriter and bat out a few lines of *Paterson* before the next patient would walk in. Very few prose writers can work that way. Certainly not novelists. It takes large doses of that old nine to three, or eight-thirty in the morning to four in the afternoon. The hours depend on your temperament, but there has to be a hunk of them together. When my children were little and I was teaching four sections of freshman something or other to get by, I would start writing at six in the evening and work until two or three in the morning.

In fact, for a novel you must often think in terms of years, not half-hours or days. As soon as I start thinking about a novel, I assume that it will be four years or so before I can see what it is I'm thinking about.

There are novelists—Mailer, Malraux, a number of good French, Mexican, and South American writers, who are also promiment public figures—who manage somehow or other to combine life with people and the composition of long pieces of narrative. But they are the exceptions who are just lucky to have that temperament.

For me—and now I'm coming back to your question—four years of work on a project is a hell of a long time to devote to one single activity. I would go absolutely crackers if I hadn't some congress with the world. I know I'm timid enough to require an official access to other people, such as a university provides. I know this from the years I've spent in Europe or on leave in America trying to write: I get bored as hell with the vocation and the loneliness of not being in human company.

What you've been saying reminds me of Camus's short story in Exile and the Kingdom *about the artist who is forced by his success to retreat to a lonely loft. The last word he scrawls is ambiguous: "solitary" or "solidarity." He couldn't work amid his milling admirers, and yet he lost contact with humanity in seeking tranquility. I am wondering how much distance you try to keep from your subject matter.*

It differs from one project to another. Nabokov, asked about the use of autobiographical material in his fiction, said that sometimes he'll bestow an autobiographical detail in one of his characters as one bestows a medal. I like the metaphor.

I, myself, have found that when I'm spiritually closest to the character, material, or passions of a piece of my fiction, I tend to place it at some radical remove. Thus, my mythical stories—for example, the stories in the *Funhouse* series directly concerned with myth—are much closer to my own imaginative concerns than the stories which are ostensibly more realistic. The Ambrose stories in that collection are the ones furthest removed from any of my own actual experiences—or so it seems to me.

Does it bother you to have readers assume that you and your characters are interchangeable?

As a writer, yes, because that's not what you are trying to communicate to a reader.

In my early bunch of novels, I have triangles in which two men share, or are rivals for, the affections of a woman. In the later fiction, it has tended to become the other way around—one man and two women in a relationship. Once, some student out of an audience at the University of Virginia, mind you, said, "I see all these adulterous triangles in your novels. Were you ever in a situation like that?" Usually, I'm not at all quick on my feet when I'm confronted by flagrant bad manners, but that time I had the presence of mind to say, "Yes, once . . . with your mother."

Are you conscious of your literary development?

Perhaps more conscious than a person should be. Particularly since I've been in my thirties and forties. I really do try to see what it is I've been up to. Especially when I'm thinking of what I want to do next, I like to look back. I don't always read everything through again, but I try to seek out patterns—the thematic and structural directions, the personality of the voices, other such things—in the books leading up to where I am at that moment. Sometimes, ten years after you've finished a piece, you can see the patterns and suggestions more clearly; perhaps you were not very aware of them at the time or were only half-intuitively groping for their formulation. I don't say that this is the only way to conduct a literary career, or even that it's a desirable method for some temperaments. I'm just reporting what I do.

I've just finished a little volume of three novellas—one each about Perseus, Bellerophon, and Scheherezade's kid sister. The fact that the heroes of the first two are rather like Aeneas is not just coincidence. I'm much impressed by the figure of Aeneas (although I don't like the *Aeneid* nearly as much as I do other classical literature).

Unlike Odysseus, who always knows exactly where he is supposed to go and what he must do, Aeneas learns where he's to go, what he's to do, and who he is in the process of going, doing, and being. For example, in Hades he finds where he is by looking at where he has been and thereby determines where he is then supposed to go. We know from Jung, from popular psychology, from the body of literature, and from our own common experience, that it's a usual phenomenon for people to take spiritual inventory at various points in life. I'm always doing that.

There's a marine animal I'm fond of. (I don't think I invented him, though maybe I improved on him.) He's a crustacean who creates his spiral shell as he goes along. The materials he encounters are assimilated into it, and at the same time he more or less intuitively directs his path toward the kinds of material shells are best made of. How I love that animal! He's the perfect image for me. He moves at a snail's pace (and I do, too). He wears his history on his back all the time, but it's not just a burden; he's living in it. His history is his house. He's constantly adding new spirals, new rings—but they're not just repetition, for he's expanding logarithmically. Its volume becomes more capacious as new material is added from the present. What he comes across is cemented with his own juices (now I know I'm making him up), and yet it's not just blind aleatoric construction because of the instinct that guides him toward the appropriate stuff for his particular shell.

Is that where your question was leading?

Well, not quite. I was aiming for a reflection, or a revision, of something you'd said in an interview with the Wisconsin Review *in 1965. You said then that you didn't see yourself as a social critic. I think that was before* Giles, Goat Boy *was finished and I was wondering whether, in writing* Giles, *your view changed.*

Parenthetically, I might comment that I didn't *say* anything in that particular interview. Interviews make me nervous, so I was supplied with a list of questions to which I jotted down answers. Strictly defined, it wasn't an interview.

But to get to your question: no, it didn't change and it hasn't changed. I've never felt responsible in the social criticism way. Of course, any book that opposes values to nihilism is in fact a form of social criticism, but the kind of thinking associated with social criticism has been, for me, a source of material rather than of themes. The people in fiction I've written, particularly in the novels, have had ideas in their heads which reflect the world they live in and they have often been ridden by those ideas. Sometimes in very naive ways, they are involved in society, just as I am and you are, but this is not the same as writing to alert readers to social malfeasances.

I suppose it would be possible to detect some changes in my "social consciousness" over the years. Obviously, anyone living through the 1960s and 1970s who's not been asleep has been breathing things more promiscuously in the air than they were in the 1950s. It would be strange indeed if they didn't register somehow or other in what I think of to write. I'm not quite as innocent of politics now as I was at age thirty, for example. How could I be, living on a campus where so much of it has been going on? Certain sensitivities have been sharpened which weren't so sharp when I was twenty-three. Looking back on the black girl who moves in *The Floating Opera* makes me sweat a little bit. But there it is, in a novel out of the 1950s, so I don't think it's inaccurate. Sure, my eyes have been opened to some things by the events of the last half decade that they had been fairly closed to, and this is reflected in my fiction.

Could you not imagine circumstances which would lead to political commitment in your writing?

Not only can I not imagine it, I would be distressed if my fiction ever became political in any way. If it came to "committed art" or "pure" art—to use the corny old terms in which the Europeans still always debate the issue—I would mount the ramparts for pure art every time. But it's a stupid dichotomy to make. All you have to do is think of the great nineteenth century Russian novelists and you see how it breaks down. Is Dostoevski a pure or a committed artist?

I hope I never write a novel the burden of which is a message like Let's get out of Viet Nam. I'd be ashamed of myself. Mind you, I don't say for a minute that a novelist who thought that's what he was doing couldn't write a good novel. I don't know the Dickens biography intimately, but he apparently thought he was writing novels the purpose of which was to change things. He thought he was a committed artist, but that's not what ravishes us in the novels.

I understand why the Left in Europe and in this country fulminates and gets apoplectic at remarks like Nabokov's "My aim is aesthetic bliss." Nabokov's apologists urge us to pay him no mind because, they assure us, there is a great deal of social criticism in his works. Well of course there is, but it's unimportant compared to what is operative in the works of, say, the big South American novelists. Nabokov no doubt does seek aesthetic bliss—and what's wrong with that?

Jane Austen wrote during an age of great social and political upheaval, yet none of it is reflected in her writing. I've always felt this lack to be a limitation of the fictional world she presents. For all her cleverness, she deals with vapid lives.

Finally, the manner and degree in which social issues are reflected depend on a particular writer's temperament. The idea of revolution floats through my recent novellas—it has to—yet that doesn't mean that I'm a revolutionist. I'm not an activist in the college, but I am fascinated by the ferment the activists manifest. For example, one of the notions I've been most preoccupied with as a private citizen is the women's lib movement. I'm not an ardent women's libber, but I am absorbed with that question. It's more fascinating in many ways than the other liberation movements. For one thing, it's more complicated—morally, psychologically, and aesthetically. Something of this concern is bound to affect my writing. Indeed, I suppose a simple-minded critic could say my trio of novellas is about women's lib. It *is* one of the themes that holds them together, although that's not at all what it's about for me.

It sounds too decadently formalist to say that political or social ideas are only grist for the mill of fiction. There's more to it than that because one has a passionate involvement with those ideas. But that's not the same as saying the product is *engagé* literature. My writing has never been *engagé*, in what seems to me to be that simpleminded sense the term is used; and although some of the literature I admire is, most of it isn't.

I believe you once stated that, far from regretting the fact that literature is not life, you really enjoy its artificiality.

Yes, I do, but I would be very upset if that were to be regarded as an apology for effetism. There's a big difference in my mind between the two.

I can readily see an artist setting himself a formal problem as his task, just as a poet who decides to write a villanelle commits himself to a very complicated formal scheme. In part, it's a matter of the simple joy of bringing off a complicated thing. Seriously, there is an element of sport in the manufacture of art. Temperamentally, I respond very strongly to this game aspect, and I would also defend it theoretically, if I were smart enough to.

It is literally true that I set two goals for myself in doing *The Sot-Weed Factor*. First, I wanted to write a novel thick enough so that the publisher could print the title across the spine instead of along it. Second, since I was working on a kind of 18th century material, I wanted to see whether I could make a plot more complicated and more formally perfect than the plot of *Tom Jones*.

I succeeded in both of these objectives. It was fat enough for the title to sit horizontal to the shelf—although I forgot to mention what I had in mind to the publisher and he, of course, put it the other way. And it has a better plot than *Tom Jones*. (I don't for a second say that it is a better novel than Fielding's but that, in the matter of simple formal symmetry, the narrative material is much more involved. There are more sub-plots and they are more complicated. And every single one of them, I promise you, is wrapped up absolutely securely.) But that doesn't mean the novel is about the game I played as its author.

Would it be fair to say that The Sot-Weed Factor *divides your work in half?*

When I look at my work, I see it falling into sets of twos. The two little novels in the beginning were both relatively realistic. Then there were two big fat ones, both relatively fantastical or irrealistical. Then there will be two volumes of related short narratives: that book of short pieces for taped voice, live voice, and print and then the current series of three novellas.

The Menelaus story in Funhouse *is very much a game, isn't it? How did it come about?*

I'd been immersed once again in frame-tale literature. With the help of a couple of graduate assistants, I'd gone through, or at least looked at, the entire corpus of frame-tale literature on the planet—from all cultures and all centuries to the extent that we could dig up the materials and find out something about them. One of the things that I noticed was that the greatest degree of narrative complexity in the history of frame-tale literature was five degrees.

It occurs several times: in the *Panchatantra,* in the *Ocean of Story,* and in a couple of other places. The relations between these framed and framing tales are usually completely gratuitous. (I could give a course on the subject, but I won't start in on it now.)

I thought it would be an interesting formal challenge to compose a work in which there were seven enveloped tales. Unlike the early practitioners, I decided to arrange them in such a fashion that each would be brought to the moment just prior to its narrative climax, then suspended for the introduction of the next. I wanted the whole thing cocked like an enormous firework, designed not only to be tripped in quick succession but so that the actual nature of the plot resolution of the insidest tale would precipitate the resolution of the next one out, and so on. They would go off like a chain of orgasms.

Never mind the spiritual or psychological reasons why one is interested in this or any other particular narrative device. Anybody who sets out to be interested just for the sake of elaborateness would be a bloody idiot. Somewhere in your artistic sense, you intuit that this is a metaphor for other things you are concerned with. You don't explain why it's a metaphor—you're no bloody critic at this point. Let someone else explain it. You just know that some concepts haunt you, speak to you, in electrical ways, and you learn to trust your intuition.

I was attracted by the engineering of the mechanical device, but there also had to be a point to it. That's the final thing, you know. You set yourself a complicated formal stunt, partly just to see if you can do it, for heaven's sake, as you do with some feat in sports, but it would be only the kind of decadence the Marxist critics sniff at if that's all there was to it.

At Buffalo, I meet with a group of apprentice writers, the more experienced of which are often into very complex experimentation. When somebody comes in with some complicated narrative gadget, we whee and ooh as it does its tricks, but if that's all there is to it, then it's a toy. One must distinguish between meretricious or gratuitous experiment and genuine experimental writing. The writer who transforms his contrivance into a powerful, effective, and appropriate metaphor for his concerns has made a piece of art, whatever its imperfections.

Richard Locke, in reviewing Updike's Rabbit Redux *in this past Sunday's* Times Book Review, *observed that Barth, Barthelme, and*

Nabokov, among others, were up to something rather different from . . .

Roth, Bellow, and Malamud.

I see you've read the review. Do you agree with his distinction?

It's about as valid as any of the distinctions we have to make. They're always imperfect, but we should not sneer at them for that reason; we have to make distinctions in order to cope with the world.

Locke used the term "reporting the secular news," which I thought was a happy phrase. He admires that class of novelists more than he does those, like Hawkes and the rest of us, who are "up to something else." I don't agree with his aesthetic preferences, of course, but I find his observation useful.

The distinction he makes, I've noticed, can only be applied to American letters. British literature presents an entirely different situation. It's really a very strange scene there. Most British novels are sterile. It's as though their writers have turned their backs on all the vital aesthetic issues of our time. There are a few British writers who don't fall into this classification—like Anthony Burgess —but they are almost Americans by this time. (Burgess by his own confession more admires what is going on aesthetically in America than in England.) Obviously, Russian literature doesn't offer an opportunity for this distinction to appear. I don't know much about current Russian literature, but an *avant garde* is proscribed. The same in China. If there's any experimental Chinese fiction, we don't know about it. Official insistence on socialist realism, which is anti-modernist, loads the dice. On the other hand, we have Western European literature. Just think for a minute of France, Germany, and Italy. The "reporter of the secular news" is virtually non-existent there, or to be found in a tiny minority.

But if we look at current American literature, we see both the experimenters and those working an older vein in substantial numbers. Despite all that has happened to distinguish our time, an impressive amount of American literature of the middle of the twentieth century, or even, for that matter, of the whole twentieth century, is nineteenth century fiction written in a more or less twentieth century idiom about twentieth century topics. Aesthetic ideals and formal notions, for these writers, haven't changed much in a hundred years.

Why is this necessarily bad?

I don't say it's a bad state of affairs, but it is very curious. History, if not real, is at least impressive. We are historical animals. The architecture of the twentieth century doesn't much resemble that of the nineteenth. Modern music, to the immediate ear, doesn't sound like the music of the nineteenth century. If you turn the radio on, you know instantly when the music you hear was composed, even if you don't know the piece or the composer. There are real, not capricious reasons for these historical differences.

It's odd how comparatively little the concepts which have influenced the modern arts, including their American representations, have touched American literature. There must be interesting reasons for it. By its nature, literature is a different kind of art: its materials, words, are referential and therefore don't lend themselves nearly as readily to abstraction as sculpture or painting. The analogies to essentially non-verbal concepts which other arts can employ tend to break down in writing. There have been some bold attempts at departure—concrete poetry, for example, which we've had since 1904 or 5, and roughly similar experiments in fiction—but in the main these have been marginal operations. Writing, then, is resistent to radical innovation, and Americans, perhaps for reasons rooted in the culture, have tended to be content with the conventions.

In Europe, on the other hand, the traditions of realism, naturalism, sociological realism, and psychological realism lost their press after the turn of the century. Not because of a naive notion of progress, but because of the preoccupations of the writers themselves, the nineteenth century vision was superseded. The metamorphosis that a Joyce goes through in his bibliography parallels in many obvious ways the metamorphoses of the painters and musicians maturing around that time.

Although there are, to be sure, novelists in France now who write the secular news reports, or modern historical novels, one doesn't think of them in connection with what's going on in French literature. But try to talk about American literature seriously without introducing writers like Bellow and the rest who, it seems to me, stem more directly from Dostoevski, Flaubert, and the other great figures of that century than from Joyce and Kafka.

John Updike once visited Buffalo. I asked him, without explaining why I asked the question, whether he admired Andrew Wyeth.

He said yes. I then introduced him as the Andrew Wyeth of our literature. I meant it half ironically, but still as a compliment. I think one has the same kind of troubled feeling confronting the phenomenon Updike, or Bellow in one of his straighter novels, or Malamud when he's not being I. B. Singer, that one has confronting a Wyeth painting. I'm not saying these aren't good paintings, but after all, we *are* living in the age of Frank Stella. I, too, rather admire Wyeth's paintings and the painter himself. His phrase "magic realism" has an intriguing quality. Still, though you like them in a half-nostalgic way, you have to wonder why anyone is painting them at this hour of the world.

I don't know what accounts for this phenomenon except the insularity of American letters. I haven't tried to think it through seriously, but every now and then it strikes me as peculiar. It's an insularity that can't be explained just by the barrier of an ocean. South American writers, by and large, have been much more cosmopolitan; they have had a much more lively sense of European intellectual movements. Maybe language helps explain it.

For the most part, the American writers you've been mentioning came to light in the 'forties and 'fifties. It was a period of fallback after an era of tremendous expansion of literary possibilities. To some extent, the task of this generation was one of consolidation. But there were American writers of the previous generation who tried to apply Cubism. Hemingway drew on the painters—particularly, he said, on Cezanne—and one can in fact see intellectual connections between Cezanne and Hemingway's style. Is your judgment of these earlier American writers really fair?

Even during the expatriate days, the Americans didn't draw nearly as much on the new possibilities as you would have expected them to. Take Hemingway. There he is, living in Paris, getting drunk with Pound and Joyce, and then just writing Hemingway, over and over again. He was right in the thick of that incredible ferment after the First World War and for all practical purposes, he was almost untouched by it. Or think of Fitzgerald.

Let me come back to the connection between the visual and literary arts. I see your work as very much part of the artistic milieu of "pop" and "op." There is a common trading on form reflecting on itself, perhaps because of a feeling that the external world has been exhausted of productive possibilities. The apocalyptic notion you mentioned earlier has a great deal to do with it. Isn't there a drawing together of the various arts in responding to this condition?

Well, I don't know. I am curious about the apocalyptic ambiance in which we live, but I'm not at all apocalyptic about the novel. I hate pop apocalypses. It's too easy, too self-indulgent a response. It's like being a phony revolutionary. I have contempt for the men who go about whispering, "The novel is dead. It's time we quit teaching literature." This is a position, by the way, that my colleague Leslie Fiedler has never maintained, often as it's attributed to him. I tell my students, "What a curious thing it is, at your age, when you're hearing on all sides that the novel—perhaps literature itself, even the printed page—is kaput, that you're committing yourselves to this moribund medium and genre instead of getting a camera or whatever you're supposed to get." The only adjective, I tell them, that can describe such a strange commitment of your one mortal life at this hour of the world is "quixotic." And it is with Quixote that the novel begins.

Have you no sense of paralysis in the contemporary scene?

Half of my bibliography is on the subject of paralysis—of one kind or another. I hate effeteness and paralysis. And yet I love the spiritual threat of it in the air. It's exciting.

We are peculiar beings: half beast, half angel. We live at a particular point in time, in one episode of human history measured from the creation to the apocalypse. But if we're intelligent and educated and we have been paying attention, we also have a hell of a lot of history under our belts. I hate the kind of primitivism that ignores history, that invents the wheel over and over again thinking it's come up with something new. I respect complexity, particularly the complexity which comes of realizing that no action is simple in the light of the history of ideas and actions. The man or woman whose style I admire most is the one who has a sophisticated awareness of alternatives; who knows the tragic futility of actions, yet doesn't yield to castration by all his sophistication.

This, of course, translates into a view of art. The artist is a sensitive, conscious animal who also belongs to a community not bounded by his particular time. He knows the history of the medium he's working in as well as the present urgent concerns of his mind and spirit, and he tries to express each in a way reflective of the other. There's a kind of entelechy involved. An artist should be aware of the effects that have been wrought in his genre and of the kinds of things that have been said so that he will appreciate the problems of saying anything freshly and originally at this late hour. He has to respect the ins and outs of the curious medium in which he's working. This catches him in something of a paradox: the more he knows, the better an artist he can theoretically become, and yet the knowledge he acquires is overwhelming—it places him in competition with the accumulated best of human history. And so, he takes a feisty stance. Nobody's going to tell *him* it's too late. He has a healthy and young, or, at least, a healthy and vigorous imagination. He has all this energy to go, and he will find a way to do it anyway. The feat becomes harder and harder to pull off, but at the same time it becomes more and more admirable to manage it successfully.

There are several ways of confronting the dilemma. One of them is to ignore it. Updike is by no means a simple-minded man; Bellow is well educated; Malamud's not a fool. They're all aware of these things. But one way to address a problem is to act as if it doesn't exist, that it's not a considerable fact of one's daily artistic life. Sometimes that works—very well, in fact. I, myself, have an uneasy feeling about that sort of address, but I suppose, finally, it's more temperament than anything else that leads me and others to take a different course, to try to confront the complexity. You'll see, after you've done a few things and been through a few experiences, that you have to confront the complexity of your own lives and accumulated histories and decide you are by no means paralyzed by that confrontation.

I'll try to illustrate the paradox in a different way: at age forty, it's not at all as easy to get really knocked out by a new writer you've discovered as it is when you're young. But that rare experience of encountering a writer who can create in you the same degree of excitement when you are forty that almost any good writer could when you were eighteen or nineteen makes it all the keener. It may also have more power and importance, because a more complicated man is being impressed than the fellow you were when you were eighteen.

What you're saying, I guess, is that in beginning a new project you are trying to achieve the Great American Novel.

No. I think that's an illusionary category. It's a category which belongs to the heroic age of the novel. I don't like talk like "The novel is passé," but certainly the heroic age of the novel is a thing of the past. That doesn't mean people don't write exciting books, or that the history of book-length fiction—which we'll call the novel because it's got to be called something or other—is finished. By no means. But really, if you read even a little bit of literary history, you realize that the kind of excitement with which people anticipated the next installment of an ongoing Dickens novel, or the way the Russian intelligentsia waited for the next thing by Dostoevski as one awaits an illumination, is unlikely to be matched today. The only thing comparable to that in popular excitement among intelligent people, I suppose, is what now happens in film. But it's a poor comparison; the best films are so much more ephemeral.

I'm not putting down literature, and I don't think it's become obsolete or that it has been relegated to the position poetry was in before poetry became re-invigorated by the return of oral reading. All I mean is that, as the audience has changed, the forms are very likely to change. The quickest look at truly contemporary literature shows it beyond question.

Walk into any art museum and you see that the stuff done in the last few decades just doesn't look like what went before it. Literature, as I said earlier, is a more complicated phenomenon; but I'm certain that a writer like Barthelme, for example, or Calvino, is a better indicator of the currents in the literature of the 1970s that I'll be interested in than the new novels by the secular news reporters. I'll read the latter for topical pleasure, the former for artistic excitement.

As a teacher of writing at Buffalo, has it been your experience that students are alert to such innovation?

Very much so. What amazes me is how students rediscover devices having an honored history of which they are apparently totally unaware. For example, one of them, who had probably never read Pirandello, must less *Tristam Shandy,* was engaged in a novel full of asides to the reader and quarrelsome intimacies with his characters. At one point he out-Sternes Sterne: he says he's so bored with writing, he's going to masturbate, and invites the reader to join him. I turned the page of his manuscript, and there it was—ample evidence to take him at his word. "Klein," I said, "I think you've got a first here! But what are you going to do if your publisher wants a press run of 160,000 copies?"

Did you ever seriously consider issuing Lost in the Funhouse *not as a conventional book but in a box or some such container with a record enclosed?*

There were some thoughts along that line. The first idea was to put a casette in with it, but I rejected it for a number of reasons. When I proposed it to Nelson Doubleday, my publisher, I expected him to be appalled. To my dismay, he wasn't. (After all, one does expect a certain measure of decent resistance to innovation. But those people in New York City really worry that McLuhan might be right, and they're all for diversifying.) Doubleday thought it was a groovy idea—perhaps he even used the adjective—at which point my own interest in it waned. There were other factors, too: it was impractical—for example, all enclosures get stolen from library copies—and what would you do in paperback editions? Also, it had too much of an air of gimmickry about it. Finally, I rejected it on aesthetic grounds. I had spent a couple of years going around on the circuit reading some of the *Funhouse* pieces in concert with the tapes because I was enchanted with the rediscovery of the oral medium. But I came to realize that, unlike the case with verse, the effect depends upon the live presence of the author.

Richard Brautigan, on a visit to Buffalo a couple of years ago, did something which he thought terribly daring and I thought terribly boring. Without an introduction, he put a tape machine in the center of the lecture hall and said, "This is a tape I made for Apple Core which has some of my verse and fiction on it." Then he turned it on, withdrew to a projection booth out of sight, and proceeded to show, gratuitously, slides of huge punctuation marks. This was an audience which had shot down Allen Ginsberg because he was "too establishment"—a very critical bunch; if it had been anybody other than Brautigan, they would have torn him apart. As it was, they listened with what seemed to me extreme patience. At the end, Brautigan came back in his dungarees, and, making a gesture toward the machine, said "Well! There it is— the twentieth century!" To which one of my students replied, "Yep: about 1914."

Isn't there a problem in being so "far out" that the artist will lose all audience?

If I were a painter, I believe I would try to find a way to be as contemporary as Frank Stella and still paint nudes, because nudes are lovely. If I were a composer, the objective I would set for myself would be to be absolutely contemporary in my mastery of means, of the grammar and syntax of modern music, of atonality, of the aleatoric thing, of the electronic arsenal, and of all the rest, and *still* make music that's ravishing to the ear. As a writer, *mutatis mutandis,* my objective has been to attempt to assimilate as well as I can the twentieth century aspects of my medium, to invent some myself, and, at the same time (and here's where I become a conservative), to preserve the appeal that narrative has always had to the imagination: the simple appeals of suspense, of *story,* with which I've been in love ever since the beginning. There's no danger that what I'll produce will be like John O'Hara's stories. It has to be different, but it will be composed of sentences; of the cadences of prose as opposed to the cadences of poetry, and, mainly, of the elements of story, of pacing, of narrative suspense, of dramatic construction—which I find simply too lovely to ignore. The trick is to have it both ways; but then, that is the trick of surviving in the twentieth century. If one wants not only to survive but to prosper artistically, one has not only to come to terms with that trick, but to be one up on it.

NOVEMBER 19, 1971

Robert Coover

In the prologue to the exemplary fictions section of Pricksongs and Descants, *you describe Cervantes as a paragon because he, like the contemporary writer, had to deal with a world undergoing radical change. When John Barth was here, he also spoke of Cervantes as a watershed figure peculiarly appropriate for our age. Obviously, there are similarities between your work and Barth's, and your common interest in Cervantes is not simple coincidence. Would you go further and say that you are part of a school?*

No, we are basically different, but it's curious how often your question recurs. Barth and I have never talked out our views (in fact, we've never met), and yet we've said the same things everywhere without knowing we were echoing one another.

I believe this can be traced to the general awareness, by writers of both North and South America, that we have come to the end of a tradition. I don't mean that we have come to the end of the novel or of fictional forms, but that our ways of looking at the world and of adjusting to it through fictions are changing. The New World is peculiarly alert to this. We are the outpost of Western culture, and it is here that we sense collapse because the waves are beating on our rocks. (Further inland—to keep within the metaphor—the structures are still protected: it will take some time before these waves have washed over the continent of Europe—and in part for this reason, there's not much life in the fiction of Europe today.)

The question is not limited to how one produces narrative art; our basic assumptions about the universe have been altered, and so change has occurred in the broad base of metaphor through which the universe is comprehended. Our old faith—one might better say our old sense of constructs derived from myths, legends, philosophies, fairy stories, histories, and other fictions which help to explain what happens to us from day to day, why our governments are the way they are, why our institutions have the character they have, why the world turns as it does—has lost its efficacy. Not necessarily is it false; it is just not as efficacious as it was.

And this climate of fundamental doubt leads us to feel at home in Cervantes's fictional world where the question of where one places one's faith is central?

Yes—not because of the content of this or that specific incident in the *Quixote* but because the fictions themselves reflect a similar on-going change in all the human activity of that time. They are full of "code words" that point to a significance beyond themselves. Spain was then a frontier of all that was going on, just as we are today.

A rather simplistic way of talking about it is to say that there was a shift from a Platonic notion of the world—the sense of the micro-cosm as an imitation of the macrocosm and that there was indeed a perfect order of which we could perceive only an imperfect illusion—toward an Aristotelian attitude which, instead of attempting a grand comprehensive view of the whole, looked at each particular subject matter and asked what was true about it. This was a widespread development of tremendous importance. We began to isolate our scientific activities, each from the other, as well as to isolate scientific from literary activity. We began to look at the world as it "really was"—and to define that "really was" in terms of the specific. It marked the beginning of realism.

Let's stay with that a moment more. Aristotelianism is basically teleological and it is biased toward a common sense acceptance of reality; in contrast, Platonism leads us to distrust our senses and to retreat from tactile experience into a cerebral, epiphenomenal uni-verse. Isn't the new fiction, in its delight with abstracting experience, moving in a Platonic direction?

No. We *are* turning back to design—I agree with you on that—and there is an attraction toward modes of inquiry and creation that we rejected as we moved into this Era of Enlightenment. Those forms we associate with Platonism have a certain beauty, and now a poten-tial for irony exists in them. But because we don't believe in a Godhead any more and the sense of a purposeful unity has vanished, a true Platonist would say we are using these things sophistically. The abstractions are empty, aren't they? Even so, they *are* useful. It is easier for me to express the ironies of our condition by the manipulation of Platonic forms than by imitation of the Aristotelian. But each writer has a different approach. Pynchon, for example, is using the more recent ones and getting almost exactly the same effect.

May we descend to the sub-lunary for a moment? You're from Iowa originally, aren't you?

Yes. And although we left when I was nine years old, in our drifting around in the Mid-West we were never very far away.

Was desire to get back to home territory part of the reason you accepted a job at the Iowa Writers' Workshop?

No, not at all. When I got away from the area after college, I never wanted to return. In fact, when Iowa solicited me, I refused at first on those grounds alone. I realized long ago that the process of asserting and creating your life is made much more difficult where the familiar vibrations are strong. I've felt a need to get away not just from my family and Iowa but from the country itself. Almost everything I've written has been done out of the country—and after midnight. I've been at Princeton this year and the writing has been going well, but this is because Princeton is virtually a foreign country.

As you've indicated, the past decade has been an explosively inventive period for fiction. How much effect does reading your contemporaries have on your writing?

An almost totally restrictive effect. I find I subtract things I might have done had they not already done them. To that extent, the more ignorant one remains, the more room there is to swing.

I'm not at all sure of the motivations that operate here. If there is a good form, why not use it, regardless of who else has used it? And yet, I must confess that the thought of doing so—once I have identified the form with someone else—inhibits me. It just does. I feel I haven't the time to do exercises in other people's forms.

This business of attributing influences is very curious. When a critic says of a work, "Aha! Clearly, this derives from X," it's an almost sure bet that the writer hasn't read X. Without exception, every single book cited as a source for either *Brunists* or the baseball book I had not read.

Are you saying that, professionally, you would prefer to read no current fiction?

No, because when I read fiction which contains new and exciting ideas, it opens up so many other new possibilities beyond or to the side of the ones I am encountering. Sometimes, too, they cast light on ideas I once had which have been dead; suddenly a "dead" idea can come alive again.

I generally wait a couple of years, though, before reading a new book.

How much of your respect for contemporary writing has to do with a fascination with structure?

That's difficult to answer. As my mind races over all the contemporary fiction I like, one writer, whom I admire as much as I do anybody, sticks out—Stanley Elkin—and he's the most formless writer of them all; in terms of structure, he just has a clothesline. And a writer who has been my friend for a long time, Sol Yurick, is quite conventional—some of his stories are almost like things out of the 'thirties—and yet I wouldn't hesitate to say that he's very, very good.

No, finally, mere design is not that appealing. I suppose I'm a bit quirky here. If, suddenly, too many writers were engaged in playing with highly complex structure, I would become suspicious and close myself off. But as long as it remains relatively fresh ground, it's exciting to get onto. The game is not intrinsically so important; *what matters is that it be generative and exciting for me while I'm creating.* I don't really care if it gets submerged and lost entirely; just as, when I'm reading, I'm not all that interested in discovering what the hidden structures are.

You've talked about Cervantes and your contemporaries, but you've not mentioned a single figure in the American literary tradition. Is there no one there whom you admire as a craftsman or whose works, had you lived x number of years ago, you might like to have written yourself?

That's too suppositious; I can't just put myself into some other set of reference. Given certain preconceptions, a particular style of language, and rather rigid expectations from the Continent as to what was to be sent back there, perhaps James Fenimore Cooper's works were indeed the only possible way to cope with the wilderness. But, historical limitations aside, there are *some* things by *some* writers that I still find very generative: Washington Irving's tales and his *Knickerbocker History*, Poe's and Hawthorne's far-out stories, and, of course, Mark Twain's books. Twain, a great writer with a stunning imagination, would have been a natural today.

But Mark Twain certainly had no sense of structure.

No, not traditional structure, but he was playful with the technical aspects of story telling. I could see him incarnated as Kurt Vonnegut.

Melville has had a very direct effect on me. By chance, I did not read *Moby Dick* until I was reworking *Brunists*. It helped me finish that book. It was a lesson in perseverance: I thought that if a writer could go that far in exploring an idea, then I could go the distance with my book.

When you read the renowned writers of the past, is it a vital encounter or do you feel as though you are visiting a museum?

Luckily, I don't have to teach anybody, so I don't have to know anything. I'm not obliged to read for any extrinsic reasons. I've never had this kind of connection to literature—I never even took lit courses. So if I pick up a book called *The Iliad* and I'm bored by it, I just put it down. If I go on reading, it's because it's alive for me now.

Fiction is alive to a fiction maker in a different way. What comes through is the dedication the guy had to his craft, the extent to which he was captivated by what he was working on, the honesty with which he faced his narrative problems, and so on. A book that is dull to others may be fascinating to a writer who can observe this other craftsman struggle and devise solutions. In contrast, some books that are quite celebrated may hit the novelist as boring because they don't engage his interest at the level of craft.

Doesn't this load the dice in favor of the recent writers who are struggling with the same conventions as you?

On the contrary. In fact, I went through a period when I didn't want to read *anybody* in the novel tradition; I felt there had been no good English novelist since, roughly, before Defoe. I assumed that the stuff that is in a sense furthest in the past—that is the most dated, irrelevant, and useless to us—is what was published last year, and that fictions become more valuable, more relevant to us as they recede from us in time. To me, the pre-Cervantean stuff seemed the most important.

I plunged into all the really ancient material, and I'm grateful to the bias I had which led me to do it. Before I had developed this hypothesis, I looked on those really old things more as mythic residue than as real fiction, but when I went back to them, I suddenly found extraordinary imaginations at work. I approached them as I would approach my own stories, and I recognized that whether it was one guy or a bunch of people writing these things, here were intelligent approaches to fictional problems. Imagine how exciting, even unsettling, it was to make this discovery. I was even turned on, briefly, to John the Seer. After having been very negative toward that sort of phony religious mentality for so long, I suddenly began to think that maybe Revelations was the best short story we had.

Needless to say, I've since backed away from that theory; I now seek my enthusiasms from the whole range of fiction. But it was a healthy attitude to hold for a time: I learned a lot and it has had a substantial influence on me.

One of the salient features of contemporary writing is the prominence given to fantasy. Just as the drama has been liberated from the convention of Ibsen's invisible fourth wall, the new writing has been freed from an obligation to realism. As in the very early fiction, the narrative line can now move easily from the realistic to the fanciful and back again.

One of the most difficult things that, from Cervantes's time, we've had to get over was a felt necessity to explain where the fiction comes from. "And he lay down and closed his eyes and commenced to dream,"—we don't have to make that sort of introductory statement any more. There was a sense that fiction was not quite proper and thus had to be excused. The more imaginative the fiction, the more dangerous it was felt to be, and consequently, the more it had to be detoxified: e.g., "I found this manuscript . . . fortunately, the author was burned as a heretic." (That device, incidentally, is still used, but for ironic purposes.) The more elaborate the attempt to hide the fiction, the creakier it became.

There seems to be a decided break in style somewhere between Origin of the Brunists *and the fictions of* Pricksongs.

Most of the pieces in *Pricksongs* precede *Brunists*.

I'm aware of that; nonetheless there is a radical difference in narrative approach in the two books. Is this attributable to inherent de-

147

mands in the novel form which call for the creation of a different kind of universe, more realistic and less tale-like?

I don't feel obliged to chase something spooky like a voice or a recognizable style. Whatever difference there is between my first novel and the bulk of the rest of my writing has little to do with development.

Before *Brunists,* I had never thought about writing a novel. I don't know why, but it had never quite occurred to me. I thought I would always go on writing these stories. It wasn't until I was nearly thirty that I first thought, "Well, what about a book?" I had several ideas—one of them, the J. Henry Waugh story on which the book was later based, had already been written and, I believe, published by then. There were also other possibilities, further out, that I'm still struggling with today, and I was intending to go straight ahead with them. But, partly because of pressure from friends, agents, and editors, and the friendly reception of my first published story in *The Noble Savage,* a mine disaster story, I went to work instead on the *Brunists.*

I thought of it, a bit, as paying dues. I didn't feel I had the right to move into more presumptuous fictions until I could prove I could handle the form as it now was in the world. In a sense, the trip down into the mine was my submerging of myself into the novel experience and then coming out again with my own revelations. In the process, I turned it into my kind of book. The basic concerns that are in everything I write are also in that book—though they look a little different, they are still there.

How did Universal Baseball Association *evolve?*

After the story (which is, essentially, the second chapter of the book) was written, I felt that I hadn't gotten everything out of the metaphor, that I hadn't yet fully understood it. So over the years that followed I set about playing with the images, working out the Association history, searching out the structure that seemed to be hidden in it.

Even though structure is not profoundly meaningful in itself, I love to use it. This has been the case ever since the earliest things I wrote when I made an arbitrary commitment to design. The reason is not that I have some notion of an underlying ideal order which fiction imitates, but a delight with the rich ironic possibilities that the use of structure affords. Any idea, even one which on the surface doesn't seem very interesting, fitted with a perfect structure, can blossom into something that even I did not suspect was there originally. Engaging in that process of discovery is the excitement of making fiction.

The Henry book came into being for me when I found a simple structural key to the metaphor of a man throwing dice for a baseball game he has made up. It suddenly occurred to me to use Genesis I.1 to II.3—seven chapters corresponding to the seven days of creation—and this in turn naturally implied an eighth, the apocalyptic day. Having decided on this basic plan, I read a lot of exegetical works on that part of the Bible in order to find out as much as I could which would reinforce and lend meaning to the division into parts.

I hit on some very good ancient works full of lore. I also found a lot of good Aramaic and Hebrew words I was able to make puns of; for example: the words for "confusion" and "emptiness," *tohu* and *bohu*, enter into the novel's funeral march scene where Rooney is leading the mourners to Purcell's music and they're going, "Tee hee hee hee hee hee, boo hoo hoo hoo. . . ."

I hate to sound like an unappreciative reader, but your intentions there missed me entirely.

Oh, but that doesn't matter to me. I don't anticipate people seeing these things; what matters is that it was generative for me. The story I had in mind became much richer. I would have had a funeral scene in any case, but now what it is really about is an evolution from the structural idea.

Henry lives in two worlds: one a real world that is forced on him and the other the one he mentally constructs through his baseball game. Is this your way of saying that, "sanity" being insane, one has to withdraw into a self-produced reality?

I'm not sympathetic with that idea, although it may emerge from Henry's game in a way meant to be ironic. The principle you have just suggested would mean that, literally and figuratively, a person should not read but only write, that we should have a universe of Henrys rolling their dice alone and making up worlds for themselves. I don't think this would be a good world to live in. I've always been contentious with my writing; I've never turned away from unpleasantness in order to provide escapism. The world itself being a construct of fictions, I believe the fiction maker's function is to furnish better fictions with which we can re-form our notions of things.

Yet there is a paradox in that very activity. In order to accomplish his ends, the writer, by the nature of his profession, must himself withdraw entirely. You could say I wrote the baseball book not for baseball buffs or even for theologians but for other writers.

May I satisfy a personal curiosity about that book which has nothing to do with metaphysics or aesthetics? When I was a boy, a friend and I worked out a frequency of incidence of different baseball plays, devised a deck of cards which corresponded to the probabilities, and invented a league. For years, I thought our game was unique. Then when I was in graduate school, I met someone who had done the same thing, except he used three dice instead of cards. When I became aware of your book through the Times *review, I was startled; the phenomenon of children extending their animistic fantasies in this way was apparently not uncommon. Did you receive much mail when the novel was published from people surprised to discover that someone else had done this?*

An amazing amount of correspondence. I had thought it was a private idea, a private book, but I soon learned that sort of activity was rather general. One guy who had read the review—but not the book—sent a letter in which he remembered his leagues, the players' names, their batting averages, everything—and, considering he'd done this before World War I, in incredible detail.

Now they even have computers doing it. They compile tapes with all the parameters—down to factors like temperament and stamina —and they distribute the printouts. It's grown to be quite a network. There is even going to be a convention of baseball parlor game players in Philadelphia. Somehow, these enthusiasts have fostered the hope that I should be the secretary for some such organization. It's been a bit of a harassment.

The title Pricksongs and Descants *intrigues me. What does it mean? Why did you choose it?*

They are musical terms. In a way, the title is redundant because a pricksong is a descant. There is a shade of difference, however. "Pricksong" derives from the physical manner in which the song was printed—the notes were literally pricked out; "descant" refers to the form of music in which there is a *cantus firmus,* a basic line,

and variations that the other voices play against it. The early descants, being improvisations, were unwritten; when they began writing them, the idea of counterpoint, of a full, beautiful harmony
emerged.

Of course, there is also the obvious sexual suggestion. In this
connection, I thought of the descants as feminine decoration around
the pricking of the basic line. Thus: the masculine thrust of narrative and the lyrical play around it.

The terms were useful to me because they were pre-Enlighten-
ment, pre-Monteverdian, and so a part of the art forms that have
been shunted aside by the developments of the last three hundred
years. The choice of title had to do with my decision to focus on
Cervantes as a turning point.

Was that decision made before or after you had written the stories?

My first thought was to publish a book of exemplary fictions. I had
about forty stories I would have included—some of which were realistic or naturalistic—similar to Cervantes's range in his exemplary
novellas. But one doesn't as a rule publish a book of stories early in
a career, I was told, so for quite a while I couldn't bring it out. Then
later, when the time was ripe, there was only a handful of the stories I still wanted to keep. Realizing I would have to write more, I
tried to come up with another organizing principle that would enable me to use some of the stuff I already had and to produce a book
that had a beginning, a middle, and an end. "The Elevator," which
is based purely on number and on musical analogues, became the
generative idea, and eventually led me to several new fictions which
brought the book together.

*To what extent were you writing to a well-formulated theory of
short fiction?*

A lot of the *Pricksongs* I wrote not knowing at all what I was doing,
not having a clue as to why I felt it was necessary to write this kind
of story. It was hit or miss. The earliest piece in the collection, "The
Panel Game," represents the turning point for me; it was written in
1957. The second oldest, "The Marker," I did in 1960; the next, in
1962. The jumps mean that a large number of fictions haven't been
included. Some things would seem very necessary, but after I would
start writing them, they seldom seemed worth the effort; they were

strange, incomplete things, often very shallow. A *few* of them did work, but I didn't know why; I was going on instinct, you see.

Well, I decided that, instinct being very unreliable, I should try to understand, to go deeper into the mechanics of the narrative form. I turned to the ancient fictions to research what had already been done and also to see what new ideas they might engender. The *Arabian Nights,* I discovered, was a gold mine of formal possibilities —and although I made specific use of none, they provided a context which made what I was writing seem real.

Going back to Ovid produced a similar response. The Ovidian stories all concern transformation; now that is not a startlingly new subject—after all, fairy tales, animal fables, and the like, deal with it—but I suddenly realized that the basic, constant struggle for all of us is against metamorphosis, against giving in to the inevitability of the process. Encountering in Ovid the same agon that underlay my own writing was liberating; I realized that what I was already doing was not only possible but essential.

Perhaps "form" is not precisely the word, but certainly the force of myth and mythopoeic thought is with us for all time. The crucial beliefs of people are mythic in nature; whether at the level of the Cinderella story or of the Resurrection, the language is mythopoeic rather than rational. To try to apply reason to such beliefs is like trying to solve a physics problem by psychoanalysis.

There's no sense in decrying this fact; on the contrary, it is a useful—even necessary—means of navigating through life. In part because individual human existence is so brief, in part because each single instant of the world is so impossibly complex, we cannot accumulate all the data needed for a complete, objective statement. To hope to behave as though this were possible is to invite paralysis through crushing despair. And so we fabricate; we invent constellations that permit an illusion of order to enable us to get from here to there. And we devise short cuts—ways of thinking without thinking through: code words that are in themselves a form of mythopoeia.

Thus, in a sense, we are all creating fictions all the time, out of necessity. We constantly test them against the experience of life. Some continue to be functional; we are content to let them be rather than try to analyze them and, in the process, forget something else that is even more important. Others outlive their usefulness. They disturb life in some unnecessary way, and so it becomes necessary to break them up and perhaps change their force.

It is a commonplace that art responds to change inaugurated by scientific or technological advances: Pope gives poetic expression to Newton, the naturalistic novel derives from Darwinism and the methods of laboratory science, etc. But might it not also be true that the poet anticipates the development of new scientific theory, that his fictions prepare our minds in such a way that they can then cope with a revolutionary concept like a saddle-shaped universe?

Yes, although it's not necessary that one become translated into the other. Essentially, both the new scientific and the new aesthetic concepts emerge because the old ones, having rigidified in forms that have lost contact with the on-goingness of the world, have become impotent.

All of us today are keenly aware that we are undergoing a radical shift in sensibilities. We are no longer convinced of the *nature* of things, of design as justification. Everything seems itself random. (The early existentialists were leading us this way; since then, we have seen the break-down of religious structures and of many of the principles of the Enlightenment which have supported our institutions.) Under these conditions of arbitrariness, the artistic impulse is directed toward putting the random parts together in any order which provides a pattern for living.

The making of fiction, then, can be an epistemological exercise. Could you illustrate how writing has affected your personal mental process?

Long ago, when I did wonder why I was pursuing this activity, I began to see that, whether or not it could be successful as a commercial enterprise, it was vital and real to me. Like a lot of young undergraduates, I had been attracted to courses in theology and the philosophy of religion. The problem of Christian belief bothered me: it wouldn't leave me alone and yet I couldn't solve it. Then I found a vibrant way to understand the matter: I imagined a character like Jesus, created him in my own mind, and carried this thing on with him. Rather than try to discuss the historical arguments for his existence or non-existence, or to investigate what had happened to the Gospel texts and how much we could depend on the various parts, I merely took the story itself and, involving myself in it, considered various variations.

At about that time, I encountered an argument between a theologian named Rudolf Bultmann and a philosopher named Karl

Jaspers. Bultmann, a dogmatist, felt that the church was reeling under the attack of the Enlightenment. (He was discovering this a little late—three hundred years after—but never mind.) He believed that Christianity ought to de-mythologize itself. Out should go the Noah story, Adam and Eve, the Virgin Birth, all those things that looked ridiculous to the modern eye—but not the Resurrection. The Resurrection had to be saved because it was that moment in which God's finger touched history. (Like Henry sticking his finger in the game and then throwing up the pizza pie.) Jaspers got into an argument with him, and it was this subsequently published correspondence that I was reading. For Jaspers, the argument was obvious: if you throw the rest out, you've got to throw the Resurrection out too. But, why throw any of it out? Why not accept it all as story; not as literal truth but simply as a story that tells us something, metaphorically, about ourselves and the world? Jaspers concluded that the only way to struggle against myth is on myth's own ground.

When I read that nearly fifteen years ago, I found in Jaspers's coherent statement a verification of what I had been writing clumsy notes to myself about. (I even copied out quite a chunk of it which, at one time, I intended to be part of the epigraph to *Brunists.*) How liberating that recognition was! I went on to write "The Reunion," a story about Thomas explaining to the other disciples why the hanged man they are waiting for won't come—and then, of course, after he's done a good job of this, the man does come, much to everybody's astonishment. (It was supposed to be in *Pricksongs,* but it had been put away in a folder for so long that I forgot it when I turned in the manuscript.)

Having shaken off the most persistent of the stories that had bothered me, I realized that other material which we take in as stories— newspaper articles, grade school histories, the things parents tell to teach us how to be good, TV programs, even societal notions that stamp some movement as good or bad—all had to be confronted in the same way. In fact, the book I'm working on now, called *The Public Burning of Julius and Ethel Rosenberg: An Historical Romance,* is a simple outgrowth of that Jesus thing I did at the beginning.

As a literary subject, the Rosenberg trial is becoming as attractive as the Sacco-Vanzetti case was to the previous generation of writers. Have you read Doctorow's Book of Daniel?

I have now, although I deliberately avoided it when I first heard about it. It sounded like the kind of transformation of real experience I wouldn't be the least interested in. But then I happened to meet Doctorow and I felt guilty about not having read so well-received a book. So I went home and read it. Well, I was enormously impressed. It's a superb, extremely wise, and mature book.

As I was afraid it might, it toned my perception of the Rosenbergs. I found myself drifting into his perception of them, and it has taken a while to get it out of my mind. The conclusions he comes to are close to quite a few of mine.

When did you start your version?

About 1966. I began it as a play, but then I thought it was awkward in that form; so, while I was finishing up the baseball book, I played with the idea as fiction. I put it off for a while because there was another book I wished to do first. Later, I wanted "The Cat in the Hat for President," written in 1968, to come out as part of a book in election-year 1972, and I needed a couple of novella-length things to go with it. I interrupted what I was doing and went back to the Rosenberg idea with that in mind, but then it expanded into something far too large for such a format.

It is the story of June 19, 1953. On that day, the Rosenbergs are burned in Times Square and all the members of the tribe are drawn to the scene. All that has happened that day happens there, in a way; everything is condensed into one big circus event.

Originally, it was the circus aspect that interested me most. Then I developed the idea of having the Vice President at the time become the first person narrator. The world has its superheroes—figures like Uncle Sam and the Phantom—and Richard Nixon, who wishes to be the incarnation of Uncle Sam but hasn't yet learned how to shazam himself into super-freakhood, is studying what is going on very carefully, picking up notes.

Sounds like you are trying to show how politics, pop culture, and religion have fused.

In a way, they've never been wholly distinct. All furnish the constructs that bind a group together.

Have you read much in cultural anthropology?

Some, yes. The discoveries we've been making about the continuity from primitive times to the present, about the relevance of primitive man to contemporary man, are fascinating.

We've just gone through an era, much maligned now, of dissection and analysis. The impressive record of the physical sciences led to a kind of scientism in other fields: e.g., analytical sociology, psychoanalysis, even literary criticism (which is based on analysis of texts). This sort of activity is typical of an age coming to its end. First there are the innocent, naive beginnings, a period of explosive creation; then there is concern with the "how" of creation, a worrying over the processes involved; finally, when this seems to run dry, there is a looking back on what's been done. There's a lot to be unhappy about in the analytical character of our recent past, but we've been enormously enriched by it: it has provided our real, operative fictions.

Some of the great creative writers of our time have been people who have pulled data into patterns. The patterns may ultimately be false in the way that art is false, but they are true in a super-real way. Levi-Strauss offers a good example of this sort of endeavor. He is an armchair anthropologist—apparently he went out into the field once, couldn't stand the mosquitos and went back home. There has been a lot of bad feeling among scientists about what he's written. They claim that what he says is much more about us than about primitive man, but that doesn't matter for our purposes. Like Freud before him, he has created a new way of putting things together, of understanding ourselves.

Another non-fiction writer of this sort, one who has had a profound influence on me, is Emile Durkheim. His long book about the elementary forms of religious life provided me with an excuse to make fictions instead of doing something more "serious." Essentially, he argued that we get our idea of religion, of a something larger than ourselves, by way of communal meetings. We live isolated lives, but when we come together in a group—for some purpose like war—we get a sense of being part of something beyond our individual existences. In part, this is repressive—in that individual freedom diminishes markedly; in part, there is an exhilaration in feeling the new power of the group. This collective effervescence, as Durkheim calls it, is the source of spiritual force.

I have always been interested in the American civil religion. I wondered where the roots were of this heresy of Western Christianity, why it developed, and why we don't recognize it or talk about it. Durkheim's constructs gave me valuable insights, and he led me to other reading about primitive societies in which festivals were set up in order to return to dream time.

In effect, dream time is an act of artistic creation, and I realize now that's what I'm doing. Most of the society's effort goes into forging the construct, the creative form in which everybody can live—a social contract of sorts. It is the job of the politicians—chiefs or whatever—to organize it. Whatever form they set up is necessarily entropic: eventually it runs down and is unable to propel itself past a certain point. When it does that, it becomes necessary to do everything that has been taboo: wear women's clothes, kill the sacred animal and eat it, screw your mother, etc. A big blast reduces everything to rubble; then something new is built. Primitive societies, wiser than we, actually set aside a time to do this on a cyclical basis.

There are a number of parallels to this kind of experience in our society. We don't exactly cordon off a period—well, we do have a shoot-em-up rite every four years, but that's not quite the same. Instead it happens in different ways. Artists re-create: they make us think about doing all the things we shouldn't do, all the impossible, apocalyptic things, and weaken and tear down structures so that they can be rebuilt, releasing new energies.

Realizing this gave me an excuse to be the anarchist I've always wanted to be. I discovered I could be an anarchist and be constructive at the same time.

But for fiction to have the dynamic relationship with society you describe, it must be read—and by more than just a few enthusiasts. In talking about your work, you have alluded to a number of figures from the past, but the distressing fact is that your potential readership is cutting itself off from its cultural vocabulary. Sometimes I fear I'm teaching a generation that (1) doesn't know anything about the past; (2) doesn't have any hope of finding out about it; and (3) doesn't care. They don't read the Bible, haven't the vaguest sense of who Kant was, and think of Cervantes as the librettist to Man of La Mancha. *Does this situation worry you when you are writing?*

I suppose it acts as a goad. The trouble is that, in creating your fiction, you tend to get more and more complicated because you are not satisfied unless you've exploited totally the complexity of your metaphor. Thus you push yourself to do things that you recognize will not be caught by the average reader. Paradoxically, as you try to make an image more wonderful for the reader, you make it more difficult for him to become attuned to it. One of the peculiar things constantly being said about contemporary American fiction is that it is deliberately forfeiting readers. Who has read John Hawkes, or John Barth, or . . .

. . . Robert Coover?

Yes, or Robert Coover. Of course this produces uneasiness. We've all read *Finnegans Wake* and been irritated by the arrogance it manifests. Who wants to be party to something like that? And yet, ultimately, I tend to give in to the demands of the metaphor—or to the grouping of metaphors that, at times, seems to be creating the fiction for me. They all seem relevant and important to me, and they would be important (or of *some* value) to people if they *could* read it.

Isn't the contemporary writer occasionally obscure because, critically, we sometimes confuse obscurantism with profundity?

It would be marvelous to find the perfect, natural, popular image to which everyone could relate. It would be ideal to have the audience feel it, get into it so that things would happen to them without their even being aware it's happening to them, and absorb through the back door the history and culture they didn't have before. Unfortunately, metaphors are seldom that productive. Most prove to be much more esoteric than you first thought.

Take the baseball image: the average American male knows baseball and can follow a character playing a baseball parlor game. Even that it is a parlor game presents no problem. So it is very useful for most readers, especially for the poorer ones, not accustomed to that kind of fiction, who read somewhere it is a good book, pick it up, and get all the way through to the end. They can say, "Gee, I was able to read a good book"; maybe, they will go on to read another good book and see if it happens a second time. Nevertheless, for most women it's a rather dull approach to a novel. And Europeans don't understand it at all: when it was published in England, no one knew what to make of it, even though I supplied a glossary.

It's hard to find the perfect metaphor—the one that reaches the almost illiterate. That's part of the greatness of the *Quixote:* it is a profound, complicated work, and yet anyone who can trace the words with his finger and figure them out can read it.

Let me have one more run at having you share my despair over the McLuhanite shape of the future. Because I'm fascinated by the to-pographies words can create, I find stories like "The Baby Sitter," "The Magic Poker," or the fictions that Barth creates exciting. So I inflict them on my students, hoping they will respond to the inge-nuity, if to nothing else. But when I enter class on the day for which they have been assigned, I'm greeted by a crowd of pained, accusing faces.

Presuming that they must be reading something with enjoyment, I pick out a dreamy-looking intellectual and ask who excites him. He says, "Brautigan." So I go home, read Brautigan, and think I must be awfully stupid because I've missed the point. The next day, I ask the student what it is he finds attractive in Brautigan. "Well," he says, "it's like, you know, wow, you know . . ."—it's the ineffable in search of the universal. Sometimes I wonder whether, twenty years from now, I'll be reduced to running videotapes of Ozzie and Harriet.

Yes, but the number of intelligent readers has always been extremely small. Even in those times when the novel was the dominant form of literature, it was read by a lot of silly people who supported an awful lot of terrible literature, while books that deserved attention weren't being read. Take a look at the reception of *Bleak House* in the U.S.: the only thing one critic could say was that Dickens had locked up *Bleak House* and thrown the key away. It was not until well along in Dickens' career that he became king of the novelists' castle.

I can't bring myself to worry over that student of yours. It's pre-sumptuous to produce a book and expect someone to give up three or four hours—and in some cases, many more—to read it. We're all victims of a short life span.

This does not mean that I think the production of literature is not worthwhile. Working with cultural givens and trying to improve on them is a rewarding endeavor. Sometimes a novel will coincide with the "Head Start" cultural vocabulary of the broad audience; sometimes it won't. There's not much to be done about it, really. So I just have to continue the enterprise for itself. There will always be some people who will read such ventures, recognize value, and try to see that it is transmitted in one way or other.

MARCH 2, 1973